Annual Editions: Business Ethics, 28/e

Eric Teoro

http://create.mheducation.com

ISBN-10: 1259883256   ISBN-13: 9781259883255

Contents

Detailed Table of Contents

Unit 3: Building an Ethical Organization

Preface

Welcome to the 28th edition of *Annual Editions: Business Ethics*. Since its inaugural issue, *Annual Editions: Business Ethics* has provided students and practitioners up-to-date articles to serve as a basis for analysis and discussion of business-related ethical issues, theories, and practices. This edition continues that legacy with a collection of articles covering a wide array of business ethics topics.

Ethics touches every facet of organizational life. Marketing managers and their staffs face ethical decisions regarding consumer research, privacy, product development, pricing, distribution, and advertising. Financial and accounting managers face challenges related to insider trading, risky financial products, money laundering, and "creative" accounting practices. Human resource and staff managers are confronted with decisions concerning layoffs, outsourcing, diversity and inclusion, employee safety, employee privacy, sexual harassment, and other forms of hostile environment. Executives in multinational companies must deal with varying cultures and ethical systems, which can produce inconsistent, and at times contradictory, ethically acceptable business practices.

In the midst of these ongoing ethical concerns, businesses today face additional ethical challenges as societal expectations regarding the nature of business changes. What role should businesses play in addressing societal problems? Note, this moves beyond a question of could to should, one that has moral imperatives. Do businesses have a responsibility to help solve discrimination, poverty, lack of education, and lack of access to basic life necessities, or should executives focus on profit maximization while maintaining basic cultural norms? Do pharmaceutical companies have a responsibility to provide inexpensive or free drugs to individuals who do not have the means to pay the current market price? How should businesses interact with the environment? Is it sufficient for them to not cause harm, or do they have a responsibility to improve the environment given their resources? How do managers balance individual and organizational rights and responsibilities? Who defines these rights and responsibilities? Questions like these become more complex for public companies in which executives and boards have fiduciary responsibilities to stockholders. Add to all of this the ethical issues and dilemmas surrounding the use of technology, such as privacy, smart "autonomous" machines and systems, the use of AI, and

the replacement of human workers, the contemporary business ethics setting can be a very confusing and challenging environment.

Accompanying the articles in this edition are resources to help students, practitioners, and researchers interact with the material more fully. Associated with each article are learning objectives, questions to generate discussion, analysis and self-appropriation, and links to additional websites for further investigation.

It is our goal to continually improve *Annual Editions: Business Ethics*. We heartily welcome your comments, opinions, and recommendations as we strive to develop a text that will encourage and equip readers to uphold the highest standard of ethical business behavior.

Eric Teoro
Editor

Editor of This Volume

Eric Teoro is Director of the Business Administration Program at Lincoln Christian University. He teaches several ethics courses including business ethics and leadership ethics. Eric's research interests are the cultivation of an ethical personal character and corporate culture, business ethics, philosophy of business, and organizational trust. He has conducted business training in Ghana and China and serves as a board member for the Greater Ashburn Community Development Corporation and as the Education Officer for Aim to Work, not-for-profits serving one of Chicago's Southside neighborhoods. Prior to teaching, Eric worked in manufacturing and served in the United States Air Force.

Academic Advisory Board Members

Members of the Academic Advisory Board are instrumental in the final selection of articles for each edition of Annual Editions. Their review of the articles for content, level, and appropriateness provides critical direction to the editors and staff. We think that you will find their careful consideration well reflected in this volume.

Joan Adams
CUNY

Suzanne Atkin
Arizona State

Brian Bartel
Mid-State Technical College

Darrell Burrell
Florida Institute of Technology

Cheryl Dale
William Carey University

Carol Decker
Tennessee Wesleyan College

Renee Eastabrooks
Marist College

Michael Essary
Athens State University

Sarah Esveldt
Carroll University

Jeffrey Fahrenwald
Rockford University

Rita Fields
Madonna University, Livonia

Jay Halfond
Boston University

Keith Harman
Oklahoma Baptist University

Kenneth Harris, Jr.
Concordia University

Carol Hughes
University of North Carolina Asheville

William J. Kehoe
University of Virginia

Dale F. Kehr
University of Memphis

Ellen Kraft
Stockton University

Kristie Loescher
University of Texas Austin

Dina Mansour-Cole
Indiana University Purdue University Fort Wayne

Joseph Matranga
Rowan University

Cheryl Moore
Argosy University

Carl Nelson
Polytechnic University

Jeanne Nicholls
Slippery Rock University

Rebecca Nichols
Boston University

Audrey Parajon
Wilmington University

Victor Parker
University of North Georgia

Pedro David Perez
Cornell University-Ithaca

Joseph A. Petrick
Wright State University

Robert K. Rowe
Park University

Michael Ryan
Texas Tech University

Pearl Steinbuch
Boston University

Shawn Taylor
Warner University

Alberta Thrash
Central State University

Melodie M. Toby
Kean University

William Walker
University of Houston

Harvey J. Weiss
Florida National College

Jonathon West
University of Miami

Unit 1

UNIT

Prepared by: Eric Teoro, *Lincoln Christian University*

Ethical Behavior in the Workplace

Ethics can be defined as a body of moral principles or rules that govern behavior. It can, also, be defined as the area of study that examines ideas about moral principles. Business ethics considers the moral conduct of individuals within organizations, as well as the conduct of organizations as a whole. It must be remembered, though, that individuals establish the behavioral norms and cultures of organizations; so as one discusses business ethics at the corporate level, one is never far from discussing ethics at the individual level.

Values are beliefs about what is important in life. Like ethics, proper values guide behavior. Individuals and cultures can disagree regarding which principles are ethically good and normative. Ethics is different from law. Not every ethical standard has been codified in law, and history teaches us that not every law was grounded in ethics. Ethics and values seek to do good, not out of legal compliance, but out of an inherent sense of moral responsibility.

The articles in this unit focus on individual ethics, with an emphasis on personal behavior. They provide guidance regarding ethical decision-making, introduce ethical challenges individuals face on a personal level, and offer suggestions on how to manage those challenges. Working through these articles provides an opportunity to examine one's personal values, recognize judgment traps and biases, consider emotional and psychological factors when confronted with ethical choices, and develop ethical tools for one's personal and professional lives.

Article

Prepared by: Eric Teoro, *Lincoln Christian University*

Did You Bring Your Ethics to Work Today?

SUSAN M. HEATHFIELD

Learning Outcomes

After reading this article, you will be able to:

- Understand that ethical breaches result in new organizational policies.

- Identify common, everyday, ethical breaches committed in organizations.

Think you are a person of integrity and that you bring your highest standards of ethics to your workplace each day? You may reassess your thinking as you explore the topic of workplace ethics in this article.

Despite hundreds of pages of policies, codes of ethics, codes of conduct, organizational values, and carefully defined work environments and company cultures, lapses in workplace ethics occur every day.

Lapses in workplace ethics result from inappropriate officer behavior such as insider stock trading, expense account fraud, sexual harassment, and involvement in conflicts of interest.

Lapses in workplace ethics do not need to rise to that level to impact the workplace environment you provide for employees, though. Lapses in workplace ethics can occur because of simple issues such as toilet paper, copy machines, and lunch signup lists.

In a nationally important workplace ethics case, Hewlett-Packard company's, successful CEO, Mark Hurd (now former H-P CEO), became embroiled in workplace ethics issues. The public statement from the company indicated that Mr. Hurd left because he violated the company's expected standards of conduct.

Cathie Lesjak, H-P's chief financial officer, who was appointed interim CEO until the company found a permanent replacement for Mr. Hurd, asked employees "to remain 'focused' and said 'Mark had failed to disclose a close personal relationship he had with the contractor that constituted a conflict of interest, failed to maintain accurate expense reports, and misused company assets.'"

While most of us don't have as far to fall as Mr. Hurd, and unfortunately, he is not the first or only high-profile executive to bite the dust over personal conduct in recent years, lapses in ethics occur in workplaces every day.

You can violate the spoken and unspoken, published and unpublished, code of conduct in your organization without a CEO title. You can also violate these rules without your actions rising to the level of conflict of interests and questionable expense accounting.

Lapses in Workplace Ethics Drive Policy Development

Policies most frequently exist because some employees are untrustworthy. For example, many in HR debate the effectiveness of a paid time off policy versus time off policies that divide available days between personal, sick days, and vacation time off.

The only reason these policies exist at all, to define the relationship between employer and employees, is because a few employees took advantage of the employer's attempts to offer sympathetic time off for legitimate life reasons.

Consequently, employers limited management discretion and decision-making about individual employee situations and instituted policies to govern the many. You can build a similar case for most organizational policies. The failure of some employees to practice principled workplace ethical decision-making results in policies that cover all employees.

Codes of conduct or business ethics exist to guide the expected behavior of honorable employees. But, much of their origination occurred for the same reason as policies. Some employees conducted themselves in ways that were unacceptable to the business.

In today's workplace, potential charges of unfair treatment, discrimination, favoritism, and hostile work environment replace much management discretion. The many suffer for the few, and sometimes, your best employees get caught in the equal treatment trap. At best, time off policies, to use just one example, require organization time and energy—hundreds of hours of tracking and accounting.

Everyday Workplace Ethics

Few employees will undergo the challenges experienced by Mr. Hurd and other senior company executives in their practice of workplace ethics. But, all employees have the opportunity daily to demonstrate the core and fiber of who they are as people. Their values, integrity, beliefs, and character speak loudly through the behavior that they engage in at work.

Lapses in the practice of workplace ethics come in all sizes, large and small, far-reaching and close to home. Some ethical lapses affect individual employees. Other ethical lapses affect whole work groups, and in particularly egregious instances, such as Mr. Hurd's, whole companies and all of the stakeholders in the company suffer as a result.

Some failures to practice everyday workplace ethics are invisible. No one but you will ever know about the decision that you made, but each lapse in ethics affects your essence as an individual, as an employee, and as a human being. Even the smallest lapse in workplace ethics diminishes the quality of the workplace for all employees.

Examples

Each failure to practice value-based workplace ethics affects your self-image and what you stand for far more than it affects your coworkers. But the effect of your behavior on your fellow employees is real, tangible, and unpredictable, too.

Following are examples of employees failing to practice fundamental workplace ethics. The solution? Change the behavior, of course. You may never have thought of these actions as problems with ethical behavior, but they are. And, all of them affect your coworkers in negative ways.

What are signs that you know that your actions are substandard? You make up excuses, give yourself reasons, and that little voice of your conscience that chatters away in your head tries to convince your ethical self that your lapse in workplace ethics is okay.

Here are 16 examples of employees failing to practice fundamental workplace ethics.

1. You are using the company restroom and use up the last roll of toilet paper, or the last piece of paper towel. Without thought for the needs of the next employee, you go back to work rather than addressing the issue.

2. You call in sick to your supervisor because it's a beautiful day and you decide to go to the beach, or shopping, or …

3. You engage in an affair with a coworker while married because no one at work will ever know, you think you're in love, you think you can get away with it, your personal matters are your own business, and the affair will not impact other employees or the workplace.

4. You place your dirty cup in the lunchroom sink. With a guilty glance around the room, you find no one watching and quickly leave the lunchroom.

5. Your company sponsors events, activities, or lunches and you sign up to attend and fail to show. Conversely, you fail to sign up and show up anyway. You make the behavior worse when you say that you took the appropriate action so someone else must have screwed up.

6. You tell potential customers that you are the vice president in charge of something. When they seek out the company VP at a trade show, you tell your boss that the customers must have made a mistake.

7. You work in a restaurant in which wait staff tips are shared equally, and you withhold a portion of your tips from the common pot before the tips are divided.

8. You have sex with a reporting staff member and then provide special treatment to your flame.

9. You take office supplies from work to use at home because you justify, you often engage in company work at home, you worked extra hours this week, and so on.

10. You spend several hours a day using your work computer to shop, check out sports scores, pay bills, do online banking, and surf the news headlines for the latest celebrity news and political opinions.

11. You use up the last paper in the communal printer and you fail to replace paper leaving the task to the next employee who uses the printer.

12. You hoard supplies in your desk drawer, so you won't run out while other employees go without supplies they need to do their work.

13. You overhear a piece of juicy gossip about another employee and then repeat it to other coworkers. Whether the gossip is true or false is not the issue.

14. You tell a customer or potential customer that your product will perform a particular action when you don't know if it will and you didn't check with an employee who does.

15. You allow a part that you know does not meet quality standards leave your workstation and hope your supervisor or the quality inspector won't notice.

16. You claim credit for the work of another employee or you fail to give public credit to a coworker's contribution when you share results, make a presentation, turn in a report, or in any other way appear to be the sole owner of a work product or results.

This list provides examples of ways in which employees fail to practice workplace ethics. It is not comprehensive as hundreds of additional examples are encountered by employees in workplaces daily.

Critical Thinking

1. What do you think about creating policies that everyone has to follow due to the misbehavior of the few?

2. What everyday ethical violations have you witnessed? Have you committed?

3. What would others say about your moral fiber, your character, based on your everyday behavior?

Internet References

Harvard Business Review
https://hbr.org/2016/12/why-ethical-people-make-unethical-choices
Markkula Center for Applied Ethics
https://www.scu.edu/ethics/ethics-resources/ethical-decision-making/everyday-ethics/
TU
https://www.tu.no/artikler/the-10-most-common-examples-of-unethical-behavior/225478

Article   Prepared by: Eric Teoro, *Lincoln Christian University*

Everyday Ethics: Tougher Than You Think

Steve Goldberg and Bruce Bettinghaus

Learning Outcomes

After reading this article, you will be able to:

- Describe various judgment traps and biases.
- Describe how to overcome judgment and decision-making traps and biases.

Management accountants' ethics training is often reduced to a list of rules to follow when making decisions. But recent research in the quickly developing area of behavioral ethics reveals an unsettling fact: The list approach isn't enough. That's because it overlooks innate biases that affect our business decisions in surprising ways. What can behavioral ethics research teach us about making less-biased decisions?

What Do People Actually Do?

Traditional ethics focus on what people should do. But the burgeoning field of behavioral ethics explores what people actually do.

That's a big difference, and it came about because the old approach didn't work well. Ann Tenbrunsel, professor of business ethics at the University of Notre Dame, asserts that ". . . efforts designed to improve ethical behavior in the workplace continue to over promise and under deliver." (See http://bit.ly/1cXD5R7.)

Those efforts fail partly because we all have unconscious ethical blind spots. In "Stumbling Into Bad Behavior" in the April 21, 2011, issue of *The New York Times,* Max H. Bazerman and Tenbrunsel wrote that ". . . we have found that much unethical conduct that goes on, whether in social life or

work life, happens because people are unconsciously fooling themselves." (See http://nyti.ms/1EGRRlV.)

Management accountants are becoming more aware of the bias problem. In 2012, the Committee of Sponsoring Organizations of the Treadway Commission (COSO) published a report by KPMG LLP, Steven M. Glover, and Douglas F. Prawitt, "Enhancing Board Oversight: Avoiding Judgment Traps and Biases" (see http://bit.ly/1bS5zdy). And a 2011 KPMG monograph, *Elevating Professional Judgment in Auditing and Accounting: The KPMG Professional Judgment Framework,* also dealt with accounting judgment issues (see http://bit.ly/1e3eJpd).

Both documents show that the accounting profession realizes that flawed decisions result from not following a sound judgment process. Management accountants also need to know that group decisions that aren't structured and conducted properly can make judgment traps and biases worse.

Why Do Biases Thrive in Accounting?

Accountants can have the best ethical intentions and believe they are meeting their responsibilities with competence and integrity. But there are known cognitive biases that can make them fall short. Unfortunately, corporate accounting and auditing are particularly prone to self-serving biases.

In their December 9, 2002, online article for Harvard Business School, "Most Accountants Aren't Crooks-Why Good Audits Go Bad," Bazerman, George Loewenstein, and Don A. Moore identified three structural aspects of accounting that create opportunity for self-serving biases (see http://hbs.me/1JKzNdW). First, biases thrive when there is *ambiguity.* Although some accounting decisions aren't ambiguous, many require considerable judgment—such as classifying an item as expense vs. capital, deciding when to recognize revenue, or estimating allowance for doubtful accounts.

Second, accountants have self-serving reasons to go along with their bosses' or clients' preferences. Psychologists refer to this as *attachment.* It's well documented that self-interest unconsciously biases decisions.

Third, as Bazerman and his colleagues note, research affirms that judgments become even more biased when people endorse others' similarly biased judgments. Psychologists call this condition *approval.* It especially can apply to external auditors, internal auditors, and financial analysts gathering evidence and expressing agreement or disagreement about proposed financial statements, budgets, or forecasts.

Our Bias-Boosting Nature. Bazerman, Loewenstein, and Moore also describe three tendencies of human nature that amplify unconscious decision bias. The first one, *familiarity,* means we are more willing to harm strangers than those with whom we have an ongoing relationship. The second, *discounting,* means that we weight immediate decision consequences more heavily than future consequences. The third tendency, *escalation,* means that we are more apt to ignore wrongdoing if it starts small and gradually escalates. This last tendency can provoke unconscious bias to evolve into conscious corruption or fraud-often despite our best intentions.

Regulators sometimes acknowledge this fact. In their article, Bazerman and his colleagues quoted then Securities & Exchange Commission (SEC) Chief Accountant Charles Niemeier, who said: "People who never intend to do something wrong end up finding themselves in situations where they are almost forced to continue to commit fraud once they have started doing this. Otherwise, it will be revealed that they had used improper accounting in the earlier periods."

Our Two Reasoning Systems. Unfortunately, judgment traps and biases have a greater effect on the decisions of competent, well-intentioned people than we realize. That's because researchers have found that we actually have two different reasoning systems in the brain, and sometimes we use the wrong one. Pioneering psychologists Keith E. Stanovich and Richard F. West named these reasoning processes "System 1" and "System 2" in their October 2000 article, "Individual differences in reasoning: Implications for the rationality debate," in *Behavioral and Brain Sciences.*

System 1 is automatic, mostly unconscious, fast, intuitive, and context sensitive. It's social in nature and is an evolutionary adaptation like our fight-or-flight instinct. System 2 is analytical, rational, based on rules, slow, not social in nature, works to achieve our goals, and is consistent with our beliefs.

System 1 reasoning comes into play when we make quick routine decisions like watching for traffic when crossing the street or moving away from signs of danger. Going through the day, it would be extremely time-consuming to apply analytical thinking to the hundreds of routine decisions we must make—such as what route to take to work, when to apply the brakes, when to use a turn signal, or when we should drink water.

We use System 2 thinking best for making thoughtful business decisions—such as choosing a raw materials supplier or what to accrue for obsolete inventory. But the more experience a decision maker has, the more he or she tends to rely on System 1 thinking. The judgment trap is that managers may rely on System 1 thinking in situations where System 2 would be more appropriate.

Five Key Judgment Steps

Talent and experience are key components of effective judgment. But consistently following a proper judgment process enhances judgment skills for both new and experienced accountants.

According to the COSO report and KPMG monograph mentioned earlier, key elements of a good judgment process include having the right mind-set; employing consultation, knowledge, and professional standards; being aware of influences and biases; and making use of reflection and coaching.

What does a good, professional judgment process look like? The five key steps are listed in "COSO's Professional Judgment Process."

COSO's Professional Judgment Process

1. Define the problem and identify fundamental objectives,
2. Consider alternatives,
3. Gather and evaluate information,
4. Reach a conclusion, and
5. Articulate and document your rationale.

For higher-quality decisions, don't cut short steps 1 and 2 of the decision process. Make sure you carefully identify the objective and consider all alternatives and diverging views. Encourage the expression of different opinions.

Source: Adapted from KPMG LLP, Steven M. Glover, and Douglas F. Prawitt, "Enhancing Board Oversight: Avoiding Judgment Traps and Biases," Committee of Sponsoring Organizations of the Treadway Commission (COSO), March 2012, http://bit.ly/1bS5zdy.

Notice that the first step is to define the problem and identify fundamental objectives. Don't assume everyone knows what they are and that you can skip the first step! Not properly defining the problem leads to a judgment trap called *solving the wrong problem* and wasting time. If you don't define the problem accurately, you could be influenced by a judgment trigger rather than a clearly defined decision objective. That's what happens when we underinvest in defining the fundamental issue.

Although the judgment process seems simple and intuitive, in the real world we encounter pressures, time constraints, limited resources, judgment traps, and self-interest biases.

Avoiding Judgment Traps and Biases

It takes hard work to avoid judgment traps and biases. For a list of the most prominent ones and how to handle them, see Table 1. Unintentional biases arise from using mental shortcuts, which are the results of System 1 thinking. Although these shortcuts are efficient and effective in some situations, they often result in predictable bias. When you cross the street in the United States, you automatically look to the left for oncoming traffic. This is

an efficient and effective automatic response. But if you cross the street in the United Kingdom, where they drive on the opposite side of the road, this automatic response could lead to damaging consequences. Once you understand the implications of a shortcut, you can take measures to mitigate its impact. But you should be aware that mitigation is difficult and often has only a limited effect. City planners in London paint directions on the streets and take other measures to remind tourists to look to the right as well as the left when crossing the street.

To make quality ethical decisions, it's important for you to have an appropriate mind-set: an inquiring mind that analyzes objectives, information, and alternatives to reach a conclusion. But you must do all that objectively, critically, creatively, and somewhat skeptically.

Now let's follow a hypothetical CFO throughout her workday to show how hidden judgment triggers and biases affect her ethical decisions and what she can do about it.

A CFO's Pitfalls

Julie Smith is the CFO of a midsize manufacturing company. It's Friday, and many things are happening at once. Today is the end of the company's second quarter, she is finishing the last round of her staff evaluations, and she has to give Human

Table 1 How to Handle Common Judgment Traps and Biases

Judgment Trap of Bias	Mitigation Technique
Rush to solve: the tendency to want to solve a problem immediately by making a quick judgment	Follow a sound judgment process. Particularly emphasize steps 1 and 2 of COSO's Professional Judgment Process: defining the problem and considering alternatives. Ask "what" and "why" questions.
Groupthink: the tendency to suppress divergent views	Emphasize the problem definition and identifying alternatives (COSO steps 1 and 2). Ask "what" and "why" questions.
Solving the wrong problem	Emphasize COSO step 1, defining the problem and identifying fundamental objectives
Confirmation tendency: looking for or interpreting evidence to support a preference	Make the opposing case. Seek disconfirming or conflicting evidence.
Anchoring: a preference for not moving far from an initial numerical value	Introduce alternative independent numerical values based on historical precedent, past experience, industry data, or other sources. Seek evaluation from an alternative source or over a longer period of time.
Overconfidence: the tendency for confidence to grow more rapidly than competence as we become more experienced	Question experts' or advisors' estimates and underlying assumptions. Test key assumptions.
Judgment triggers and framing: the tendency to look at a problem from a limited perspective	Consider alternative frames or perspectives.
Availability: the tendency to only consider easily accessible information and ignore other relevant information	Define the problem and objectives (COSO step 1). Consider all identifiable alternatives (COSO step 2). Ask what would be most relevant.

Resources (HR) her final decision on the new hire for the controller's office. Instead of looking forward to a relaxing weekend, she's worried about tomorrow's emergency board meeting to approve the acquisition of the company's main raw materials supplier. In addition, her children's spring school break starts next week. Her whole family plans to get up early on Sunday and fly to Florida for a vacation.

Julie is a CMA® (Certified Management Accountant) and a member of IMA® (Institute of Management Accountants). She diligently tries to follow the *IMA Statement of Ethical Professional Practice* (see http://bit.ly/IMAStatement). But even if Julie were aware of all of her decision biases, behavioral research shows that it's difficult or impossible to eliminate them! Like most executives, Julie has little formal training in psychology, in how to make good judgments, or in how to spot human tendencies that threaten good judgment. Her bachelor's and master's degrees in accounting focused on technical knowledge needed to pass the CMA and CPA (Certified Public Accountant) exams. And her MBA focused only on managing change and strategic planning.

Julie has several important decisions to make before leaving on her vacation. This artificial deadline could lead to the judgment trap called *rush to solve* (see Table 1). Because she is rushed, Julie might not adequately consider all the job candidates and their qualifications before making a hiring decision. If she knows the previous salary of a job applicant, Julie's salary offer may be affected by a bias trap called *anchoring*—a preference to stay close to an initially named numerical value. Knowing the candidate's salary before the candidate earns an MBA may cause Julie's offer to fall short of what the candidate is really worth now.

The emergency board meeting presents other problems. Julie, the CEO, and the board chair are all urging the acquisition of their raw materials supplier for a price of $600 million. But business decisions made in a group setting like the board meeting can be biased because participants often suppress divergent views. In this case, no one wants to disagree with Julie and the CEO. The board doesn't encourage people to voice different opinions, which results in shallow thinking.

Also, the board may mistakenly believe that an early consensus is a sign of strength. It may not spend enough time defining the problem, clarifying issues and objectives, or considering alternative actions.

To see how Julie should have handled the acquisition issue using the COSO Professional Judgment Process to reduce decision-making bias, see Figure 1.

Don't Limit Perspectives

At the emergency board meeting, Julie presented the potential acquisition as a "slam dunk" move with low risk. But she didn't present any alternative viewpoints. That's a red flag!

Julie needs to understand the concept of *frames*—mental structures or perspectives used to determine the importance of information. Imagine you're in a house where each window gives you a different view. By considering all the windows—the frames—you get a better understanding of where the house is situated. Julie considered only one frame—that the acquisition was a "slam dunk." Better decision makers are aware when they are dangerously limiting the number of frames.

The board made this problem worse by not defining its objectives carefully. Is the objective securing a long-term source of raw materials? If so, did the board consider other actions—such as a long-term supply contract, purchasing alternative suppliers, or purchasing less than 100 percent of the current supplier? The board's narrow framing of the issue creates a *judgment trigger*. Executives pounce on one action but not necessarily the best one. As the KPMG monograph notes, studies show that we become more confident as we become more experienced and successful. But our confidence actually increases more rapidly than our competence. If board members realized this, they might be more skeptical of the "slam dunk" recommendation.

I've Made Up My Mind

We all know people who say, "Don't bother me with the facts. I've already made up my mind." This attitude illustrates our unconscious *confirmation tendency*. We tend to look for evidence confirming our viewpoint instead of being evenhanded. If board members are pressured into accepting Julie's viewpoint, their research may turn up supporting data only.

And the fact that Julie has already suggested it will cost $600 million to acquire the supplier makes the board vulnerable to the *anchoring* judgment trap—our tendency to not move far from an initially named numerical value. So even if buying the supplier is a good idea, Julie has biased the board to spend about $600 million on it.

But what if Julie didn't name a figure and assigns someone to investigate the supplier? The researcher finds that the supplier has been profitable for the past 10 years but that some older, difficult-to-find information hints at major unsolved problems. In that case, a judgment trap called *availability* might trip up both the researcher and the board because there's a tendency for decision makers to consider information that's easier to retrieve as being more relevant to a decision than less accessible information. Auditors can fall prey to this trap also. An auditor may follow an approach used in previous years or on a recent engagement even if other approaches may be more effective. Our "desires" heavily influence the way we interpret information.

In addition to considering alternatives, the way the board examines them can bias a decision. The board should consider

Decision Process →	→	→	→	→	→
COSO Professional Judgment Steps	**Step 1: Define Problem and Objective**	**Step 2: Consider Alternatives**	**Step 3: Gather/Evaluate Information**	**Step 4: Reach Conclusion**	**Step 5: Document Rationale**
INITIAL ISSUE: Should Julie's company purchase its main raw materials supplier for $600 million?	**INITIAL PROBLEM DEFINITION:** whether or not to acquire supplier **REVISED FRAMING:** securing long-term source of materials	• Purchasing supplier • Long-term supply contract • Purchasing alternative suppliers • Purchasing less than 100% of supplier	• Primary analysis by CFO and CEO	• Board decision	
Typical traps and biases	• Solving the wrong problem • Judgment triggers • Narrow framing • Incomplete problem definition	• Judgment triggers • Narrow framing	• Confirmation tendency • Overconfidence • Availability • Anchoring • Rush to solve	• Groupthink • Rush to solve	
Mitigation techniques	• Be aware of framing, judgment traps, and biases • Define the objective clearly • Ask "what" and "why" questions	• Be aware of judgment traps and biases • Consider alternative frames	• Be aware of judgment traps and biases • Question acquisition cost figure– seek alternative estimates • Question underlying assumptions • Seek out the most relevant information • Make the opposing case and seek support	• Be aware of judgment traps and biases • Encourage diverse views • Follow a sound judgment process	• Be aware of judgment traps and biases. • Document each step. • Avoid conflicts of interest. • Include discarded alternatives.

Figure 1 How to Reduce Decision-Making Bias   Julie Smith, the hypothetical CFO of a midsize manufacturing company, was urging the board of directors to rush into acquiring the company's main raw materials supplier. Let's look at the way she should have handled the issue. Each step in the formal COSO decision-making process is shown below, along with judgment traps and biases that would come up and techniques to mitigate them. Note that the biases, judgment traps, and mitigation techniques apply at multiple steps in the decision process. We have minimized repetition for this example.

multiple options at the same time rather than one option at a time. If options are considered consecutively, there's a tendency to approve a suboptimal option and then not give equal consideration to other options, according to Kathrine L. Milkman, Dolly Chugh, and Max H. Bazerman in "How Can Decision Making Be Improved?" in *Perspectives on Psychological Science.*

Julie and the board also should consider all stakeholders' points of view. As Julie documents her conclusion, she should assess whether it makes sense and whether the underlying information supports it.

Thus Julie and the management team are facing judgment traps and unconscious biases in a variety of areas. But the biggest problem is that they aren't even aware of them.

- Reduce conflicts of interest, and
- Try to recognize situations causing vulnerability to bias.

Then you have to follow up and continue to work at it. Behavioral research consistently demonstrates that being aware of judgment biases is only a first step in reducing their effects. Even with awareness, it's very difficult to overcome biases. And other things can bias our decisions, such as anger, tiredness, stress, and how many issues we handle at the same time.

But working on this will pay big dividends. By following a sound judgment process, you can replace knee-jerk reactions with formal analysis. That's the way to make your everyday ethics excel and protect yourself, your company, and all its stakeholders.

Critical Thinking

1. Describe judgment traps and biases that you struggle with. What concrete steps can you take to overcome them?

2. Describe a situation and its associated judgment biases and traps. Work through the 5-step decision-making process, describing how one can overcome the biases and traps.

Internet References

Ethics Unwrapped
   http://ethicsunwrapped.utexas.edu/video/self-serving-bias
Frontiers in Systems Neuroscience
   http://journal.frontiersin.org/article/10.3389/fnsys.2014.00195/full
Mind Tools
   https://www.mindtools.com/pages/article/avoiding-psychological-bias.htm

---

STEVE GOLDBERG, **CPA**, **PHD**, is a full professor of accounting at the School of Accounting, Seidman College of Business at Grand Valley State University in Grand Rapids, Mich. He teaches and does research in international accounting and ethics and has taught auditing, financial accounting, and managerial accounting. **BRUCE BETTINGHAUS**, **PHD**, is an associate professor of accounting at the School of Accounting, Seidman College of Business at Grand Valley State University. He teaches and does research in accounting ethics, financial reporting theory, and managerial accounting.

Resources: Improving Your Ethical Judgment

Dan Ariely, *The (Honest) Truth About Dishonesty: How We Lie to Everyone Especially Ourselves*, Harper Collins, New York, N.Y., 2013.
Using original experiments and research, the author explains how and why we lie.

Max H. Bazerman and Ann E. Tenbrunsel, *Blind Spots: Why We Fail to Do What's Right and What to Do about It*, Princeton University Press, Princeton, N.J., 2013.
Learn about the ways we overestimate our ability to do what is right, acting unethically despite our best intentions.

Max H. Bazerman, George Loewenstein, and Don A. Moore, "Why Good Accountants Do Bad Audits," *Harvard Business Review*, November 2002, http://bit.ly/1K87CsM.
The authors argue that eliminating or lessening unconscious bias will require fundamental changes in the way accounting firms and their clients operate.

Francesca Gino, *Sidetracked: Why Our Decisions Get Derailed, and How We Can Stick to the Plan*, Harvard Business Review Press, Boston, Mass., 2013.
The author reveals how simple, irrelevant factors can have profound consequences on our decisions and behavior.

Daniel Kahneman, *Thinking, Fast and Slow*, Farrar, Straus and Giroux, New York, N.Y., 2011.
A major *New York Times* best seller, this book offers deep insights about our judgments and reactions.

Reducing Bias

The good news is that everyone can start reducing bias with four simple steps:

- Follow a sound judgment process,
- Be aware of judgment traps and biases,

Article   Prepared by: Eric Teoro, *Lincoln Christian University*

The PLUS Ethical Decision-making Model

ETHICS RESEARCH CENTER

Learning Outcomes

After reading this article, you will be able to:

- Understand and utilize the steps of an effective decision-making model.

- Understand how to incorporate ethical considerations into the decision-making model.

Seven Steps to Ethical Decision-Making

Step 1: Define the problem
Step 2: Seek out relevant assistance, guidance, and support
Step 3: Identify alternatives
Step 4: Evaluate the alternatives
Step 5: Make the decision
Step 6: Implement the decision
Step 7: Evaluate the decision

Introduction

Organizations struggle to develop a simple set of guidelines that makes it easier for individual employees, regardless of position or level, to be confident that his/her decisions meet all of the competing standards for effective and ethical decision-making used by the organization. Such a model must take into account two realities:

- Every employee is called upon to make decisions in the normal course of doing his/her job. Organizations cannot function effectively if employees are not empowered to make decisions consistent with their positions and responsibilities.

- For the decision maker to be confident in the decision's soundness, every decision should be tested against the organization's policies and values, applicable laws and regulations, as well as the individual employee's definition of what is right, fair, good, and acceptable.

The decision-making process described below has been carefully constructed to be:

- Fundamentally sound based on current theories and understandings of both decision-making processes and ethics.

- Simple and straightforward enough to be easily integrated into every employee's thought processes.

- Descriptive (detailing how ethical decision are made naturally) rather than prescriptive (defining unnatural ways of making choices).

Step 1: Define the Problem

The most significant step in any decision-making process is to determine why a decision is called for and identify the desired outcome(s). How you define a problem shapes your understanding of its causes and where you will search for solutions?

First, explore the difference between what you expect and/or desire and the current reality. By defining the problem in terms of outcomes, you can clearly state the problem.

Consider this example: Tenants at an older office building are complaining that their employees are getting angry and frustrated because there is always a long delay getting an elevator to the lobby at rush hour. Many possible solutions exist, and all are predicated on a particular understanding the problem:

- Flexible hours—so all the tenants' employees are not at the elevators at the same time.

- Faster elevators—so each elevator can carry more people in a given time period.

- Bigger elevators—so each elevator can carry more people per trip.
- Elevator banks—so each elevator only stops on certain floors, increasing efficiency.
- Better elevator controls—so each elevator is used more efficiently.
- More elevators—so that overall carrying capacity can be increased.
- Improved elevator maintenance—so each elevator is more efficient.
- Encourage employees to use the stairs—so fewer people use the elevators.

The real-life decision makers defined the problem as "people complaining about having to wait." Their solution was to make the wait less frustrating by piping music into the elevator lobbies. The complaints stopped. There is no way that the eventual solution could have been reached if, for example, the problem had been defined as "too few elevators."

How you define the problem determines where you go to look for alternatives/solutions—so define the problem carefully.

Step 2: Seek Out Relevant Assistance, Guidance, and Support

Once the problem is defined, it is critical to search out resources that may be of assistance in making the decision. Resources can include people (i.e., a mentor, coworkers, external colleagues, or friends and family) as well professional guidelines and organizational policies and codes. Such resources are critical for determining parameters, generating solutions, clarifying priorities, and providing support, both while implementing the solution and dealing with the repercussions of the solution.

Step 3: Identify Available Alternative Solutions to the Problem

The key to this step is to not limit yourself to obvious alternatives or merely what has worked in the past. Be open to new and better alternatives. Consider as many as solutions as possible—five or more in most cases, three at the barest minimum. This gets away from the trap of seeing "both sides of the situation" and limiting one's alternatives to two opposing choices (i.e., either this or that).

Step 4: Evaluate the Identified Alternatives

As you evaluate each alternative, identify the likely positive and negative consequence of each. It is unusual to find one alternative that would completely resolve the problem and is

significantly better than all others. As you consider positive and negative consequences, you must be careful to differentiate between what you know for a fact and what you believe might be the case. Consulting resources, including written guidelines and standards, can help you ascertain which consequences are of greater (and lesser) import.

You should think through not just what results each alternative could yield, but the likelihood it is that such impact will occur. You will only have all the facts in simple cases. It is reasonable and usually even necessary to supplement the facts you have with realistic assumptions and informed beliefs. Nonetheless, keep in mind that the more the evaluation is fact-based, the more confident you can be that the expected outcome will occur. Knowing the ratio of fact-based evaluation versus non-fact-based evaluation allows you to gauge how confident you can be in the proposed impact of each alternative.

Step 5: Make the Decision

When acting alone, this is the natural next step after selecting the best alternative. When you are working in a team environment, this is where a proposal is made to the team, complete with a clear definition of the problem, a clear list of the alternatives that were considered, and a clear rationale for the proposed solution.

Step 6: Implement the Decision

While this might seem obvious, it is necessary to make the point that deciding on the best alternative is not the same as doing something. The action itself is the first real, tangible step in changing the situation. It is not enough to think about it or talk about it or even decide to do it. A decision only counts when it is implemented. As Lou Gerstner (former CEO of IBM) said, "There are no more prizes for predicting rain. There are only prizes for building arks."

Step 7: Evaluate the Decision

Every decision is intended to fix a problem. The final test of any decision is whether or not the problem was fixed. Did it go away? Did it change appreciably? Is it better now, or worse, or the same? What new problems did the solution create?

Ethics Filters

The ethical component of the decision-making process takes the form of a set of "filters." Their purpose is to surface the ethics considerations and implications of the decision at hand. When decisions are classified as being "business" decisions (rather than "ethics" issues), values can quickly be left out of consideration and ethical lapses can occur.

At key steps in the process, you should stop and work through these filters, ensuring that the ethics issues imbedded in the decision are given consideration.

We group the considerations into the mnemonic PLUS.

- **P** = Policies
  Is it consistent with my organization's policies, procedures, and guidelines?
- **L** = Legal
  Is it acceptable under the applicable laws and regulations?
- **U** = Universal
  Does it conform to the universal principles/values my organization has adopted?
- **S** = Self
  Does it satisfy my personal definition of right, good, and fair?

The PLUS filters work as an integral part of steps 1, 4, and 7 of the decision-making process. The decision maker applies the four PLUS filters to determine if the ethical component(s) of the decision are being surfaced/addressed/satisfied.

- Step 1: Define the problem (use PLUS to surface the ethics issues)
  - Does the existing situation violate any of the PLUS considerations?
- Step 2: Seek out relevant assistance, guidance, and support
- Step 3: Identify available alternative solutions to the problem
- Step 4: Evaluate the identified alternatives (use PLUS to assess their ethical impact)
  - Will the alternative I am considering resolve the PLUS violations?
  - Will the alternative being considered create any new PLUS considerations?
  - Are the ethical trade-offs acceptable?
- Step 5: Make the decision
- Step 6: Implement the decision
- Step 7: Evaluate the decision (PLUS surface any remaining/new ethics issues)
  - Does the resultant situation resolve the earlier PLUS considerations?
  - Are there any new PLUS considerations to be addressed?

The PLUS filters do not guarantee an ethically sound decision. They merely ensure that the ethics components of the situation will be surfaced so that they might be considered.

How Organizations Can Support Ethical Decision-Making

Organizations empower employees with the knowledge and tools they need to make ethical decisions by

- Intentionally and regularly communicating to all employees.
- Organizational policies and procedures as they apply to the common workplace ethics issues.
- Applicable laws and regulations.
- Agreed-upon set of "universal" values (i.e., Empathy, Patience, Integrity, Courage).
  Providing a formal mechanism (i.e., a code and a helpline, giving employees access to a definitive interpretation of the policies, laws, and universal values when they need additional guidance before making a decision).

Critical Thinking

1. Utilize the PLUS Ethical Decision-making Model to determine the ethically right course of action regarding a personal decision in an organization.
2. Utilize the PLUS Ethical Decision-making Model to determine the ethically right course of action regarding a corporate-level business decision.
3. What are the strengths and weaknesses of the Model's four filters?

Internet References

Board of Innovation
  https://www.boardofinnovation.com/blog/2017/08/02/16-cognitive-biases-that-kill-innovative-thinking/

Core
  https://core.ac.uk/download/pdf/52077506.pdf

Josephson Institute
  http://josephsoninstitute.org/med-introtoc/

Status Net
  https://status.net/articles/ethical-decision-making-process-model-framework/

Article

Prepared by: Eric Teoro, *Lincoln Christian University*

Three Simple Rules to Stop Yourself from Lying

NATALIE KITROEFF

Learning Outcomes

After reading this article, you will be able to:

- Recognize that "small" lies can lead to more serious ethical breaches.
- Describe several basic steps to avoid lying.

Start by being honest when someone has something in their teeth.

The squirmiest part of Yael Melamede's new documentary about lying comes about 30 minutes in, when a 2007 news report about the resignation of the dean of admissions at MIT is featured. The dean had just resigned after lying for 28 years about having a college degree, reported NBC anchor Brian Williams. Viewers can watch Williams recount her ethical breach with a weird kind of clairvoyance. In February of this year (2015), the anchor was suspended from NBC for repeating a fabricated tale about taking fire while in a helicopter during the 2003 U.S. invasion of Iraq.

The idea that everyone lies is not surprising. It's still interesting to hear people explain the first lie in a string of lies that sent them to jail or see a fibber tell the world about the demise of another fibber. Melamede's documentary, *(Dis)Honesty—The Truth About Lies,* which began showing at film festivals in April and is now available to stream on demand, delivers all of the above scenes, with an assist from Duke behavioral economist Dan Ariely.

Melamede takes a tour through Ariely's research, which shows, broadly, that when people can justify it to themselves or see others behaving similarly, they have no qualms about lying. The movie features a wife who started cheating on her husband out of boredom, a pro cyclist who doped out of necessity, and an accountant who fudged his company's books first out of fear and then out of greed. Watching people unspool their lies will not make you feel better about yourself. It will make you feel as though you're one lie away from being very publicly humiliated.

Most of the liars interviewed in *(Dis)Honesty* did not make huge mistakes from the get-go. They started small, with a quick visit to AshleyMadison.com or a conversation with a friend about how to get faster on a bike. The disgraced MIT admissions dean, Marilee Jones, said that at first, she simply didn't bother correcting people who assumed that she was a PhD Brian Williams said his memory failed him and that he confused the plane he was traveling on with another one. Ariely, who has spent his career studying lies, says that's typical: Often people who get into major trouble for dishonesty were at one point relatively low-key liars.

Bloomberg asked Ariely how people who tell little lies can keep from turning into people whose lies land them on television. He offered a couple of easy strategies. For a friend.

1. Stop telling people you want to meet up with them if you don't.

    The classic "let's meet up" lie, where two people pretend that they are planning on hanging out, can spiral out of control, Ariely says.

    "You basically don't want to tell this person that you aren't interested in meeting each other again," Ariely says. "It is really similar to other kinds of lies. We don't want to deal with unpleasantness right now, so we end up worse down the road."

    Telling someone that you must do drinks, then canceling drinks and repeating that process for months is the kind of habitual lie that Ariely says "lead you to be a bigger liar."

It also costs you time, causes guilt, and doesn't actually make the person on the other end of the line feel better. The next time you run into an old friend whom you would rather not see on purpose, preempt your desire to please them.

"Saying something like, 'I'm really buried at work for the next month, if things change I will let you know'," is a better approach, Ariely says.

That may be untrue, but unlike "let's meet up," a fib about your workload is unlikely to set off a chain reaction of untruths. "That's the kind of lie that doesn't cost you as much."

2. Tell your friends when you don't like the person they're dating.

Do you hate your bestie's bae? Make it known. "It's one of those things that people don't say enough. We don't get enough feedback," says Ariely. Offering a dispassionate opinion about something so subjective can help your pals and might also make you less self-delusional.

"When we are in our own little realm, it is very hard for us to see past our emotions and past our immediate incentives. When you give advice to someone else, you take the outside view. We do think more long-term," Ariely says. Facing an inconvenient opinion head on by blurting it out can make you more likely to take an objective stance about your own problems. Just be strategic about how significant of an other you target.

"Married without kids, go for it; married with kids, don't go for it," says Ariely.

3. Make easy-to-follow rules.

"I am a big believer in rules, because they help us be who we want without having to contemplate it every time," Ariely says. For example, he decided always to tell someone when they had something in their teeth. "Before that, it was 'should I say something? Should I not?'" he says. Now he realizes he should never have hesitated. "One hundred percent of the time people are grateful. They realize I am not going to be the last person they talk to."

Sure, answering "bloated" when someone asks how you're feeling, or saying "no" when they ask to hang out is uncomfortable. Do it anyway. Even Omar Little had a code.

Critical Thinking

1. Describe a time when you lied. Why did you do so? How did you justify it?

2. Develop several concrete steps you can take to avoid lying.

3. Is lying ever ethical? Why or why not?

Internet References

About.com
http://philosophy.about.com/od/Philosophical-Questions-Puzzle/a/The-Ethics-Of-Lying.htm

Harvard University
http://dash.harvard.edu/bitstream/handle/1/3209557/Korsgaard_Two ArgumentsLying.pdf?sequence=2

Santa Clara University
http://www.scu.edu/ethics/publications/iie/v6n1/lying.html

The (Dis)honesty Project
http://thedishonestyproject.com/

Article   Prepared by: Eric Teoro, *Lincoln Christian University*

Be Clear on Employee Technology and Social Media Use Policies

Numbers of Surveys Confirm That Social Media and Technology Use among Employees Leads to a Loss of Productivity. But, More Importantly, Legal and Security Concerns Are on the Rise Because of It, As Well.

LESLIE RUHLAND

Learning Outcomes

After reading this article, you will be able to:

- Understand the problems associated with personal technology usage in the workplace.
- Understand the importance of company policies regarding personal technology usage in the workplace.

Technology has great potential for businesses in almost every realm of their organizations. However, its personal use by employees has also become the number one employment legal risk for employers. In fact, according to a recent study, businesses report that about 25 percent of outgoing e-mail contains content that could pose a legal, financial, or regulatory risk.

Balancing Privacy with Maintaining Productivity

For many employers, the larger issue with their worker's use of personal technology is the loss of productivity. A study by OfficeTeam revealed that, among workers and senior office managers who were questioned, most of them used their cellphones to answer e-mails and visit social media sites, while spending an additional average of about 42 minutes a day on other personal tasks.

Basing their calculations on Department of Labor figures, the study's authors noted that,

If these numbers were true for every full-time worker in the US, that would add up to $15.5 billion in lost productivity every week due to professionals using their mobile devices for nonwork activities.

According to the study, the average office employee spends almost five hours every week on a cellphone. In addition to social media sites, workers use their phones to visit sports and entertainment sites, play mobile games, and shop. The study concluded that,

All in all, the average employee could be wasting more than eight hours per work week on activities unrelated to the job.

Another survey by CareerBuilders backs up these statistics. That survey found that 19 percent of employers questioned think that their workers are productive fewer than 5 hours a day. And 55 percent of employers pointed to employee texting and cell phone use as the biggest source of distraction.

According to an article about the survey results,

...there's a high cost of low productivity. Almost half of employers (48%) said smartphone distractions compromised the quality of work. Other negative consequences included: a lower morale because other workers have to pick up the slack (38%), a negative impact on the boss/ employee relationship (28%), and missed deadlines (27%).

While as many as 85 percent of businesses in the United States have some degree of Internet restrictions and others actively monitor employee's use of company technology, there are problematic issues with privacy. And, in addition to the very real loss of productivity, there is ever present and growing threat of cyber security breaches.

Establishing Policies That Protect Privacy and Security Needs

One of the problems with the issue of technology and social media use is the rampant lack of policies and guidelines that are comprehensive and sensible.

An article from *The Balance* points out the benefits of a well-thought-out policy,

> *An effective internet and email policy that will help employees understand what is expected of them as it affects their work is a must for employers. You want to go on record to define what employees can do from work provided devices or employee-owned devices that are used for or involve your employees, your workplace, or your company.*

> *Employees don't mind guidelines because they don't want to act inappropriately and cross a line that they didn't know existed. So, the development of a fair, understandable, sensible policy is strongly recommended.*

According to FindLaw.com, employees have basic rights in the workplace including the right to privacy. However, they also note that an employee's right to privacy in the workplace has become a controversial legal topic.

Technology now enables employers to monitor most workplace communications made by employees using company computers. They point out that, while employees may feel that this monitoring is a violation of their privacy rights, that often is not the case.

In regard to Internet use and e-mail, Findlaw.com states,

> *An employee's activities while using an employer's computer system are largely unprotected by personal privacy laws. Emails are considered to be company property if they are sent using the company's computer system. Employers generally have the right to monitor and view employee email, so long as they have a valid business purpose for doing so.*

This does not mean that companies are exempt from disclosing their monitoring activities. In fact, the mere fact that employees are aware that their technology communications at work may be monitored to minimize abuse and security lapses.

Telephone communications while at work is more protected, however. There are wider limitations on an employer's right

to monitor its employees' telephone usage at work. According to the Electronics Communications Privacy Act (ECPA), an employer may not monitor an employee's personal phone calls, even those made from telephones on work premises.

However, an employer may monitor a personal call if the employee knows the call is being monitored and has consented to it. The ECPA also protects an employee's voicemail messages at work. In fact, an employer may face legal liability if they read, disclose, delete, or prevent access to an employee's voicemail messages.

Up-to-date Company Policies and Employee Handbooks

A company's employee handbook is its blueprint for internal conduct. It is a written guide to how the company interacts with employees and the employees with one another. Policies should cover all aspects of what a business expects from employees such as attendance, safety rules, legal compliance with employment laws, facilities management, and dress codes.

Policies are guidelines that define company rules and procedure, and should include the consequences for not following them. And because of the dynamic nature of labor law and regulations, the employee handbook should be regularly reviewed and updated when necessary.

One of the most important aspects of any employee handbook is that it is kept up to date.

Laws change, new issues arise, and businesses evolve over time. And if your handbook is in multiple languages, each version needs to be updated, as well.

Protect Your Company and Your Employees

Company policies reinforce and clarify the standards expected of employees and help employers manage staff more effectively by defining acceptable and unacceptable behavior in the workplace.

And an employee handbook that is comprehensive and up to date will provide the documentation for businesses faced with possible litigation arising from employee disputes.

If you have questions regarding this or other HR compliance issues and practices, let us help you in managing your HR needs, payroll processes, and staying on top of compliance demands. Get your Free Download: Payroll Outsourcing Guide to help you make an informed decision or call Accuchex Payroll Management Services at 877-422-2824.

Critical Thinking

1. What forms of personal technology usage have you witnessed or engaged in in the workplace?
2. What are the ethical issues involved with personal technology usage in the workplace?
3. Create a standard/policy for balancing personal privacy and organizational needs for security and productivity.

Internet References

Pew Research Center
http://www.pewinternet.org/2016/06/22/social-media-and-the-workplace/
Techvera
https://techvera.com/technology-acceptable-use-policy-business/
The Olson Group
https://theolsongroup.com/5-reasons-social-media-workplace-can-help-employees/

Unit 2

Prepared by: Eric Teoro, *Lincoln Christian University*

UNIT

Corporate Social Responsibility and the Nature of Business

Contemporary businesses face several significant challenges in the today's global marketplace. World trends are changing the expectations that individuals and whole societies have of business. No longer is the traditional product or service value proposition considered sufficient; today's company must also demonstrate moral values and a commitment to social good if it is to engender trust.

Corporate Social Responsibility (CSR) refers to the obligation that a business has to operate in a manner that will benefit society at large. When companies engage in charitable activities, they engage employees at deeper levels, attract better talent, and build positive reputations. Companies engaged in CSR take sustainability seriously, not only with respect to environmental issues but also with respect to human capital development. They adhere to fiduciary principles, recognizing their responsibility to create lasting value for all their stakeholders.

Some, however, counter popular notions of CSR. They ask why offering a product or service that improves the quality of lives, treating employees fairly, conducting business dealings honestly, cleaning up one's own messes, following laws, and paying taxes are not sufficient, in and of themselves, to constitute a sociably responsible company. They advocate the inherent worth of business, and question the ability, even the rightness, of executives at publicly traded companies to focus on issues other than profit maximization, assuming such a focus remains within ethical norms. In essence, they ask why the normal operations of business are not considered sufficiently ethical or socially responsible in themselves.

Article   Prepared by: Eric Teoro, *Lincoln Christian University*

Ethics Training Is Missing the Mark: Here's Why

S. L. YOUNG

Learning Outcomes

After reading this article, you will be able to:

- Recognize that ethics training and ethical decision-making need to incorporate emotional, psychological, and moral considerations.

- Recognize that ethical decision-making impacts individuals' emotional, psychological, and moral health.

Ethics is a topic that's often discussed by parents, schools, organizations, and employers. These discussions usually teach individuals about the importance of being ethical: what does it mean; why is it important; what are the costs of unethical activities? This subject matter must be taught; however, the toughest parts of being ethical are almost never discussed. That is . . . what are the emotional, physiological, and moral challenges that individuals who don't want to be complicit to unethical behavior experience?

Before exploring the affects of wanting to be ethical, the reason that ethics is important must be reviewed.

Ethics are behavioral standards that individuals, organizations, and societies apply and generally adhere to as acceptable. Without ethical standards, there can be numerous variables used to determine if something is right or wrong, good or bad. Notwithstanding these random variables, there are always individual considerations based on experiential learning; however, an individual's ethical standards are normally defined and developed by family, religious beliefs, friends, and societal practices. These standards provide common operating practices that are used to define the limits of acceptable behavior.

Generally, individuals know whether something is right or wrong. Although, there are times that ethical decisions will require additional consideration, input, or sometimes assistance to make the appropriate choice. The challenge—many times—is whenever a decision is within an unclear range or the biggest test is making a decision about whether to get involved to resolve a known ethical issue. During these times, individuals can experience an internal battle while attempting to make an ethical decision.

The internal impacts of making tough ethical choices can impact individuals:

- Emotionally—a feeling someone has related to a particular situation, event, or consideration;
- Physiologically—a body's reaction to making a tough decision, which could be stress, anxiety, sweat, depression, etc.;
- Morally—a challenge to an individual's belief system weighed against the things an individual believes to be true—but may be altered while making a tough decision.

These internal impacts are seldom (if ever) discussed during ethics training. This omission is unfortunate because an ability to process these intangible elements are important factors while individuals determine whether to be ethical during certain moments.

In a time that winning at almost any cost is more pervasive, there must be an increased focus given to educating individuals about the significance of internal processing in ethical decision making—beyond the mental processing. Otherwise, a larger number of individuals are more likely to bend the limits of standards, rules, policies, or laws to receive an unfair or personal advantage.

After the allegations of ball deflation by the New England Patriots prior to Super Bowl XLIX, my nephew and I discussed the potential ethical issues. During our conversation, my nephew made a couple of points to support his argument: 1) the deflation was found in the first half, but didn't impact the game's outcome and 2) everyone cheats at some point. What?!?!

The rationale used in his positioning is troubling for several reasons:

- First, a determination of whether something is ethical should never be decided based on an outcome, but instead by an evaluation of a consideration, situation, or an event;
- Second, a choice to be unethical cannot be validated based on attempting to justify the behavior by rationalizing the actions or activities of another;
- Third, individuals must be accountable and responsible for their actions—including complicit acceptance of wrongdoings by allowing known unethical behavior to continue unchallenged.

There is a cost to individuals, organizations, and societies if unethical activities aren't resolved in a timely manner. However, there are also costs to individuals' emotional, physiological, and moral health while making a choice whether to get involved with the prevention of unethical behavior.

Decisions individuals make cannot be necessarily managed by external factors; although, if ethical training helps individuals to understand and prepare for the internal factors that might be experienced while dealing with ethical dilemmas, then more individuals will be better prepared to handle the internal impacts that can be experienced while attempting to behave ethically.

Critical Thinking

1. Describe how ethical decision-making impacts the decision maker's emotional, psychological, and moral health.
2. What concrete steps can individuals take to incorporate emotional and psychological considerations into ethical decision-making?
3. What concrete steps can individuals take to incorporate emotional and psychological considerations into ethical training?

Internet References

A Guide to Ethics (St. Olaf College)
http://pages.stolaf.edu/ein/themes/emotions-and-reason/
Practical Ethics (University of Oxford)
http://blog.practicalethics.ox.ac.uk/2013/12/happiness-meaning-and-well-being/
Psychology Today
https://www.psychologytoday.com/blog/hot-thought/201006/ethical-thinking-should-be-rational-and-emotional
Virtue Ethics Info Centre
http://virtueethicsinfocentre.blogspot.com/2008/02/morality-and-emotions.html

Article   Prepared by: Eric Teoro, *Lincoln Christian University*

A Time for Ethical Self-Assessment

Peter Drucker's literature on business scruples and the Ethics of Prudence is newly timely, and not just because of the holidays.

RICK WARTZMAN

Learning Outcomes

After reading this article, you will be able to:

- Understand the importance and value of answering the following question: When you look in the mirror in the morning, what kind of person do you want to see?

- Recognize that management deals with the nature of "Man, and with Good and Evil."

This may be the season of giving, but it sure feels like everybody is suddenly on the take.

Siemens (SI), the German engineering giant, agreed this month to pay a record $1.6 billion to US and European authorities to settle charges that it routinely used bribes and kickbacks to secure public works contracts across the globe. Prominent New York attorney Marc Dreier—called by one US prosecutor a "Houdini of impersonation and false documents"—has been accused by the feds of defrauding hedge funds and other investors out of $380 million.

And then, of course, there's financier Bernard L. Madoff, who is said to have confessed to a Ponzi scheme of truly epic proportions: a swindle of $50 billion, an amount roughly equal to the GPD of Luxembourg.

All told, it begs the question that Peter Drucker first raised in a provocative 1981 essay in the journal *The Public Interest* and that later became the title of a chapter in his book, *The Ecological Vision*: "Can there be 'business ethics'?"

Drucker didn't pose this to suggest that business was inherently incapable of demonstrating ethical behavior. Nor was he positing that the workplace should somehow be exempt from moral concerns. Rather, his worry was that to speak of "business ethics" as a distinct concept was to twist it into something that "is not compatible with what ethics always was supposed to be."

What Drucker feared, specifically, was that executives could say they were meeting their social responsibilities as business leaders—protecting jobs and generating wealth—while engaging in practices that were plainly abhorrent. "Ethics for them," Drucker wrote, "is a cost-benefit calculation . . . and that means that the rulers are exempt from the demands of ethics, if only their behavior can be argued to confer benefits on other people."

It's hard to imagine that a Madoff or a Dreier would even attempt to get away with such tortured logic: an ends-justify-the-means attitude that Drucker labeled "casuistry." But we all know managers who've tried to rationalize an unscrupulous act by claiming that it served some greater good.

The Mirror Test

In his book *Resisting Corporate Corruption*, Stephen Arbogast notes that when Enron higher-ups sought an exemption from the company's ethics policy so that they could move forward with certain dubious financial dealings, the arrangement was made to "seem a sacrifice for the benefit of Enron." Reinhard Siekaczek, a former Siemens executive, told *The New York Times* (NYT) that the company's showering of foreign officials with bribes "was about keeping the business unit alive and not jeopardizing thousands of jobs overnight."

For Drucker, the best way for a business—indeed, for any organization—to create an ethical environment is for its people to partake in what he came to call in a 1999 article "the mirror test." In his 1981 piece, Drucker had a fancier name for this idea: He termed it "The Ethics of Prudence." But either way, it boils down to the same thing: When you look in the mirror in the morning, what kind of person do you want to see?

The Ethics of Prudence, Drucker wrote, "does not spell out what 'right' behavior is." It assumes, instead, "that what is wrong behavior is clear enough—and if there is any doubt, it is 'questionable' and to be avoided." Drucker added that "by following prudence, everyone regardless of status becomes a leader" and remains so by "avoiding any act which would make one the kind of person one does not want to be, does not respect."

Drucker went on: "If you don't want to see a pimp when you look in the shaving mirror in the morning, don't hire call girls the night before to entertain congressmen, customers, or salesmen. On any other basis, hiring call girls may be condemned as vulgar and tasteless, and may be shunned as something fastidious people do not do. It may be frowned upon as uncouth. It may even be illegal. But only in prudence is it ethically relevant. This is what Kierkegaard, the sternest moralist of the 19th century, meant when he said that aesthetics is the true ethics."

Time to Reflect

Drucker cautioned that the Ethics of Prudence "can easily degenerate" into hollow appearances and "the hypocrisy of public relations." Yet despite this danger, Drucker believed that "the Ethics of Prudence is surely appropriate to a society of organizations" in which "an extraordinarily large number of people are in positions of high visibility, if only within one organization. They enjoy this visibility not, like the Christian Prince, by virtue of birth, nor by virtue of wealth—that is, not because they are personages. They are functionaries and important only through their responsibility to take right action. But this is exactly what the Ethics of Prudence is all about."

Now is the time of year when many of us find ourselves sitting in church or in synagogue, or, if we're not religious, simply taking stock of who we are and where we want to be as the calendar turns. But what's even more critical is that we continue this sort of honest self-assessment when we return to our jobs in early 2009.

"I have learned more theology as a practicing management consultant than when I taught religion," Drucker once said. This, he explained, is because "management always deals with the nature of Man and (as all of us with any practical experience have learned), with Good and Evil as well."

So take the mirror test now—and then keep taking it well after the Christmas ornaments have been packed away and the Hanukkah candles have burned down to the nub. In the meantime, happy holidays to all.

Critical Thinking

1. Explain the meaning of Drucker's question "can there be business ethics?"
2. Defend the position that there can be business ethics.
3. What is the mirror test?
4. What is the ethics of prudence?
5. What is meant by "aesthetics is the true ethics"?

Internet References

American Management Association
   http://www.amanet.org/training/articles/Ethical-Leadership-Self-Assessment-How-Machiavellian-Are-You.aspx

National Association Medical Staff Services
   http://www.namss.org/Portals/0/Ethics%20Files/Self-assessment%20Tool.pdf

---

RICK WARTZMAN is the director of the Drucker Institute at Claremont Graduate University.

Article   Prepared by: Eric Teoro, *Lincoln Christian University*

The Social Responsibility of Business Is to Increase Its Profits

MILTON FRIEDMAN

Learning Outcomes

After reading this article, you will be able to:

- Describe Friedman's position regarding the primary responsibility of a corporate executive.
- Describe Friedman's concerns regarding the popular understanding of social responsibility.

When I hear businessmen speak eloquently about the "social responsibilities of business in a free-enterprise system," I am reminded of the wonderful line about the Frenchman who discovered at the age of 70 that he had been speaking prose all his life. The businessmen believe that they are defending free enterprise when they declaim that business is not concerned "merely" with profit but also with promoting desirable "social" ends; that business has a "social conscience" and takes seriously its responsibilities for providing employment, eliminating discrimination, avoiding pollution and whatever else may be the catchwords of the contemporary crop of reformers. In fact they are—or would be if they or anyone else took them seriously—preaching pure and unadulterated socialism. Businessmen who talk this way are unwitting puppets of the intellectual forces that have been undermining the basis of a free society these past decades.

The discussions of the "social responsibilities of business" are notable for their analytical looseness and lack of rigor. What does it mean to say that "business" has responsibilities? Only people can have responsibilities. A corporation is an artificial person and in this sense may have artificial responsibilities, but "business" as a whole cannot be said to have responsibilities, even in this vague sense. The first step toward clarity in examining the doctrine of the social responsibility of business is to ask precisely what it implies for whom.

Presumably, the individuals who are to be responsible are businessmen, which means individual proprietors or corporate executives. Most of the discussion of social responsibility is directed at corporations, so in what follows I shall mostly neglect the individual proprietors and speak of corporate executives.

In a free-enterprise, private-property system, a corporate executive is an employee of the owners of the business. He has direct responsibility to his employers. That responsibility is to conduct the business in accordance with their desires, which generally will be to make as much money as possible while conforming to the basic rules of the society, both those embodied in law and those embodied in ethical custom. Of course, in some cases his employers may have a different objective. A group of persons might establish a corporation for an eleemosynary purpose—for example, a hospital or a school. The manager of such a corporation will not have money profit as his objective but the rendering of certain services.

In either case, the key point is that, in his capacity as a corporate executive, the manager is the agent of the individuals who own the corporation or establish the eleemosynary institution, and his primary responsibility is to them.

Needless to say, this does not mean that it is easy to judge how well he is performing his task. But at least the criterion of performance is straight-forward, and the persons among whom a voluntary contractual arrangement exists are clearly defined.

Of course, the corporate executive is also a person in his own right. As a person, he may have many other responsibilities that he recognizes or assumes voluntarily—to his family, his conscience, his feelings of charity, his church, his clubs, his city, his country. He may feel impelled by these responsibilities to devote part of his income to causes he regards as worthy, to refuse to work for particular corporations, even to leave his job, for example, to join his country's armed forces. If we wish, we may refer to some of these responsibilities as "social responsibilities." But in these respects he is acting as a principal, not an agent; he is spending his own money or time or energy, not the money of his employers or the time or energy he has contracted to devote to their purposes. If these are "social responsibilities," they are the social responsibilities of individuals, not of business.

What does it mean to say that the corporate executive has a "social responsibility" in his capacity as businessman? If this statement is not pure rhetoric, it must mean that he is to act in some way that is not in the interest of his employers. For example, that he is to refrain from increasing the price of the product in order to contribute to the social objective of preventing inflation, even though a price increase would be in the best interests of the corporation. Or that he is to make expenditures on reducing pollution beyond the amount that is in the best interests of the corporation or that is required by law in order to contribute to the social objective of improving the environment. Or that, at the expense of corporate profits, he is to hire "hardcore" unemployed instead of better qualified available workmen to contribute to the social objective of reducing poverty.

In each of these cases, the corporate executive would be spending someone else's money for a general social interest. Insofar as his actions in accord with his "social responsibility" reduce returns to stockholders, he is spending their money. Insofar as his actions raise the price to customers, he is spending the customers' money. Insofar as his actions lower the wages of some employees, he is spending their money.

The stockholders or the customers or the employees could separately spend their own money on the particular action if they wished to do so. The executive is exercising a distinct "social responsibility," rather than serving as an agent of the stockholders or the customers or the employees, only if he spends the money in a different way than they would have spent it.

But if he does this, he is in effect imposing taxes, on the one hand, and deciding how the tax proceeds shall be spent, on the other.

This process raises political questions on two levels: principle and consequences. On the level of political principle, the imposition of taxes and the expenditure of tax proceeds are governmental functions. We have established elaborate constitutional, parliamentary and judicial provisions to control these functions, to assure that taxes are imposed so far as possible

in accordance with the preferences and desires of the public—after all, "taxation without representation" was one of the battle cries of the American Revolution. We have a system of checks and balances to separate the legislative function of imposing taxes and enacting expenditures from the executive function of collecting taxes and administering expenditure programs and from the judicial function of mediating disputes and interpreting the law.

Here the businessman—self-selected or appointed directly or indirectly by stockholders—is to be simultaneously legislator, executive and jurist. He is to decide whom to tax by how much and for what purpose, and he is to spend the proceeds—all this guided only by general exhortations from on high to restrain inflation, improve the environment, fight poverty and so on and on.

The whole justification for permitting the corporate executive to be selected by the stockholders is that the executive is an agent serving the interests of his principal. This justification disappears when the corporate executive imposes taxes and spends the proceeds for "social" purposes. He becomes in effect a public employee, a civil servant, even though he remains in name an employee of a private enterprise. On grounds of political principle, it is intolerable that such civil servants—insofar as their actions in the name of social responsibility are real and not just window-dressing—should be selected as they are now. If they are to be civil servants, then they must be elected through a political process. If they are to impose taxes and make expenditures to foster "social" objectives, then political machinery must be set up to make the assessment of taxes and to determine through a political process the objectives to be served.

This is the basic reason why the doctrine of "social responsibility" involves the acceptance of the socialist view that political mechanisms, not market mechanisms, are the appropriate way to determine the allocation of scarce resources to alternative uses.

On the grounds of consequences, can the corporate executive in fact discharge his alleged "social responsibilities?" On the other hand, suppose he could get away with spending the stockholders' or customers' or employees' money. How is he to know how to spend it? He is told that he must contribute to fighting inflation. How is he to know what action of his will contribute to that end? He is presumably an expert in running his company—in producing a product or selling it or financing it. But nothing about his selection makes him an expert on inflation. Will his holding down the price of his product reduce inflationary pressure? Or, by leaving more spending power in the hands of his customers, simply divert it elsewhere? Or, by forcing him to produce less because of the lower price, will it simply contribute to shortages? Even if he could answer these questions, how much cost is he justified in imposing on his stockholders, customers and employees for this social purpose? What is his appropriate share and what is the appropriate share of others?

And, whether he wants to or not, can he get away with spending his stockholders', customers' or employees' money? Will not the stockholders fire him? (Either the present ones or those who take over when his actions in the name of social responsibility have reduced the corporation's profits and the price of its stock.) His customers and his employees can desert him for other producers and employers less scrupulous in exercising their social responsibilities.

This facet of "social responsibility" doctrine is brought into sharp relief when the doctrine is used to justify wage restraint by trade unions. The conflict of interest is naked and clear when union officials are asked to subordinate the interest of their members to some more general purpose. If the union officials try to enforce wage restraint, the consequence is likely to be wildcat strikes, rank-and-file revolts and the emergence of strong competitors for their jobs. We thus have the ironic phenomenon that union leaders—at least in the U.S.—have objected to Government interference with the market far more consistently and courageously than have business leaders.

The difficulty of exercising "social responsibility" illustrates, of course, the great virtue of private competitive enterprise—it forces people to be responsible for their own actions and makes it difficult for them to "exploit" other people for either selfish or unselfish purposes. They can do good—but only at their own expense.

Many a reader who has followed the argument this far may be tempted to remonstrate that it is all well and good to speak of Government's having the responsibility to impose taxes and determine expenditures for such "social" purposes as controlling pollution or training the hard-core unemployed, but that the problems are too urgent to wait on the slow course of political processes, that the exercise of social responsibility by businessmen is a quicker and surer way to solve pressing current problems.

Aside from the question of fact—I share Adam Smith's skepticism about the benefits that can be expected from "those who affected to trade for the public good"—this argument must be rejected on the grounds of principle. What it amounts to is an assertion that those who favor the taxes and expenditures in question have failed to persuade a majority of their fellow citizens to be of like mind and that they are seeking to attain by undemocratic procedures what they cannot attain by democratic procedures. In a free society, it is hard for "evil" people to do "evil," especially since one man's good is another's evil.

I have, for simplicity, concentrated on the special case of the corporate executive, except only for the brief digression on trade unions. But precisely the same argument applies to the newer phenomenon of calling upon stockholders to require corporations to exercise social responsibility (the recent G.M crusade, for example). In most of these cases, what is in effect involved is some stockholders trying to get other stockholders (or customers or employees) to contribute against their will to "social" causes favored by the activists. Insofar as they succeed, they are again imposing taxes and spending the proceeds.

The situation of the individual proprietor is somewhat different. If he acts to reduce the returns of his enterprise in order to exercise his "social responsibility," he is spending his own money, not someone else's. If he wishes to spend his money on such purposes, that is his right and I cannot see that there is any objection to his doing so. In the process, he, too, may impose costs on employees and customers. However, because he is far less likely than a large corporation or union to have monopolistic power, any such side effects will tend to be minor.

Of course, in practice the doctrine of social responsibility is frequently a cloak for actions that are justified on other grounds rather than a reason for those actions.

To illustrate, it may well be in the long-run interest of a corporation that is a major employer in a small community to devote resources to providing amenities to that community or to improving its government. That may make it easier to attract desirable employees, it may reduce the wage bill or lessen losses from pilferage and sabotage or have other worthwhile effects. Or it may be that, given the laws about the deductibility of corporate charitable contributions, the stockholders can contribute more to charities they favor by having the corporation make the gift than by doing it themselves, since they can in that way contribute an amount that would otherwise have been paid as corporate taxes.

In each of these—and many similar—cases, there is a strong temptation to rationalize these actions as an exercise of "social responsibility." In the present climate of opinion, with its widespread aversion to "capitalism," "profits," the "soulless corporation" and so on, this is one way for a corporation to generate goodwill as a by-product of expenditures that are entirely justified on its own self-interest.

It would be inconsistent of me to call on corporate executives to refrain from this hypocritical window-dressing because it harms the foundation of a free society. That would be to call on them to exercise a "social responsibility"! If our institutions, and the attitudes of the public make it in their self-interest to cloak their actions in this way, I cannot summon much indignation to denounce them. At the same time, I can express admiration for those individual proprietors or owners of closely held corporations or stockholders of more broadly held corporations who disdain such tactics as approaching fraud.

Whether blameworthy or not, the use of the cloak of social responsibility, and the nonsense spoken in its name by influential and prestigious businessmen, does clearly harm the foundations of a free society. I have been impressed time and again by the schizophrenic character of many businessmen. They are capable of being extremely far-sighted and clearheaded in matters that are internal to their businesses. They are incredibly short-sighted and muddle-headed in matters that are outside their businesses but affect the possible survival of business in general. This shortsightedness is strikingly exemplified in the calls from many businessmen for wage and price guidelines or controls or income policies. There is nothing that could do more in a brief period to destroy a market system and replace it by a centrally controlled system than effective governmental control of prices and wages.

The short-sightedness is also exemplified in speeches by businessmen on social responsibility. This may gain them kudos in the short run. But it helps to strengthen the already too prevalent view that the pursuit of profits is wicked and immoral and must be curbed and controlled by external forces. Once this view is adopted, the external forces that curb the market will not be the social consciences, however highly developed, of the pontificating executives; it will be the iron fist of Government bureaucrats. Here, as with price and wage controls, businessmen seem to me to reveal a suicidal impulse.

The political principle that underlies the market mechanism is unanimity. In an ideal free market resting on private property, no individual can coerce any other, all cooperation is voluntary, all parties to such cooperation benefit or they need not participate. There are no values, no "social" responsibilities in any sense other than the shared values and responsibilities of individuals. Society is a collection of individuals and of the various groups they voluntarily form.

The political principle that underlies the political mechanism is conformity. The individual must serve a more general social interest—whether that be determined by a church or a dictator or a majority. The individual may have a vote and say in what is to be done, but if he is overruled, he must conform.

It is appropriate for some to require others to contribute to a general social purpose whether they wish to or not.

Unfortunately, unanimity is not always feasible. There are some respects in which conformity appears unavoidable, so I do not see how one can avoid the use of the political mechanism altogether.

But the doctrine of "social responsibility" taken seriously would extend the scope of the political mechanism to every human activity. It does not differ in philosophy from the most explicitly collectivist doctrine. It differs only by professing to believe that collectivist ends can be attained without collectivist means. That is why, in my book *Capitalism and Freedom,* I have called it a "fundamentally subversive doctrine" in a free society, and have said that in such a society, "there is one and only one social responsibility of business—to use its resources and engage in activities designed to increase its profits so long as it stays within the rules of the game, which is to say, engages in open and free competition without deception or fraud."

Critical Thinking

1. Do you agree with Friedman's position? Why or why not?
2. Does Friedman advocate maximizing profits regardless of cost or behavior? Defend your answer.
3. Would Friedman support popular notions of corporate social responsibility if such behaviors maximized profits? Why or why not?

Internet References

Becker Friedman Institute (University of Chicago)
  https://bfi.uchicago.edu/feature-story/corporate-social-responsibilty-friedmans-view
Huffington Post
  http://www.huffingtonpost.com/john-friedman/milton-friedman-was-wrong_b_3417866.html
PhilPapers
  http://philpapers.org/archive/COSDMF.pdf

Article   Prepared by: Eric Teoro, *Lincoln Christian University*

Corporate America Needs to Get Back to Thinking about More than Just Profits

Marina v. N. Whitman

Learning Outcomes

After reading this article, you will be able to:

- Understand factors that explain swings between business focusing on profits and focusing on social or public good.
- Understand the author's argument for business to engage in social or public good.

Disclosure Statement

Marina v. N. Whitman does not work for, consult, own shares in, or receive funding from any company or organization that would benefit from this article, and has disclosed no relevant affiliations beyond their academic appointment.

Should companies be doing more to make the world a better place?

The world's biggest money manager thinks so. He recently urged companies to contribute more to society if they want BlackRock as an investor.

"A company's ability to manage environmental, social, and governance matters demonstrates the leadership and good governance that is so essential to sustainable growth," BlackRock's chief Larry Fink wrote in his annual letter to CEOs, "which is why we are increasingly integrating these issues into our investment process."

Fink's letter, seen by some as an ultimatum to "be good" or be excluded from BlackRock's US$5.7 trillion in assets,

symbolizes the tightrope companies must walk. On one side are those insisting companies focus on raising their share price in the short term—even if it means hurting the environment, workers, and communities in the long run. On the other, a growing chorus are demanding that doing "good" (or at least, as Google might put it, not doing evil) be their top priority and let profits follow.

This battle isn't new. It was front and center in the 1970s as economist Milton Friedman insisted a corporation's only obligation was to maximize profits for the shareholder. What is new is that the "forces of good" appear to be rising again.

Earlier in my career, in the 1980s, when companies were putting shareholder value first and profits were tight, I was a senior executive at General Motors during a period of wrenching downsizing. I convinced my bosses that doing a little good, even amid plant closings and layoffs, could make a real difference for hard-hit communities, and so we donated to local charities to mitigate some of the pain.

Years later, at the University of Michigan, my experience at GM helped me shape a graduate course on corporate social responsibility that examined the tension between Friedman's view and the one expressed by Fink.

Today, I believe that companies, awash in profits, can once again afford to make money while doing good.

The "Good Corporation" Is Born

A lack of competition is one of the main reasons U.S. companies became known for serving the public good in the decades after World War II.

Domestically, whole industries were dominated by just one or a handful of companies, such as AT&T in communications and the "Big Three" (GM, Ford, and Chrysler) in automobiles. Meanwhile, Europe and Japan were struggling to recover from the massive destruction of years of war, while the rest of Asia had not yet developed enough to provide competition.

So American businesses became very profitable. At the same time, three pressures helped imbue them with a sense of a public purpose: more powerful unions, partnerships between business and government forged during World War II, and the need to raise capital from public markets to fuel expansion.

Yes, shareholders were to be rewarded, but it was also the case that big companies provided workers with stable, well-paid jobs and secure pensions. This was back when Americans were more likely to have one or two jobs for life.

Communities and the public in general often benefited as companies financed public interest research like AT&T's Bell Labs or developed products with broadly positive impacts like GM's crash dummy.

Put simply, profitability and a bit of prodding to serve a public purpose prompted U.S. companies to do good.

The Good Company: RIP

This stable world began to unravel during the 1970s in the aftermath of two oil shocks and the disintegration of the international monetary system that had been forged at Bretton Woods near the end of World War II. Growth slowed in virtually all industrialized nations. At home, inflation and unemployment both worsened sharply.

At the same time, those "oligopolistic rents" in the 1950s and 1960s began to shrink steadily as U.S. companies faced increased competition in global markets after Europe and Japan recovered and rebuilt from wartime devastation and other Asian countries climbed the development ladder to the point where they, too, could create competitive companies and industries.

This made it harder for U.S. companies to meet the expectations of their many stakeholders. American businesses' profit margins shrank, and companies were broken up, cutting short the previously safe seats of chief executives. The views of conservative economists like Friedman took hold, dictating that a corporation's sole obligation should be to stockholders.

In 1993, journalist Robert Samuelson drove the point home by publishing an "obituary" in Newsweek headlined "R.I.P.: The Good Corporation," concluding bleakly that, "We thought all companies could marry efficiency and social responsibility. We were wrong."

Institutional Investors Strike Back

Well, turns out Samuelson may have called the death of the good company prematurely as activists and even investors like BlackRock bombard executives with demands that they bear more responsibility for social good. In fact, 60 percent of the companies that responded to a 2016 survey of 92 major corporations reported rising stakeholder pressure to get engaged on issues, from human rights to climate change.

While environmental and other more traditional activists have had some impact, it's the major institutional investors that are the more effective conduit to force corporate change since they manage nearly 70 percent of all publicly listed U.S. securities.

For example, on climate change, financial firms that collectively own more than $26 trillion in assets have been pressuring the world's biggest emitters to cut emissions and disclose more of the risks. Their pressure has worked, as oil companies such as Exxon Mobil and others have promised to do both.

For today's CEOs, managing the delicate balancing act between these stakeholders and the equally powerful "activist" investors that primarily want a quick gain has perhaps never before been such a challenge. Billionaire investor Carl Icahn and other hedge fund managers have become more aggressive pushing companies to maximize profits or face the consequences. Just ask Ford's Mark Fields, DuPont's Ellen Kullman, or the former CEOs at General Electric, U.S. Steel, CSX, J.Crew, and Yahoo, all of whom lost their jobs because they didn't do what the activists wanted in 2017.

Fat with Profits

I would argue, however, that today the choice between satisfying shareholders and serving a public service should be an easier one for most companies. That's because the biggest companies in the United States are sitting on a record pile of cash and making some of the biggest profits on record.

And that's before they start to see the tremendous gains from the sharp reduction in the corporate tax rate from 35 to 21 percent.

In other words, companies can afford to do a little good and heed Larry Fink's message. Some companies, including AT&T, Boeing, and several large banks, have already announced that they plan to use the windfall from the tax cut to invest more in their communities and give raises or bonuses to workers.

It's a good start to bringing the good corporation back from the dead.

Critical Thinking

1. Do businesses have a responsibility to engage in social or public good? If so, are there limits as to what should be expected?

2. Choose an industry and describe what forms of social or public good it should engage in. Defend your suggestions.

3. Provide examples of personal and social goods and needs. How can you, as an individual, balance the competing claims for personal and social goods and needs?

Internet References

Journal of Corporate Responsibility and Leadership
http://jcrl.umk.pl/files/7815/0102/1176/ksiezak.pdf

Smart Recruiters
https://www.smartrecruiters.com/blog/top-20-corporate-social-responsibility-initiatives-of-2018/

Article   Prepared by: Eric Teoro, *Lincoln Christian University*

Fiduciary Principles: Corporate Responsibilities to Stakeholders

SUSAN C. ATHERTON, MARK S. BLODGETT, AND CHARLES A. ATHERTON

Learning Outcomes

After reading this article, you will be able to:

- Describe the history of fiduciary theory and court opinion.
- Understand the relationship between fiduciary and corporate social responsibilities.

Introduction

The lack of trust in American corporations and in corporate management over the recent scandals and financial crisis has increased public and legislative outcry for accountability in business decisions. Frustration is rampant, with "seemingly unending examples of mismanagement, ethical misconduct, and patterned dishonesty of a society dubbed 'the cheating culture.'"[1] International competition created tremendous risks and rewards but forced companies to attract investors through creative accounting practices to raise share value. As a result, three decades of corporate greed, inappropriate financial risk-taking and personal misconduct eroded trust in corporate decision-making.[2]

Corporate governance reform initiatives beginning in 2002 were designed to increase financial disclosure and responsibility; however, such legislation is insufficient to rebuild public trust in business. Restoring trust requires that those individuals who manage corporations, that is, the board of directors and senior officers, comply with requirements for greater accountability and transparency, *and* abide by the legal norms to which boards of directors and management are already subject, as directors and officers are legally bound as fiduciaries owing duties of care and loyalty to the corporation.[3] However, centuries of legal and religious formalization and codification have diminished the actual meaning and

purpose of fiduciaries, with the result that modern corporate fiduciaries have limited responsibility toward stakeholders and the greater society. Restoring the original definitions and roles of fiduciaries may legitimize and guide the corporation in developing new relationships with stakeholders.

This paper does not focus on illegal conduct by corporate individuals, although many criminal violations of fiduciary norms involve intentional assessment of the risk of penalties versus potential profits.[4] Rather, the paper examines the limitations of today's corporate fiduciary duties given the original intent of the fiduciary relationship. In particular, we examine the definitions of fiduciaries and fiduciary responsibilities to determine the extent to which formalization and codification have led to avoidance of corporate responsibility. We then revisit the historical and religious origins of fiduciaries in commercial transactions that defined and shaped the integration of moral and ethical duties in business today yet were so narrowly defined that corporate liability became increasingly limited. We propose a modest but well-defined, consistent and universal definition of "fiduciary duties," that could offer corporate managers guidance in developing new approaches to stakeholder relationships—relationships built on expectations of corporate trust and decision-making that maximize shareholder wealth while protecting stakeholders.

The Modern Fiduciary

Most business students and executives today are introduced to the concept of a "fiduciary" in the context of agency law, where a fiduciary is defined as "one who has a duty to act primarily for another person's benefit," and agency is generally defined as "the fiduciary relation that results from the manifestation of consent by one person (a 'principal') to another (an 'agent') that the agent shall act on the principal's behalf and subject to the principal's control, and the agent manifests or otherwise consents so to act."[5] Restatement (Third) of Agency states that proof of an agency relationship requires the existence of the manifestation by the principal that the agent shall act for him; the agent's acceptance of the undertaking; and, the understanding that the principal is in control of the undertaking. The agency relationship that results is founded on trust, confidence, and good faith by one person in the integrity and fidelity of another, creating certain duties owed by each party established in the agency agreement and implied by law.[6] Within the relationship, fiduciaries have a duty of loyalty—the duty to act primarily for another in matters related to the activity and not for the fiduciary's own personal interest.

Fiduciaries also have a duty of good faith—the duty to act with scrupulous good faith and candor; complete fairness, without influencing or taking advantage of the client. The fiduciary relationship, as defined by history and case law, exists in every business transaction. Moreover, the relationship is defined by the specific role or function of the agent toward the principal, that is, the relationship of corporate management and boards of directors to shareholders, lawyer to client, or broker to client, and governed by the laws associated with those transactions, including criminal and labor law, securities and corporate law, contracts, partnerships, and trusts.[7] The roles of trustees, administrators, and bailees as fiduciaries were of ancient origin, whereas agents appeared only at the end of the eighteenth century.[8] Partners, corporate boards of directors, and corporate officers held fiduciary duties originating with the formation of modern partnerships and corporations, as did majority shareholders, while union leaders held fiduciary roles only when unions were granted power by statute to represent workers in negotiations with management.[9] While modern definitions of these duties remain intact, the scope of the duties greatly varies based on the fiduciary's role, which increases the complexity of analysis required to understand violations of those duties.

The modern definition of "agent" as a fiduciary was first rationalized and clarified as a legal doctrine in 1933:[10] "When the person acting is to represent the other in contractual negotiations, bargainings or transactions involved in business dealings with third persons, or is to appear for or represent the other in hearings or proceedings in which he may be interested, he is termed an 'agent,' and the person for whom he is to act is termed the 'principal.'" The element of continuous subjection to the will of the principal distinguishes the agent from other fiduciaries and the agency agreement from other agreements.[11] This implies that corporate officers and directors are also agents. However, in law and practice today, the fiduciary roles of corporate officers and directors are not "continuous subjection to the will of the principal (shareholders)" but more flexible as officers and directors make many decisions not approved by shareholders.

Further, the duties of officers and directors are distinct from those of other corporate employees. Corporate officers and directors owe fiduciary duties to shareholders (as defined by state case law and Delaware corporate law) while employees as agents owe duties to employers, suppliers, vendors, or customers in a wide variety of relationships involving trust.[12] This distinction has created a two-tiered definition of fiduciaries, each with different duties, and varying liabilities for breaches of those duties, and is supported by economic theory. Such differentiation in fiduciary roles does not appear to be the intention, either historically or in modern corporate law. In 1928, Judge Benjamin Cardozo, then Chief Judge of the New York Court of Appeals, eloquently recognized the significance and sanctity of fiduciary principles in *Meinhard v. Salmon:*[13]

> [J]oint adventurers, like copartners, owe to one another . . . the duty of the finest loyalty . . . and the level of conduct for fiduciaries has been kept at a higher level than that trodden by the crowd. It will not consciously be lowered by any judgment of this court.

Cardozo's opinion reflects three important principles that reinforce a long line of precedent in defining a *special level of fidelity for all fiduciaries:* (1) fiduciary matters demand a higher standard than normal marketplace transactions; (2) exceptions to the fiduciary standard undermine the duty of loyalty; and (3) neither courts nor regulators who interpret, enforce or modify the fiduciary standard should consciously weaken it.[14] Supreme Court Justice Brandeis later noted that a fiduciary "is an occupation which is pursued largely for others and not merely for oneself . . . in which the amount of financial return is not the accepted measure of success."[15]

Fiduciary Duties: The Required Triad

The Delaware Supreme Court, renowned for its corporate governance decisions and the source of the primary legal standards for the duties and liabilities of corporate officers, ruled in 1993, reaffirmed in 2006, and again in 2010, that the "triad" of duties includes the duty of loyalty, due care and good faith, where "good faith" and "full and fair disclosure" are considered to be the essential elements of, or prerequisites for proper conduct, by a director.[16] Violation of the duty of good faith could remove directors' protections from liability. The Delaware Court also ruled that corporate officers owe the same fiduciary duties as corporate directors, noting that it is not possible to discharge properly either the duty of care or the duty of loyalty without acting in good faith with respect to the interests of the companies' constituents.[17] Major legislation such as The Sarbanes-Oxley Act of 2002[18], or The Dodd–Frank Act[19] of 2010 support these legal standards *and* require that directors and their corporations return to these fundamental principles to which they were formally subject already: individual integrity and responsibility in corporate governance; and, accountable and transparent disclosure of important financial and other information on which investors and the stability of the capital markets depend.[20]

The Court has long held that the board of directors is ultimately responsible for the management of the corporation,[21] although boards often delegate major decisions to corporate officers with more expertise and information on a particular subject. Under Delaware corporate law, officers are granted titles and duties through the corporation's bylaws or the board's resolutions and employees who are not granted this power are deemed agents.[22] Additionally, Delaware law dictates that the terms "officers" or "agents" are by no means interchangeable: officers are the corporation, but an agent is an employee and does not have the equivalent status of an officer.[23] Agents' specific duties include loyalty, performance, obedience, notification, and accounting.

Again, we see this distinction between officers as managers of the corporation and agents as employees as contrary to the historical and case law definitions espoused by two leading Chief Justices. It is noteworthy that agents as employees (and fiduciaries) are not required to act in a manner that ensures that organizational activities are conducted in good faith and with care for stakeholder's interests. Also noteworthy is the omission in corporate law of the duty of obedience (to obey the law), which appeared to occupy a recognized place in corporations through 1946 but eventually was eliminated. As recent courts have made clear that corporate actors cannot consciously violate, or permit the corporation to violate, corporate and noncorporate norms, even when it may be profitable for the corporation, this duty may be resurfacing.[24] The recent *Disney* decision specifically defines the current required triad of fiduciary duties.[25]

The Duty of Loyalty

"[T]he duty of loyalty mandates that the best interests of the corporation and its shareholders takes precedence over any interest possessed by a director, officer or controlling shareholder and . . . is not limited to cases involving a financial or other cognizable fiduciary conflict of interest. It also encompasses cases where the fiduciary fails to act in good faith."[26] The duty of loyalty is often described as a obligation of directors to protect the interests of the company and its stockholders, to refrain from decisions that would injure the company or deprive the company of profit or an advantage that might properly be brought to the company for it to pursue, and to act in a manner that he or she believes is in good faith to be in the best interests of the company and its stockholders.[27] Recent case law also adds that the duty of loyalty requires boards to act *affirmatively and in good faith.*[28]

The Duty of Care

The duty of care is defined as " . . . that amount of care which ordinarily careful and prudent men would use in similar circumstances."[29] Courts review the standard of care in directors' decision-making *process,* not the substance of decisions thus limiting director liability for failure in risky decisions. A breach of the duty of care may be found when a director is grossly negligent if the substance of the board's informed decision cannot be "attributed to any rational business purpose."[30] In response to the financial crisis, legislation has specifically addressed the need for increased risk assessment in our financial institutions, requiring increased disclosure to ensure that effective reporting systems are in place and that all relevant information has been evaluated to ensure financial and economic stability. The duty of care is often perceived as a minimal standard, but addressing the impact of risk could increase the importance of this standard.

The Duty to Act in Good Faith

In the *Disney* case, the court stated that "Good faith has been said to require an 'honesty of purpose,' and a genuine care for the fiduciary's constituents . . ."[31] A director acts in "subjective bad faith" when his actions are "motivated by an actual intent to do harm" to the corporation, and bad faith can take different forms with varying degrees of culpability.[32] The court clearly ruled that the duty of good faith cannot be satisfied if directors act in subjective bad faith, consciously disregard their duties, actually intend to harm the corporation, or cause the corporation to knowingly violated the law.[33]

Most legal scholars disagree as to the practical importance of the duty of good faith, but proponents of managerial accountability in corporate governance look to the doctrine of good faith because the traditional duties of care and loyalty do very little to discipline boards, even if allegations of self-dealing were made (i.e., violations of duty of loyalty).[34] The Disney decision was critical for corporate governance since the court recognized that conduct that benefits the corporation must be done with proper motives in order to satisfy the duty of good faith, thus making boards and senior managers more accountable for their decisions. Implicit in these recent cases is the assumption that new rules of "conduct" may be useful in restoring trust to a doubting public. To more fully understand these new rules of ethical conduct we must turn to the historical origins of fiduciary principles.

Origins of Fiduciary Principles
Biblical and Early History

If you would understand anything, observe its beginning and its development.

Aristotle, 4th Century BCE [35]

The historical definition of a "fiduciary" was stated in terms of "an essential code of conduct for those who have been entrusted to care for other peoples' property," carry out transactions, work for another, or aid persons who were vulnerable and dependent upon others.[36] The breadth and complexity of early trust relationships is implicit in today's corporate organizational structure and business relationships. As early as 1790 B.C., the Code of Hammurabi (a Babylonian code of laws) established rules of law governing business conduct, or fiduciary considerations, for the behavior of agents (employees) entrusted with property.[37] For example, a merchant's agent was required to keep receipts and to pay triple damages for failing to provide promised goods, although an exception was allowed if losses were due to enemy attack during a journey.[38] The insightful research of several scholars traces the religious roots of the fiduciary principle to the Old and New Testaments.[39] For example, the Lord told Moses that it is a sin not to restore that which is delivered unto a man to keep safely, and penalties must be paid for the violation,[40] (i.e., duties of loyalty and due care); the right to fair treatment in the marketplace,[41] implying a responsibility to conduct transactions in good faith; and the unjust steward who, expecting to be fired, curries favor with his master's debtors by allowing them to repay less than their full debts, illustrating the precept that one cannot serve two masters.[42] Additionally, the law on pledges obligates everyone to establish his own trustworthiness by carrying out the agreements he has made and by being sensitive to the needs of those who depend on him to meet their needs (i.e., loyalty of master to servant, employer to employee, seller to buyer, powerful to vulnerable).[43]

Fiduciary roles were likened to the roles of stewards in early religious and business history as well as in later corporate development. In this context, "Fiduciary law secularized a particular religious tradition and applied it to commercial pursuits," where the shepherd tending his flocks may be likened to a fiduciary (steward or employer) or an agent (servant or employee) tending the sheep for the owner of the flock.[44] The "steward," may be described as a moral agent or representative of "God," a corporate partner or stakeholder whose profits could be distributed by the steward to the poor at year's end.[45] Also, the King (as steward) was described as God's representative responsible for administering the covenant (agreements) for the people, and who must avoid preoccupation with the trappings of office while observing the law.[46] Thus, the king may be described as a model of godliness to the people by governing in a way that conforms to the requirements of the covenant.[47]

The increasing complexity in fiduciary relationships over time is equated to the increasing complexity in the relationship between man and God (as owner) in early biblical history. The relationships change as a function of the increase in the complexity of the duties demanded of the steward (manager of covenants). Similarly, the steward is the precursor to the modern professional fiduciary as well as to those corporate directors or officers who owe a duty of care to the owners (shareholders) of the corporation as well as a duty of loyalty to all stakeholders and to the larger society. Stewards, or fiduciaries, "hold offices with authority, power and privileges set by law or custom, separate from individual personalities, and such office demands moral duties in private conduct, requiring new decision-making habits and reflective capacities that transcend selfishness."[48] Similar to the descriptions of fiduciaries by Justices Cardozo and Brandeis, the description of stewards implies an inherent willingness to serve others (a moral duty), and a willingness to subordinate one's interests to that of others by acceptance of the duty to serve. Both in early law and today, the fiduciary, or steward, is evaluated and compensated for his performance and understands that failure to fulfill his duties will result in penalties. While today's corporations seldom attribute morality to a deity in fiduciary law, acceptance of fiduciary duties does require selflessness and a willingness to subordinate the fiduciary's interests to that of another. Aristotle, who lived from 384 B.C. to 322 B.C., influenced the development of fiduciary principles, recognizing that in economics and business, people must be bound by high obligations of loyalty, honesty and fairness, and that when such obligations aren't required or followed, society suffers.[49]

Fiduciaries in Ancient Law
Modern fiduciary law is traceable to developments in Ancient Roman law and early English law. Ancient Roman law defined fiduciary relationships as both moral and legal relationships of trust. For centuries until the end of the eighteenth century, Roman law refined and formalized fiduciary law, recognizing various "trust" (*fiducia*) contracts in which a person held property in safekeeping or otherwise acted on another's behalf (the core duties of loyalty and due care), and acted in good "faith" (*fides*) (core duties of honesty, full disclosure and applied diligence). Failure to uphold such trust could result in monetary penalties as well as a formal "infamy" (*infamia*), in which one lost rights to hold public office or to be a witness in a legal case.[50] These fiduciary relationships in early Roman law were later incorporated into British courts of equity and then into Anglo-American law, providing standards for modern corporate law.[51]

Early English law established the role of steward or agent with the granting of the Magna Carta, an English legal charter issued in 1215 which allowed the King to grant charters (companies) yet retain sovereignty (ownership) in the charter while recognizing the recipient's limited rights.[52] The King served as steward, with fiduciary rights (ownership) in the management of his property but was required to place the interests of his subjects (inferior rights) above his own—a fiduciary relationship. Increasing population growth caused the King to transfer his role as steward to town leaders, creating an early form of agency (master to servant). Scholars describe the king's stewardship duties as similar to the legal or fiduciary duties ascribed primarily to boards of directors and senior officers.[53] Town leaders were similar to "agents" or employees who owed duties to their "stewards" or employers (managers). The continued development of Charter companies and later private companies, during the era of industrialization and specialization in business of the 1700s–1800s, formalized the role of fiduciaries and their specific duties.

Early common law separated management from ownership (investors), creating the office of "manager" to protect the interests of investors and to prevent corporate self-dealing.[54] Subsequently, fiduciary duties were attached to such office, and stewardship duties were borrowed from early law and applied to positions of responsibility to promote financial goals. Thus, although a "fiduciary" is a term described by legal statute, case law or professional codes of conduct, this term also describes ethical obligations and duties in a wide variety of business and personal activities and encompasses a "legal or moral recognition of trust, reliance, or dependence and of responsibility often ignored." [55]

A Modest Proposal: New Rules of Fiduciary Conduct

Legal standards for management behavior can be traced to "deeply rooted moral standards" that shaped the "fiduciary principle, a principle of natural law incorporated into the Anglo-American legal tradition underlying the duties of good faith, loyalty and care that apply to corporate directors and officers."[56] Scholars examined early fiduciary history as a potential solution to understanding corporate misconduct, suggesting that revisiting those early fiduciary principles might answer the questions: To what standards should managers be held? What are the historical and conceptual bases for these standards?[57] Alternatively, if one assumes that fiduciaries are responsible to the company's shareholders as well as to a wider set of constituents, one might ask questions such as: In whose interests does the company presently function? In whose interests should it function in the future?[58] The latter set of questions not only asks who is served by the company, but also suggests that stakeholders bear some general rights as citizens, and should be protected against an abuse of power or violation that causes injury, as citizens.

If the role of a fiduciary is ascribed only to corporate boards and officers or to licensed professionals, corporate misconduct at other levels may go undetected. Despite this, corporate management argues that directors and officers are responsible only to shareholders, and that corporate management cannot serve two masters, that is multiple groups of stakeholders. To the contrary, history has demonstrated that fiduciary duties have been and can be the responsibility of all corporate members, and these duties may be extended to all stakeholders and the larger society. Research supports the theory that the corporation

should have one set of duties for multiple stakeholders, an argument made by managers in the 1990s that managers had the skills and independence to mediate fairly among the firm's stakeholders, and could assemble innovative teams capable of expanding wealth and economic opportunity.[59] Managers sustained this claim well into the 1990s, both within their firms and within their major business associations but by 1997 pressure from the global commodity and national financial markets persuaded managers to revise their stakeholder standard. The perception is that managers moved from a focus on a single duty of loyalty to shareholders, to a narrower focus on making their principals (shareholders) and themselves rich, while disassociating themselves from the ideal of widening economic opportunity and improving living standards for the many.[60] The Clarkson Principles, a set of principles for stakeholder management, are considered to be a critical academic effort to revive the idea that managers should be obligated to expand material opportunities for the many through economic growth.[61] Additionally, compliance with fiduciary duties can reduce the principal's costs of monitoring and disciplining agents and lessens the need for government regulation.[62]

Today, although most major corporations support the idea of corporate social responsibility (CSR), and believe that CSR and profit maximization work together, they continue to support the Freidman view that "The social responsibility of business is to increase its profits."[63] A top executive of a major oil company illustrates this view in the comment that "a socially responsible way or working is not . . . a distraction from our core business. Nor does it in any way conflict with our promise and our duty to deliver value to our shareholders."[64]

We propose that adherence to a *new understanding and rule* of fiduciary principles goes hand in hand with CSR and profit maximization and is perhaps the missing link in today's corporate governance. The essential definition of a fiduciary does not change—a fiduciary is a person who has a duty to act primarily for the benefit of another. However, the role of the fiduciary should extend to all corporate members, and the duties of the fiduciary should not differ regardless of the specific function or distinction in roles. The primary focus of all corporate members continues to be to the shareholders (owners of the corporation), but duties toward other stakeholders should be consistent with those duties to shareholders. Any differentiation lowers the high standard of fidelity required of fiduciaries. Thus, the duties of loyalty, good faith, due care and obedience to the law should be incorporated fully into all fiduciary relationships, regardless of role or function within the corporation.

Concluding Thoughts

"Many of the most shocking examples of corporate misbehaviors involve conduct that violates existing law."[65] This result occurs when most cost-benefit analysis weighs the potential harm and subsequent penalties against the potential profits, resulting in an ethical question often ignored because of the focus on maximizing shareholder profitability. Therefore, reform initiatives for boards of directors and corporate governance "without proper attention to ethical obligations will likely prove ineffectual."[66] Schwartz et al. found that board and officer leadership by example and action are roles central to the overall ethical and governance environment of their firms, a leadership role that is reinforced by board members' legal responsibilities to provide oversight of the financial performance of their firms—based on the assumption that ethical corporate leadership results in the best long-term interests of the firm.

Thus, Schwartz et al.'s study of corporate boards of directors demonstrated that boards have a professional duty expressed as a fiduciary duty to make ethics-based decisions. We contend that ethics and morals in line with fiduciary principles *must* permeate the entire corporate culture, if corporate governance reform is to succeed. A return to those central values inherent in ethical and fiduciary duties extended to the greater community as well as to shareholders may provide more socially responsible guidelines for corporations in this period of stakeholder demand for increased government regulation. Defining and providing examples of fiduciary values of honesty, loyalty, integrity responsibility, fairness, and citizenship can provide guidance for corporate fiduciary relationships with all stakeholders, and provide a more efficient voluntary control mechanism. Thus, we contend that consistent fiduciary principles should be implemented throughout the firm, regardless of the corporate member's function or role.[67] This view is consistent with Friedman's view, that a corporate executive is an employee of the owners of the business, owes responsibility to his employers to conduct the business in accordance with their desires, which generally will be to make as much money as possible while conforming to the basic rules of society, embodied both in law and ethical custom.[68]

Our review of the historical and religious origins of fiduciary relationships demonstrates that the concept of fiduciary was intended to be both a societal and a legal principle, and this is consistent with Friedman's view of obeying the law and social custom. The leaders of organizations, as stewards, were responsible to the whole organization, and to society, not just to themselves or shareholders. Perhaps a revitalization of the stewardship principle is part of the new perspective required to create sustainable competitive advantage in today's economy. We believe that there is room for stakeholder-focused management that does no harm to shareholder interests while also benefiting a larger constituency, *and* that fiduciary duties require the exercise of care, loyalty, obedience, and good faith with regard to shareholders as well as to all stakeholders and the larger community.[69]

References

1. See David Callahan, *The Cheating Culture: Why More Americans are Doing Wrong to Get Ahead* (Florida: Harcourt, Inc., 2004), 12.
2. See LaRue Tone Hosmer, *The Ethics of Management, 6th Ed.* (New York: McGraw-Hill, 2008).
3. Peter C. Kostant, *Meaningful Good Faith: Managerial Motives and the Duty to Obey the Law,* 55 N.Y.L.S.L. Rev., 421 (2010).
4. Alan R. Palmiter, *Duty of Obedience: The Forgotten Duty,* 55 N.Y.L.S.L. Rev., 457 (2010).
5. Restatement (Third) of Agency, 3rd Ed. §1(1). (2006), Restatement Third of Agency is a set of principles issues by the American Law Institute, frequently cited by judges as well as attorneys and scholars in making legal arguments.
6. Nancy Kubasek et al., *Dynamic Business Law* (New York: McGraw-Hill/Irwin, 2009), 856,857.
7. Tamar Frankel, *Fiduciary Law,* 71 Cal. L. Rev. 795, 797–802 (1983).
8. See Tamar Frankel, *Fiduciary Law,* 71 Cal. L. Rev., 801–802.
9. See note 8.
10. Deborah A. DeMott, "The First Restatement of Agency: What Was the Agenda?," 32 *S. Ill. U.L.J.,* (2007). Restatement (Second) of Agency, 1958, the American Law Institute, is now out of print and has been completely superseded and replaced by Restatement of the Law Third, Agency, 2006. However, some courts will continue to cite to The Restatement of the Law Second, Agency.
11. Deborah A. DeMott, "The First Restatement of Agency: What Was the Agenda?," 31.
12. Kenneth M. Rosen, *Meador Lecture Series 2005–2006: Fiduciaries,* 58 Ala. L. Rev., 1041 (2007).
13. Kenneth M. Rosen, *Meador Lecture Series 2005–2006: Fiduciaries,* citing *Meinhard v. Salmon,* 164 N.E. 545 (N.Y. 1928).
14. Kenneth M. Rosen, *Meador Lecture Series 2005–2006: Fiduciaries,* 1041.
15. See Kenneth M. Rosen, "*Meador Lecture Series 2005–2006: Fiduciaries.*"
16. *See In re* Walt Disney Co. Deriv. Litig., 907 A.2d 693, 753–57 (Del. Ch. 2005) (identifying possible duty of good faith), *aff'd,* 906 A.2d 693 (Del. 2006) (affirming the decision of the Chancellor).
17. Michael Follett, "Note: *Gantler V. Stephens:* Big Epiphany or Big Failure? A look at the current state of officers' fiduciary duties and advice for potential protection," *35 Del. J. Corp. L.,* 563 (2010).
18. Sarbanes-Oxley Act of 2002, PL 107–204, 116 Stat 745. Sarbanes-Oxley requires corporate officers to be responsible for earnings reports, prohibits accounting firms from acting as consultants to accounting clients (a conflict of interest) and increases penalties for fraud.
19. The Dodd-Frank Wall Street Reform and Consumer Protection Act, Pub.L. 111–203, H.R. 4173, (2010).

20. Kilpatrick Stockton LLP, *Directors Fiduciary Duties After Sarbanes-Oxley* (Atlanta: Kilpatrick Stockton LLP), 2003.

21. Delaware General Corporation Law section 141(a) provides that "[t]he business and affairs of every corporation organized under this chapter shall be managed by or under the direction of a board of directors, except as may be otherwise provided in this chapter or in its certificate of incorporation." DEL. CODE ANN. Tit. 8, § 141(a)(2006).

22. See Michael Follett, note 57.

23. Michael Follett, note 57.

24. Alan R. Palmiter, citing *Stone v. Ritter,* 911 A.2d 362, 364–65 (Del. 2006), *Graham V. Allis-Chalmers Mfg. Co.,* 188 A.2d 125, 130 (Del. 1963), and *Caremark Int'l Inc. Deriv. Litig.,* 698 A.2d 959, 971 (Del. Ch. 1996), where directors breached the duty of care for "sustained or systematic failure" to assure existence of reporting systems that identify illegal corporate conduct, for example, medical referral kickbacks, 459.

25. *In re* Walt Disney Co. Deriv. Litig., 907 A.2d 693, 753 (Del. Ch. 2005), aff'd. 906 A.2d 27 (Del. 2006).

26. Thomas A. Uebler, "Shareholder Police Power: Shareholders' Ability to Hold Directors Accountable for Intentional Violations of Law," 33 Del. J. Corp. L., 199 (2008).

27. Thomas A. Uebler, "Shareholder Police Power: Shareholders' Ability to Hold Directors Accountable for Intentional Violations of Law," 201.

28. See Thomas A. Uebler.

29. *In re* Walt Disney Co. Deriv. Litig., 907 A.2d 693, 753–57 (Del. Ch. 2005), *aff'd,* 906 A.2d 693 (Del. 2006) .

30. *In re* Walt Disney Co. Deriv. Litig., 907 A.2d 693, 753 (Del. Ch. 2005), aff'd. 906 A.2d 27 (Del. 2006)), quoting *Sinclair Oil Corp. v. Levien,* 280 A.2d 717, 720 (Del. 1971), and *Smith v. Van Gorkom,* 488 A.2d 858, 873 (Del. 1985),

31. *In re* Walt Disney.

32. *In re* Walt Disney, at 55.

33. Peter C. Kostant , "Meaningful Good Faith: Managerial Motives and the Duty to Obey the Law," 424,426.

34. See Peter C. Kostant, 426–427.

35. Amanda H. Podany, "Why Study History? A View from the Past," Presented at The History Summit I, California State University Dominguez Hills, May 29, 2008.

36. See Kenneth Silber, "Fiduciary Matters," www.AdvisorOne.com/article/fiduciarymatters, June 28, 2011.

37. Joseph F. Johnston, Jr., "Natural Law and the Fiduciary Duties of Managers," *Journal of Markets & Morality* (2005), 8:27–51.

38. Kenneth Silber, "Fiduciary Matters."

39. See Brian P. Schaefer, "Shareholders Social Responsibility," *Journal of Business Ethics* (2008), 81:297–312; and Stephen B. Young, "Fiduciary Duties as a Helpful Guide to Ethical Decision-Making in Business," *Journal of Business Ethics* (2007), 74:1–15.

40. John H. Walton, Deuteronomy: An Exposition of the Spirit of the Law, *Grace Theological Journal* 8, 2(1987), 213–25, quoting Leviticus 6:2–5.

41. See John H. Walton, quoting Deuteronomy 25:13–16.

42. John H. Walton notes that the precept that one cannot serve two masters in Luke 16:1–13 was later cited by scholar Austin Scott in an influential 1949 paper "The Fiduciary Principle," which describes boards' and officers' responsibility to shareholders and not to other constituents.

43. John H. Walton, "Deuteronomy: An Exposition of the Spirit of the Law," quoting Deuteronomy 24:14–15.

44. See Stephen B. Young, "Fiduciary Duties as a Helpful Guide to Ethical Decision-Making in Business."

45. Sarah Key, "Toward a New Theory of the Firm: A Critique of Stakeholder 'Theory'," *Management Decision* (1999), 37:317–328.

46. John H. Walton, quoting Deuteronomy 17:14–20, 216.

47. Stephen B. Young details the link between fiduciary and ethical duties in the four covenants, or agreements, between God and man in the Old Testament that establishes and expands man's duties of care. These covenants allow stewards to impose ethical duties on those who obey them (i.e., agents or employees) and reflect the core of modern agency and fiduciary relationships: (1) The first covenant establishes Noah as steward of God's will to care for creation, and if Noah and his descendents take good care of creation it would not be destroyed (duty of care for the owner's property); (2) The second covenant requires Abraham to accept the duty to behave according to a code of holy behavior in return for protection (protection from liability for accepting the responsibilities of duty of loyalty and care); (3) The third covenant requires the children of Israel to behave morally with religious devotion in return for protection of all of society (extending fiduciary duties of loyalty and care from an individual to society, i.e., to all stakeholders); and (4) The fourth covenant expanded these promises–if the conduct of all mankind is ethical and moral and not based on material temptations, Jesus will protect them on earth and grant them entry into heaven (fiduciary duties are deeply rooted in moral principles).

48. See Stephen B. Young and Joseph F. Johnston, Jr.

49. John H. Walton, "Deuteronomy: An Exposition of the Spirit of the Law."

50. See Kenneth Silber, "Fiduciary Matters."

51. See Kenneth M. Rosen, *Meador Lecture Series 2005–2006: Fiduciaries.*

52. See Stephen B. Young, "Fiduciary Duties as a Helpful Guide to Ethical Decision-Making in Business."

53. See Kenneth M. Rosen, "Meador Lecture Series 2005–2006: Fiduciaries."

54. Richard Marens and Andrew Wicks, "Getting Real: Stakeholder Theory, Managerial Practice, and the General Irrelevance of Fiduciary Duties Owed to Shareholders," *Business Ethics Quarterly* (1999), 273–293.

55. Sarah W. Holtman, "Fiduciary Relationships," in The Encyclopedia of Ethics, 2nd Ed, eds. Lawrence C. Becker and Charlotte B. Becker (NY: Routledge, 2001), 545–49.

56. See Joseph F. Johnston, Jr., "Natural Law and the Fiduciary Duties of Business Managers."

57. See Joseph F. Johnston, Jr. "Natural Law and the Fiduciary Duties of Business Managers."

58. Sheldon Leader, "Participation and Property Rights," *Journal of Business Ethics* 21:97–109, (1999), 98–99.

59. Allan Kaufman, "Managers' Double Fiduciary Duty," *Business Ethics Quarterly* 12:189–214 (2002), 189.

Fiduciary Principles: Corporate Responsibilities to Stakeholders by Susan C. Atherton, Mark S. Blodgett, and Charles A. Atherton

47

60. Allan Kaufman, "Managers' Double Fiduciary Duty," 190.

61. Allan Kaufman, "Managers' Double Fiduciary Duty," 190–193.

62. Kaufman, "Managers' Double Fiduciary Duty."

63. See Peter C. Kolstad, 137–138, citing Milton Friedman, "The Social Responsibility of Business is to Increase Its Profits," The New York Times Magazine (New York: 1970).

64. See Allan Kaufman, 192.

65. See David Callahan, "The Cheating Culture: Why More Americans are Doing Wrong to Get Ahead."

66. Mark S. Schwartz et al., "Tone at the Top: An Ethics Code for Directors?," *Journal of Business Ethics* (2005), 58:79–100.

67. R. Edward Freeman, in "The Politics of Stakeholder Theory: Some Future Directors," *Business Ethics Quarterly* (1994) 4:409–421, suggested that "multi-fiduciary stakeholder analysis is simply incompatible with widely-held moral convictions about the special fiduciary obligations owed by management to stockholders. At the center of the objections is the belief that the obligations of agents to principals are stronger or different in kind from those of agents to third parties." This view is not supported by historical development of the fiduciary principle, and may be perceived more as a function of corporate management choosing those functions that support personal, not fiduciary, goals.

68. See Milton Friedman, 51.

69. Bradley R. Agle and Ronald K. Mitchell, "Introduction: Recent Research and New Questions," in Agle et al., "Dialogue: Toward Superior Stakeholder Theory," *Business Ethics Quarterly* (2008), 18:153–190.

Critical Thinking

1. Describe the fiduciary duties of officers and directors? of managers? of employees?

2. What safeguards should be employed to assure the fulfillment of the above fiduciary duties?

3. What ethical principles undergird fiduciary principles?

Internet References

Business for Social Responsibility
http://www.bsr.org/reports/BSR_AW_Corporate-Boards.pdf

Forbes
http://www.forbes.com/sites/csr/2010/10/28/friend-or-foe-fiduciary-duties-meet-sociallyresponsible-investments/

United States Department of Labor
http://www.dol.gov/ebsa/publications/fiduciaryresponsibility.html

Article

Prepared by: Eric Teoro, *Lincoln Christian University*

The Four Principles of 'Conscious Capitalism'

R. MICHAEL ANDERSON

Learning Outcomes

After reading this article, you will be able to:

- Recognize that doing business the "right way" is not incompatible with being profitable.
- Describe the four principles of Conscious Capitalism.

If you had a chance to implement a system that would bring in 10 times more profit than similar firms in your market, would your first thought be about what you'd have to give up to do so? What part of your soul you'd have to sell?

The truth is that by doing business the right way—being truly authentic, sticking wholeheartedly to your ethics and morals, and caring more about your customers and employees than your shareholders—you can achieve that gain *without* losing your soul.

Conscious Capitalism is the system that lets you do this. I know, because we launched Conscious Capitalism San Diego last week (disclosure: I'm president of the board of directors). As the 20th local chapter worldwide, the results are clear: Conscious Capitalism companies don't only outperform the market by 10.5 times, they even outperformed the Good to Great companies such as Fannie Mae and Walgreens by 300 percent—by doing business the "right way."

Imagine that: you don't have to give anything up to become a market leader.

In fact, you can be the good guy.

There are four principles of Conscious Capitalism.

1. Conscious leadership

Organizations mirror the actions and personality of the individual at the top. This is the kind of person people want to follow. The authentic, open person. Conscious Leaders are the ones who inspire loyalty and consistent high performance in their teams.

2. Stakeholder orientation

Conscious leaders know the importance of taking into account *all* of their stakeholders. You're never going to become a premium brand by only focusing on the shareholders. The really important factors for long-term business success are the employees and customers, and often the vendors and community as well. Take care of them and they will take care of you.

3. Conscious culture

A values-based culture is one that is intentional about how people act and perform. When a culture is not defined and enforced, your people aren't all moving in the same direction.

For example, Greg Koch, the CEO of Stone Brewing Co. and one of the speakers at our inaugural event, talked about how he would rather leave a key position unfilled than bring in someone not 100 percent aligned with his firm's values and mission. He explained that not having that position filled hurt, but it was better than the alternative. Stone Brewing Co. is now one of the top micro-brewing house[s] in the U.S.—it's even expanding into Germany.

4. Higher purpose

Finally, the company should be in business to do more than just make money. Great leaders realize that in order to become successful over the long term, you must provide true value. That comes from passionate people getting inspired about their work. How inspiring is your company's purpose? For example, would you want to work for a company whose mission it is to "deliver maximum value to the shareholders"?

I wouldn't either.

Coach John Wooden famously never talked about winning. He talked about doing your best. And you know what? He won. More than anyone.

That's what we're talking about with Conscious Capitalism. Quit trying to play someone else's game. Be true to yourself, your customers, your employees. And you will be rewarded.

Those who chase the almighty dollar never find it.

Andrew Hewitt of Game Changers 500, another speaker at the launch, puts it in perspective: "A 2013 Cone Communications-Echo study found that only 20 percent of brands worldwide are seen to meaningfully and positively impact people's lives, yet 91 percent of global consumers would switch brands if a different brand of similar price and quality supported a good cause."

"With this huge gap between societal values and corporate values it's no wonder that purpose-driven organizations are far outperforming the pack. Doing good has become good business, not only because of changing consumer values but also because good companies are attracting the top talent, particularly millennials who are estimated to make up 75 percent of the global workforce by 2025."

The fact is, many business leaders are already living these principles without even knowing it. If you're one of them, now you know you're not alone.

It isn't just the "right" thing to do.

It's also the *profitable* thing to do.

Critical Thinking

1. What does it take to become a conscious leader?

2. What values would characterize a conscious corporate culture?

3. Choose five companies in five different industries. Write higher purpose statements for each company.

Internet References

Bloomberg Business

http://www.bloomberg.com/news/articles/2015-02-19/container-store-conscious-capitalism-and-the-perils-of-going-public

Fast Company

http://www.fastcompany.com/3031509/the-future-of-work/5-myths-about-the-freshest-iteration-of-capitalism

Forbes

http://www.forbes.com/sites/danschawbel/2013/01/15/john-mackey-why-companies-should-embrace-conscious-capitalism/

Article

Prepared by: Eric Teoro, *Lincoln Christian University*

Doing More Good

Here are several ways your company can become a better corporate citizen.

JODI CHAVEZ

Learning Outcomes

After reading this article, you will be able to:

- Describe the business benefits of good corporate citizenship.
- Describe steps for implementing corporate social responsibility.

Today's challenging economic climate has forced many organizations to reduce spending, release workers, and raise fees to consumers. The result is that businesses of all shapes and sizes are being painted in an unfavorable light, inviting criticism from the public and politicians alike.

But the picture being painted—that of a business culture that abandons the public in pursuit of profits—isn't an accurate one. The most effective counter to this depiction is the rise of corporate responsibility initiatives.

The Committee Encouraging Corporate Philanthropy (CECP), an international forum of business leaders focused on measuring and encouraging corporate philanthropy, recently released its *Giving in Numbers* report for 2011. In the report, the CECP noted that one out of every two businesses had actually increased the amount of funds contributed to charity or community organizations since the onset of the recession in 2007. As a matter of fact, a quarter of companies reported increasing their giving by more than 25 percent. Furthermore, the CECP tracked aggregate total contributions for 110 high-performing companies in 2007–2010 and found that aggregate total giving rose by 23 percent.

Clearly, many successful businesses are actually augmenting their contributions to society and taking the challenge of good corporate citizenship seriously. But why? Of course, the ability to "do more good" for more people carries intrinsic value and tremendous appeal. Yet there are other significant business benefits that arise out of doing more good.

Here we'll explore some of these benefits, and I'll offer practical ways you can begin to make a difference in your company and, ultimately, society.

The Business Case for Being Charitable

The rise of corporate responsibility and citizenship has been two decades in the making. As detailed in "Responsibility: The New Business Imperative," published in the May 2002 issue of *The Academy of Management Executive,* during the 1990s: "Numerous exposés of labor practices in global supply chains pressured multinational brands and retailers to adopt corporate codes of conduct. Later in the decade, pressure—and expectations—increased further, driving firms not only to introduce codes but also to ensure compliance with these codes by their suppliers." Finally, the fall of businesses like Enron and the recent financial collapse and mortgage crisis forced businesses to reexamine their "anything goes" approach to profitability.

All these are crucial steps in the evolution of corporate responsibility. But today the most important driver of corporate responsibility is the belief that good citizenship makes good business sense.

There are several ways it can give you a competitive advantage.

Building a reputation: Companies large and small impact the neighborhoods, cities, and countries they do business in. By aligning your goals with the goals of the community in which you operate, you're more likely to build a mutually beneficial relationship with potential stakeholders, including employees, customers, investors, suppliers, and business partners.

Setting your company apart: Like an innovative product or a new service offering, a strong record of corporate responsibility is a competitive advantage that you can leverage against others in your industry.

Attracting investment: Businesses with strong records of corporate responsibility generate more interest from investors when compared with apathetic competitors. In a study titled "Institutional and Social Investors Find Common Ground," originally published in the *Journal of Investing* and later cited in the comprehensive article "The Business Case for Corporate Social Responsibility" in the *International Journal of Management Review,* author Timothy Smith lays out why this is the case. "Many institutional investors 'avoid' companies or industries that violate their organizational mission, values, or principles . . . [They also] seek companies with good records on employee relations, environmental stewardship, community involvement, and corporate governance."

Reducing costs and risks: Companies that make a concerted effort to contribute to and advance society are more likely to avoid potential penalties or exposure to legal fines and government intervention. This is especially important in a climate of increased regulation and scrutiny. A strong record of corporate citizenship can also help you avoid harm to your reputation and sales that may arise without notice.

Attracting better talent: Great people want to work for great companies. By demonstrating your strong commitment to teamwork, responsibility, community, etc., you can attract employees who share those same values. Furthermore, now may be the opportune time to start reevaluating your corporate responsibility profile so you can connect with future leaders. Research indicates that the Millennial generation, currently entering the workforce in record numbers, is particularly civic minded. Members of this generation want more from their job than just a paycheck—they want an opportunity to make a difference. Why not give it to them and give yourself an edge in the process?

Increasing motivation and retention: In addition to attracting new talent, a demonstrated commitment to corporate responsibility can enhance engagement across your current workforce. It can also help you identify leaders who want to spearhead these important initiatives. This can help you reduce the expenses inherent in high turnover, including recruiting, training, and onboarding, and eliminate productivity gaps that occur when an employee leaves your company.

The Millennial generation wants more from their job than just a paycheck—they want an opportunity to make a difference.

Fostering innovation: By looking beyond the walls of your buildings and understanding the wider impact of your business, you can open your eyes to new opportunities and new avenues for growth. A primary example of this is Xerox, which has shown a continued commitment to sustainability and citizenship in designing "waste free" products and investing in "waste free" facilities. This commitment has led to the development of new products that appeal to corporations, fuel profitability, and set Xerox apart in the marketplace. Toyota is another example of a company that recognized the impact of its business—vehicle emissions—and built a profitable solution to the problem in the form of the popular Prius hybrid. Though other auto manufacturers have followed suit, the development of the Prius and its status as the first commercially viable hybrid gave Toyota a competitive advantage and a leg up on the competition. No matter what product or service you offer, a new perspective gleaned from a commitment to corporate responsibility can help you do the same.

Putting Responsibility into Action

Today, corporate responsibility encompasses many forms, including education about social issues and advancement of different cultures (social responsibility), ensuring the health of the environment (sustainability), and donating funds or time to charitable causes (philanthropy). Corporate responsibility is also concerned with the health and safety of the workforce and providing good working conditions for employees.

With corporate responsibility taking on so many facets, it may be difficult to determine how your company can begin making an impact. The International Institute for Sustainable Development (IISD) recently published *Corporate Social Responsibility: An Implementation Guide for Business* to help companies adapt and facilitate corporate social responsibility. Here is their recommended framework for implementation.

Conduct a corporate social responsibility (CSR) assessment: Gather and examine relevant information about your products, services, decision-making processes, and activities to determine your current CSR activity. An effective assessment should give you an accurate understanding of your values and ethics, the CSR issues that are affecting your business now or in the future, key stakeholders, and your leadership's ability to deliver a more effective CSR approach.

Develop a CSR strategy: Using your assessment as a starting point, begin to determine your objectives. Develop a realistic strategy that can help you reach your goals. The IISD recommends these five steps to developing an effective strategy:

- Build support with the CEO, senior management, and employees.
- Research what others (including competitors) are doing.
- Prepare a matrix of proposed CSR actions.
- Develop options for proceeding and the business case for them.
- Decide on direction, approach, boundaries, and focus areas.

***Develop commitments*:** Create a task force to review your objectives and finalize your strategy. The task force should solicit input from key stakeholders—the CEO, department heads, top management, etc.—to gauge their interest and ensure future participation. Using this feedback, prepare a preliminary draft of your CSR commitment, and review this again with those employees who will be affected or who can help effect change. At this point, you can revise and publish your commitments for your internal audience, customers, investors, and potential employees.

***Implement CSR commitments*:** This is the phase where your planning begins to give way to reality. Though each company should approach this critical step in accordance with its unique values and culture, the IISD offers these universal best practices:

- Prepare a CSR business plan.
- Set measurable targets, and identify performance measures.
- Engage employees and others to whom CSR commitments apply.
- Design and conduct CSR training.
- Establish mechanisms for addressing resistance.
- Create internal and external communications plans.
- Make commitments public.

***Document progress*:** It's imperative that you're able to communicate the impact of your efforts to internal and external stakeholders. Reporting tools provide insight into the costs of your initiatives as well as the hard and soft benefits derived from your corporate responsibility program.

Reporting on responsibility initiatives has actually given rise to an entirely new financial model called social accounting. Social accounting is the process of measuring, monitoring, and reporting to stakeholders the social and environmental effects of an organization's actions. Social accounting is conducted by accountants who employ the same tools and knowledge used in traditional financial reporting. Though many larger organizations utilize social accounting, all businesses can benefit from being able to demonstrate the true value of their actions.

In fact, robust social accounting and responsibility reporting is fast becoming the standard for businesses, not the exception. KPMG conducted an *International Survey of Corporate Responsibility Reporting 2011* to review trends of 3,400 companies worldwide, including the top 250 global companies (the G250). The survey indicated that corporate responsibility reporting is undertaken by 95 percent of the G250 and 64 percent of the 100 largest companies across the 34 countries surveyed.

"[Corporate responsibility] has moved from being a moral imperative to a critical business imperative. The time has now come to enhance [corporate responsibility] reporting information systems to bring them up to the level that is equal to financial reporting, including a comparable quality of governance controls and management," said Wim Bartels, global head of KPMG's Sustainability Assurance.

***Evaluate and improve*:** Using the reports and metrics generated, continue to refine your corporate responsibility initiatives. This is critical. Evaluate your performance objectively, identify opportunities for improvement, and engage key stakeholders to plot a course for the future.

The reality of today's economic, political, and social climate necessitates that business leaders rise above their bottom lines and look to make an impact outside their organization. Doing so presents an opportunity to elevate others while elevating your organization.

Critical Thinking

1. If a company focuses on the business benefits of good corporate citizenship, is it, in fact, being a good corporate citizen? Why or why not?

2. Describe a company that you believe is a good corporate citizen. Justify your belief.

3. What steps can you take as an employee to promote good corporate citizenship?

Internet References

CSRwire
http://www.csrwire.com/pdf/JustGoodBusinessCSRwireExcerpt.pdf

Forbes
http://www.forbes.com/sites/richardlevick/2012/01/11/corporate-social-responsibility-for-profit/

Journal of Economics, Business, and Management
http://www.joebm.com/index.php?m=content&c=index&a=show&catid=43&id=535

Jodi Chavez is senior vice president of Accounting Principals.

Article   Prepared by: Eric Teoro, *Lincoln Christian University*

Exploring a New Agenda for Corporate Sustainability

GAEL O'BRIEN

Learning Outcomes

After reading this article, you will be able to:

- Understand the difference between incorporating sustainability into business strategies and making sustainability a foundational aspect of business strategy from the outset.

- Understand the role of futures thinking in sustainability efforts.

- Understand the role of CEOs in sustainability efforts.

For hundreds of CEOs, 2017 galvanized their speaking out when changes in public policy ran counter to company values on diversity, social issues, or how to address climate change. However, the role of business in society isn't on every CEO or Board agenda, nor is sustainability routinely considered a cornerstone in business strategy.

Nevertheless, business as usual has been upended. We can count on uncertainty, change, and disruption continuing to affect business in 2018 and beyond requiring companies to reinvent themselves. Government's role in addressing social and environmental challenges is unclear. While short-term thinking hasn't loosened its grip, it is increasingly clear it offers no solutions to some of the key problems confronting business. So the question is, will companies (and leaders) in shoring themselves up to deal with rapid change recognize the increased importance of what sustainability offers?

Drawn to the conference title "How Business Leads," I attended the annual fall conference of Business for Social Responsibility (BSR), a nonprofit organization whose members include many of the largest businesses in the world—companies like Microsoft, Boeing, The Walt Disney Company,

MacDonald's, and Target—who were represented by nearly 1,000 of their sustainability officers, team members, and partners. I wanted to understand the global nonprofit's take on where sustainability leadership is heading.

The broad scope and complexity of the sustainability field was brought home when I needed to choose breakout sessions from among the 30 offered: topics ranged from the ethics of artificial intelligence to human trafficking and from products and climate resilience to discussion of the 21st-century social contract.

Celebrating BSR's 25th anniversary, CEO Aaron Cramer framed the conference by outlining the need to redefine sustainable business with a new agenda, approach, and advocacy going forward—themes elaborated on in a subsequent report, "The Future of Sustainable Business: New Agenda, New Approach, New Advocacy."

My takeaways from the conference included: (1) redefining sustainable business takes continuous improvement to the next level to increase relevance, impact, value, and collaboration; (2) if the right players are involved, the collaboration involved in "futures thinking" (a process to map possible scenarios) puts sustainability and ethical considerations into business planning and strategy from the outset to benefit stakeholders; and (3) the new advocacy, modeled by hundreds of CEOs in 2017, happens authentically when CEOs grasp the value of their sustainability teams and operate out of a company's values, mission, and connection and commitment to stakeholders.

Redefining Sustainable Business

Cramer told BSR members that an unprecedented era of change and disruption was ushering in a new business environment and it was time to redefine sustainable business around the roadmap already established. "In the last five years," he said, "we've had the Paris Agreement, Sustainable Development Goals, and the UN Guiding Principles on Business and Human Rights." We have a roadmap, he continued, "and it is universally accepted that business is central to that."

He indicated the *new agenda* is being driven by areas where sustainability and business have converged and new topics emerged (such as climate resilience, new technology, and its ethical implications and automation affecting work). The *new approach* he indicated would change an operating assumption and evolve the role of chief sustainability officers. Rather than integrating sustainability into regular business strategy, he said, smart companies have sustainability as a foundation from the beginning. "We're seeing companies look at questions related to climate, social acceptance of new technologies, and that enable economic vitality and security as the building blocks of success." The *new advocacy*, he explained, is a need for a new voice for business which many CEOs already demonstrated in responding to 2017 issues.

The BSR report indicates that over the next year, the organization will be engaging with member companies "on what is changing—and what needs to change—to achieve a just and sustainable world" and asking a series of questions that will help advance relevance, value, and collaboration.

Futures Thinking

I participated in the breakout session "Redefining Sustainable Business: A Futures-Thinking Design Sprint" with a group of CSR executives who worked on a futures proposition Marks and Spencer the multinational British retailer, raised for our input. The exercise gave us exposure to "Futures Thinking" tools and how they can help companies deal effectively with rapid change, uncertainty, and complexity. The purpose is to be able to spot early signs of change and identify multiple possible future outcomes to explore. Forecasts aren't reliable. Our 20-minute maiden exercise didn't help Marks and Spencer, but the experience reinforced for me how greatly companies would benefit from very diverse teams that include both sustainability and ethics officers when business strategies, decisions, or "Futures Thinking" are addressed with marketing, finance, and other key areas.

Both the sustainability and ethics functions within organizations have multidimensional ways of seeing and relating to stakeholders, unintended consequences, and potential ways of making authentic connections. In line with this, one of the BSR report's questions for member discussion in BSR's

process of redefining sustainable business in 2018 is: "How can sustainability teams use their core competencies and networks to help their companies anticipate and address new issues that will be created by rapid changes in the global climate, technology, and the role of business?"

The New Advocacy

The CEOs who've been the most effective speaking out against racism and on behalf of diversity, fairness, human rights, climate change, gender equity, and other issues are those whose corporate policies reflect and reinforce the behaviors and actions that give weight to their words. These issues, rather than separate from business, are interconnected; business isn't an inanimate entity—it is inextricably connected to people—those who create, make, deliver, buy, and use products and services. Issues of sustainability, acknowledged or not, are at the heart of every stage of the process.

We badly need champions like those CEOs who use their voices for principles not politics. In a recent Harvard Business Review article, "The New CEO Activists," which offers a playbook, business school professors Aaron K. Chatterji and Michael W. Toffel write: "As more and more business leaders choose to speak out on contentious political and social matters, CEOs will increasingly be called on to help shape the debate of those issues." Employees and customers deserve this kind of leadership as do the communities in which the companies operate. Granted, these are difficult issues and mistakes happen. And leaders make choices about how mistakes are addressed; the degree to which they actively support and reinforce a company's culture; and the degree to which they fuel their potential leadership by using sustainability and ethics teams as a critical resource in dealing with the business landscape.

In the reinvention that is an inherent part of change, exploring what would have to happen to have sustainability as a foundation for business strategy would be a great start.

Critical Thinking

1. Choose an industry. What forms of sustainable activity should companies in that industry engage in? What are the boundaries or limits of such engagement?

2. What sustainability activities can you engage in as an individual? Do you have the responsibility to engage in such activities? Why or why not?

Internet References

Forbes

https://www.forbes.com/sites/stevebanker/2018/05/08/balancing-green-a-practical-guide-to-corporate-sustainability/#1a484fc432cc

Harvard Business Review

https://hbr.org/ideacast/2018/03/mckinseys-head-on-why-corporate-sustainability-efforts-are-falling-short.html

Ivey Business Journal

https://iveybusinessjournal.com/publication/corporate-sustainability-what-is-it-and-where-does-it-come-from/

World Business Council for Sustainable Development

http://wbcsdpublications.org/a-guide-to-futures-thinking/

GAEL O'BRIEN, a Business Ethics Magazine columnist, is an executive coach and presenter focused on building leadership, trust, and reputation. She publishes *The Week in Ethics* and is a Kallman Executive Fellow, Hoffman Center for Business Ethics, Bentley University.

Article   Prepared by: Eric Teoro, *Lincoln Christian University*

Are Business Ethics Missing from Corporate Social Responsibility?

Shahar Silbershatz

Learning Outcomes

After reading this article, you will be able to:

- Understand the three main pillars of corporate social responsibility.

- Understand the difference between integrity and responsibility, and how to incorporate integrity into corporate social responsibility programs.

The notion of Corporate Social Responsibility (CSR) has been around for decades—arguably since as far back as 1953 when Howard Bowen published his book "Social responsibilities of the businessman."

The controversy surrounding this notion has raged for just as long, in its essence pitting Milton Friedman against Edward Freeman—the former claiming that a business's sole responsibility is to create value for its shareholders, while the latter contending that the responsibility for value creation exists toward all stakeholders.

With the investment community increasingly embracing Socially Responsible Investment criteria in recent years, it's becoming clear that Freeman's argument is gaining the upper hand. What's less clear is whether business ethics enthusiasts should cheer this development.

There can be no doubt that from a moral perspective, CSR has been an enormously positive trend: companies today are dramatically more considerate of the societies and communities around them, and of their environmental impact than they've ever been. But that does not necessarily make them more ethical.

Business Ethics and Corporate Social Responsibility Explained

One way of looking at CSR is through the ESG lens, reflecting the Environmental, Social, and Governance criteria used by the investment community to measure a company's sustainability.

According to that approach, there are three main pillars that make up a company's moral responsibility (or in other words, the responsibilities it has beyond its economic and legal ones):

1. **Environment:** Also known as Planet from the triple-bottom-line (TBL) model of People, Planet, Profit, this covers the most often talked-about elements of a company's CSR and sustainability profile as it relates to its impact on the environment: CO_2 emissions, pollution, waste, energy effectiveness, renewability, recyclability, water intensity, circular economy, and so on.

2. **Social:** From the good old corporate philanthropy (think reducing poverty in Africa or sponsoring the local football team) all the way to the more up-to-date corporate efforts around human rights, diversity, community involvement, employee wellbeing, animal welfare, and so on. This component can also be seen as People in the above-mentioned TBL model.

3. **Governance:** This third element differs from the previous two in that it does not describe specific activities or strategies. It rather describes the way the company structures itself, manages its decisions, and in general—how it behaves.

This ranges from "hard" principles of corporate governance like transparency, disclosure, accountability, control, and so on—to the "softer" principles around fairness, ethics, and integrity (that are mostly aimed at preventing negative phenomena such as corruption).

The imbalance mentioned above between these three pillars—where the first two are action-oriented and the third one is behavior-oriented—does not end there; it is also reflected in the way these pillars have developed in recent years.

While the first two have gradually become more proactively managed and incorporated in strategy, the third one is still mostly managed defensively and is rarely seen as part of a company's strategy, positioning, or point of differentiation. And herein lies the problem.

As environmental and social strategies are starting to be seen by executive management teams and boards of directors as part of the company's value creation, they are becoming a higher priority and relevant to the entire organization. Yet, as long as corporate governance remains a defensive "tick-box exercise," it will not be seen as creating business value. Therefore, it will remain the exclusive domain of compliance and legal teams—rather than become incorporated in the company's operations.

Business Ethics and Integrity as Part of Corporate Social Responsibility Strategies

Some may ask whether it is at all possible for topics like ethics and integrity to become part of a company's strategy and value creation. In my opinion, it most certainly is. And while there is no easy formula for that, there are several basic principles companies and leaders should follow to make that happen:

Shift Focus from Responsibility to Integrity

It may be seen as semantics by some, but while responsibility is intuitively connected to duties and expectations from others, integrity suggests an internal moral code.

While the former is a formal role-based construct driven by legislation, the latter is a behavioral people-based construct that is driven by culture. As such, it applies to both intentions and actions, and creates a more direct link between the company and the individuals that comprise it; after all, the behavior of the company is the sum of the behaviors of its individuals.

IBM, for example, bases its CSR ideology on personal rather than corporate responsibility (being one of its three values). Similarly, Unilever places integrity at the heart of its corporate responsibility commitments.

Another good example is Siemens—while it was forced to so following its corruption scandal in 2006, its $100 million Integrity Initiative and other integrity-related practices have since become a role model approach.

Be Purpose-led

Purpose is becoming somewhat of a buzzword. Yet, the notion that a company needs to be driven by an idea that is bigger and higher than a commercial goal is not new.

When companies are truly committed to such an idea, they can more easily and effectively shape their actions and behavior in a coordinated way. This way, "doing good" and "making money" don't become two disconnected forces pulling the company and its ethics in opposite directions.

Companies like Unilever, Whole Foods, Patagonia, CVS, REI, Zappos.com, The Body Shop, Toms, Etsy, Novo Nordisk, and countless others have been vigorously demonstrating in recent years, how and why it pays to be purpose-driven (in dollars, not just brownie points).

Lead by Example

In any hierarchical organization, leaders act as role models, and companies are no different.

When leaders and managers practice and demonstrate ethical behavior and when they reward such behavior among others (and punish its absence), an ethical culture will emerge. This is so much more important than having an exemplary code of ethics and conduct. While many companies have such a code, they also demonstrate work practices that turn out to be highly unethical.

Building a culture of integrity top-down requires tools like leadership development, training, award and recognition programs, and the incorporation of integrity as a key criterion in performance evaluation and KPIs.

Another way to get leaders to role model integrity is by involving the board of directors and making it the ultimate guardian. Not just of the company's performance, but of its character too. Companies like UBS, Citigroup, and Centrica are showing the way by having dedicated board committees dealing specifically with culture and ethics.

Summing Up Integrity and Corporate Social Responsibility

In simple words, the above-mentioned principles aim to build a culture of integrity that permeates the company's DNA and becomes part of the way it creates value.

Whether you subscribe to Friedman's or Freeman's views on the responsibility of corporations, you will surely agree that a case like Dieselgate—where Volkswagen was found to be cheating emissions tests of Diesel cars in the United States in 2015—shows how the failure of doing so by a CSR champion turned out to be highly irresponsible and led to substantial damage to both shareholders and stakeholders.

It's not the domain of CSR that is unethical—but the way it's being practiced by many companies today. If companies learn how to include the building of a genuine culture of integrity as part of practicing CSR, both society and investors will be the better for it.

Critical Thinking

1. Describe instances of companies adhering to and violating the three pillars of CSR.
2. Define integrity. What elements comprise integrity?
3. How can individuals and companies develop and incorporate integrity?

Internet References

Council for Corporate Responsibility
   http://uscorporateresponsibility.org/about/the-seven-pillars-of-corporate-responsibility/
Foreign Policy News
   http://foreignpolicynews.org/2016/04/18/ethics-foundation-corporate-social-responsibility/
International Center for Ethics, Justice and Public Life
   https://www.brandeis.edu/ethics/ethicalinquiry/2013/November.html

SHAHAR SILBERSHATZ, as CEO of Caliber, a Copenhagen-based brand and reputation consultancy, helps his clients build a strong and lasting corporate character by providing a mix of strategic consulting and stakeholder insight. He has an MBA from Columbia Business School and over 20 years of experience working at leading consultancies in New York, London, and Copenhagen, and advising some of the world's largest companies in the areas of marketing, communications, business strategy, and stakeholder relations.

Unit 3

UNIT

Prepared by: Eric Teoro, *Lincoln Christian University*

Building an Ethical Organization

Ethos can be defined as the fundamental character, spirit, or disposition of an individual, group, or culture. It informs, and is manifested in, one's beliefs, customs, aspirations, or practices. For business ethics ultimately to be meaningful, it must transcend momentary reactions or responses to ethical scandals. For business ethics ultimately to be meaningful, it must become part of an organization's ethos. It should guide member behavior on a daily, ongoing basis. It should impact strategic decision-making and shape an organization's interactions with all stakeholders. Business ethics should start at the top of an organization and filter its way throughout every level. It is not a tactic to prevent legal action against an organization, though it might result in fewer lawsuits or governmental regulations and interventions. By its nature, business ethics should be proactive and normative, promoting the good for its own sake.

It is important, therefore, to understand how an organization can embed ethics into its corporate ethos. Leaders need to measure the success of their ethics and compliance programs, ensuring the programs inculcate the necessary values at every level of the organization. They need to recognize the ambiguity that surrounds many business decisions, equipping their employees to do the right thing. Leaders need to promote equity for, and expect honest from, all employees. Employees should be able to go to work free from harassment and bullying. Managers need to pay attention to character while hiring, and continually improve corporate training in terms of content and delivery.

Article   Prepared by: Eric Teoro, *Lincoln Christian University*

Creating an Ethical Culture

Values-based ethics programs can help employees judge right from wrong.

David Gebler, JD

Learning Outcomes

After reading this article, you will be able to:

- Describe the seven levels of corporate values and how they relate to each other.
- Develop a program for creating an ethical corporate culture.

While the fate of former Enron leaders Kenneth Lay and Jeffrey Skilling is being determined in what has been labeled the "Trial of the Century," former WorldCom managers are in jail for pulling off one of the largest frauds in history.

Yes, criminal activity definitely took place in these companies and in dozens more that have been in the news in recent years, but what's really important is to take stock of the nature of many of the perpetrators.

Some quotes from former WorldCom executives paint a different picture of corporate criminals than we came to know in other eras:

"I'm sorry for the hurt that has been caused by my cowardly behavior."
—*Scott Sullivan, CFO*

"Faced with a decision that required strong moral courage, I took the easy way out. . . . There are no words to describe my shame."
—*Buford Yates, director of general accounting*

"At the time I consider the single most critical character-defining moment of my life, I failed. It's something I'll take with me the rest of my life."
—*David Myers, controller*

These are the statements of good people gone bad. But probably most disturbing was the conviction of Betty Vinson, the senior manager in the accounting department who booked billions of dollars in false expenses. At her sentencing, US District Judge Barbara Jones noted that Vinson was among the lowest-ranking members of the conspiracy that led to the $11 billion fraud that sank the telecommunications company in 2002. Still, she said, "Had Ms. Vinson refused to do what she was asked, it's possible this conspiracy might have been nipped in the bud."

Judge Jones added that although Ms. Vinson "was among the least culpable members of the conspiracy" and acted under extreme pressure, "that does not excuse what she did."

Vinson said she improperly covered up expenses by drawing down reserve accounts—some completely unrelated to the expenses—and by moving expenses off income statements and listing them as assets on the balance sheet.

Also the company's former director of corporate reporting, Vinson testified at Bernie Ebbers's trial that, in choosing which accounts to alter, "I just really pulled some out of the air. I used some spreadsheets." She said she repeatedly brought her concerns to colleagues and supervisors, once describing the entries to a coworker as "just crazy." In spring 2002, she noted, she told one boss she would no longer make the entries. "I said that I thought the entries were just being made to make the income statement look like Scott wanted it to look."

Standing before the judge at her sentencing, Vinson said: "I never expected to be here, and I certainly won't do anything like this again." She was sentenced to 5 months in prison and 5 months of house arrest.

Pressure Reigns

While the judge correctly said that her lack of culpability didn't excuse her actions, we must carefully note that Betty

Vinson, as well as many of her codefendants, didn't start out as criminals seeking to defraud the organization. Under typical antifraud screening tools, she and others like her wouldn't have raised any red flags as being potential committers of corporate fraud.

Scott Sullivan was a powerful leader with a well-known reputation for integrity. If any of us were in Betty Vinson's shoes, could we say with 100 percent confidence that we would say "no" to the CFO if he asked us to do something and promised that he would take full responsibility for any fallout from the actions we were going to take?

Today's white-collar criminals are more likely to be those among us who are unable to withstand the blistering pressures placed on managers to meet higher and tougher goals. In this environment, companies looking to protect themselves from corporate fraud must take a hard look at their own culture. Does it promote ethical behavior, or does it emphasize something else?

In most companies, "ethics" programs are really no more than compliance programs with a veneer of "do the right thing" messaging to create an apparent link to the company's values. To be effective, they have to go deeper than outlining steps to take to report misconduct. Organizations must understand what causes misconduct in the first place.

We can't forget that Enron had a Code of Ethics. And it wasn't as if WorldCom lacked extensive internal controls. But both had cultures where engaging in unethical conduct was tacitly condoned, if not encouraged.

Building the Right Culture

Now the focus has shifted toward looking at what is going on inside organizations that's either keeping people from doing the right thing or, just as importantly, keeping people from doing something about misconduct they observe. If an organization wants to reduce the risk of unethical conduct, it must focus more effort on building the right culture than on building a compliance infrastructure.

The Ethics Resource Center's 2005 National Business Ethics Survey (NBES) clearly confirms this trend toward recognizing the role of corporate culture. Based on interviews with more than 3,000 employees and managers in the United States the survey disclosed that, despite the increase in the number of ethics and compliance program elements being implemented, desired outcomes, such as reduced levels of observed misconduct, haven't changed since 1994. Even more striking is the revelation that, although formal ethics and compliance programs have some impact, organizational culture has the greatest influence in determining program outcomes.

The Securities & Exchange Commission (SEC) and the Department of Justice have also been watching these trends.

Stephen Cutler, the recently retired SEC director of the Division of Enforcement, was matter of fact about the importance of looking at culture when it came to decisions of whether or not to bring an action. "We're trying to induce companies to address matters of tone and culture. . . . What we're asking of that CEO, CFO, or General Counsel goes beyond what a perp walk or an enforcement action against another company executive might impel her to do. We're hoping that if she sees that a failure of corporate culture can result in a fine that significantly exceeds the proverbial 'cost of doing business,' and reflects a failure on her watch—and a failure on terms that everyone can understand: the company's bottom line—she may have a little more incentive to pay attention to the environment in which her company's employees do their jobs."

Measuring Success

Only lagging companies still measure the success of their ethics and compliance programs just by tallying the percentage of employees who have certified that they read the Code of Conduct and attended ethics and compliance training. The true indicator of success is whether the company has made significant progress in achieving key program outcomes. The National Business Ethics Survey listed four key outcomes that help determine the success of a program:

- Reduced misconduct observed by employees,
- Reduced pressure to engage in unethical conduct,
- Increased willingness of employees to report misconduct, and
- Greater satisfaction with organizational response to reports of misconduct.

What's going to move these outcomes in the right direction? Establishing the right culture.

Most compliance programs are generated from "corporate" and disseminated down through the organization. As such, measurement of the success of the program is often based on criteria important to the corporate office: how many employees certified the Code of Conduct, how many employees went through the training, or how many calls the hotline received.

Culture is different—and is measured differently. An organization's culture isn't something that's created by senior leadership and then rolled out. A culture is an objective picture of the organization, for better or worse. It's the sum total of all the collective values and behaviors of all employees, managers, and leaders. By definition, it can only be measured by criteria that reflect the individual values of all employees, so understandingcultural vulnerabilities that can lead to ethics issues requires knowledge of what motivates employees in the organization.

Leadership must know how the myriad human behaviors and interactions fit together like puzzle pieces to create a whole picture. An organization moves toward an ethical culture only if it understands the full range of values and behaviors needed to meet its ethical goals. The "full-spectrum" organization is one that creates a positive sense of engagement and purpose that drives ethical behavior.

> **Leadership must know how the myriad human behaviors and interactions fit together like puzzle pieces to create a whole picture. An organization moves toward an ethical culture only if it understands the full range of values and behaviors needed to meet its ethical goals.**

Why is understanding the culture so important in determining the success of a compliance program? Here's an example: Most organizations have a policy that prohibits retaliation against those who bring forward concerns or claims. But creating a culture where employees feel safe enough to admit mistakes and to raise uncomfortable issues requires more than a policy and "Code training." To truly develop an ethical culture, the organization must be aware of how its managers deal

with these issues up and down the line and how the values they demonstrate impact desired behaviors. The organization must understand the pressures its people are under and how they react to those pressures. And it must know how its managers communicate and whether employees have a sense of accountability and purpose.

Categorizing Values

Determining whether an organization has the capabilities to put such a culture in place requires careful examination. Do employees and managers demonstrate values such as respect? Do employees feel accountable for their actions and feel that they have a stake in the success of the organization?

How does an organization make such a determination? One approach is to categorize different types of values in a way that lends itself to determining specific strengths and weaknesses that can be assessed and then corrected or enhanced.

The Culture Risk Assessment model presented in Figure 1 has been adapted from the Cultural Transformation Tools® developed by Richard Barrett & Associates. Such tools provide a comprehensive framework for measuring cultures by mapping values. More than 1,000 organizations in 24 countries have used this technique in the past 6 years. In fact, the international management consulting firm McKinsey & Co. has adopted it as its method of choice for mapping corporate cultures and measuring progress toward achieving culture change.

SUSTAINABLITY	7	Resilience to withstand integrity challenges
SOCIAL RESPONSIBILITY	6	Strategic alliances with external stakeholders
ALIGNMENT	5	Shared values guide decision making
ACCOUNTABILITY	4	Responsibilty and initiative
SYSTEMS AND PROCESSES	3	Compliance systems and processes
COMMUNICATION	2	Relationships that support the organization
FINANCIAL STABILITY	1	Pursuit of profit and stability

Based on Cultural Transformation Tools Seven Levels of Consciousness Model, Copyright Barrett Values Centre

Figure 1   Seven levels of an ethical organization

The model is based on the principle, substantiated through practice, that all values can be assigned to one of seven categories:

Levels 1, 2, and 3—The Organization's Basic Needs

Does the organization support values that enable it to run smoothly and effectively? From an ethics perspective, is the environment one in which employees feel physically and emotionally safe to report unethical behavior and to do the right thing?

Level 1—Financial Stability. Every organization needs to make financial stability a primary concern. Companies that are consumed with just surviving struggle to focus enough attention on how they conduct themselves. This may, in fact, create a negative cycle that makes survival much more difficult. Managers may exercise excessive control, so employees may be working in an environment of fear.

In these circumstances, unethical or even illegal conduct can be rationalized. When asked to conform to regulations, organizations do the minimum with an attitude of begrudging compliance.

Organizations with challenges at this level need to be confident that managers know and stand within clear ethical boundaries.

Level 2—Communication. Without good relationships with employees, customers, and suppliers, integrity is compromised. The critical issue at this level is to create a sense of loyalty and belonging among employees and a sense of caring and connection between the organization and its customers.

The most critical link in the chain is between employees and their direct supervisors. If direct supervisors can't effectively reinforce messages coming from senior leadership, those messages might be diluted and confused by the time they reach line employees. When faced with conflicting messages, employees will usually choose to follow the lead of their direct supervisor over the words of the CEO that have been conveyed through an impersonal communication channel. Disconnects in how local managers "manage" these messages often mean that employees can face tremendous pressure in following the lead established by leadership.

Fears about belonging and lack of respect lead to fragmentation, dissension, and disloyalty. When leaders meet behind closed doors or fail to communicate openly, employees suspect the worst. Cliques form, and gossip becomes rife. When leaders are more focused on their own success, rather than the success of the organization, they begin to compete with each other.

Level 3—Systems and Processes. At this level, the organization is focused on becoming the best it can be through the adoption of best practices and a focus on quality, productivity, and efficiency.

Level 3 organizations have succeeded in implementing strong internal controls and have enacted clear standards of conduct. Those that succeed at this level are the ones that see internal controls as an opportunity to create better, more efficient processes. But even those that have successfully deployed business processes and practices need to be alert to potentially limiting aspects of being too focused on processes. All organizations need to be alert to resorting to a "check-the-box" attitude that assumes compliance comes naturally from just implementing standards and procedures. Being efficient all too often leads to bureaucracy and inconsistent application of the rules. When this goes badly, employees lose respect for the system and resort to self-help to get things done. This can lead to shortcuts and, in the worst case, engaging in unethical conduct under the guise of doing what it takes to succeed.

Level 4—Accountability

The focus of the fourth level is on creating an environment in which employees and managers begin to take responsibility for their own actions. They want to be held accountable, not micromanaged and supervised every moment of every day. For an ethics and compliance program to be successful, all employees must feel that they have a personal responsibility for the integrity of the organization. Everyone must feel that his or her voice is being heard. This requires managers and leaders to admit that they don't have all the answers and invite employee participation.

Levels 5, 6, and 7—Common Good

Does the organization support values that create a collective sense of belonging where employees feel that they have a stake in the success of the ethics program?

Level 5—Alignment. The critical issue at this level is developing a shared vision of the future and a shared set of values. The shared vision clarifies the intentions of the organization and gives employees a unifying purpose and direction. The shared values provide guidance for making decisions.

The organization develops the ability to align decision making around a set of shared values. The values and behaviors must be reflected in all of the organization's processes and systems, with appropriate consequences for those who aren't willing to walk the talk. A precondition for success at this level is building a climate of trust.

Level 6—Social Responsibility. At this level, the organization is able to use its relationships with stakeholders to sustain itself through crises and change. Employees and customers see that the organization is making a difference in the world through its products and services, its involvement in the local community, or its willingness to fight for causes that improve humanity. They must feel that the company cares about them and their future. Companies operating at this level go the extra mile to make sure they are being responsible citizens. They support and encourage employees' activities in the community by providing time off for volunteer work and/or making a financial contribution to the charities that employees are involved in.

Level 7—Sustainability. To be successful at Level 7, organizations must embrace the highest ethical standards in all their interactions with employees, suppliers, customers, shareholders, and the community. They must always consider the longterm impact of their decisions and actions.

Employee values are distributed across all seven levels. Through surveys, organizations learn which values employees bring to the workplace and which values are missing. Organizations don't operate from any one level of values: They tend to be clustered around three or four levels. Most are focused on the first three: profit and growth (Level 1), customer satisfaction (Level 2), and productivity, efficiency, and quality (Level 3). The most successful organizations operate across the full spectrum with particular focus in the upper levels of consciousness—the common good—accountability, leading to learning and innovation (Level 4), alignment (Level 5), social responsibility (Level 6), and sustainability (Level 7).

Some organizations have fully developed values around Levels 1, 2, and 3 but are lacking in Levels 5, 6, and 7. They may have a complete infrastructure of controls and procedures but may lack the accountability and commitment of employees and leaders to go further than what is required.

Similarly, some organizations have fully developed values around Levels 5, 6, and 7 but are deficient in Levels 1, 2, and 3. These organizations may have visionary leaders and externally focused social responsibility programs, but they may be lacking in core systems that will ensure that the higher-level commitments are embedded into day-to-day processes.

Once an organization understands its values' strengths and weaknesses, it can take specific steps to correct deficient behavior.

Starting the Process

Could a deeper understanding of values have saved WorldCom? We will never know, but if the culture had encouraged open communication and fostered trust, people like Betty Vinson might have been more willing to confront orders that they knew were wrong. Moreover, if the culture had embodied values that encouraged transparency, mid-level managers wouldn't have been asked to engage in such activity in the first place.

The significance of culture issues such as these is also being reflected in major employee surveys that highlight what causes unethical behavior. According to the NBES, "Where top management displays certain ethics-related actions, employees are 50 percentage points less likely to observe misconduct." No other factor in any ethics survey can demonstrate such a drastic influence.

So how do compliance leaders move their organizations to these new directions?

1. *The criteria for success of an ethics program must be outcomes based.* Merely checking off program elements isn't enough to change behavior.

2. *Each organization must identify the key indicators of its culture.* Only by assessing its own ethical culture can a company know what behaviors are the most influential in effecting change.

3. *The organization must gauge how all levels of employees perceive adherence to values by others within the company.* One of the surprising findings of the NBES was that managers, especially senior managers, were out of touch with how nonmanagement employees perceived their adherence to ethical behaviors. Nonmanagers are 27 percentage points less likely than senior managers to indicate that executives engage in all of the ethics-related actions outlined in the survey.

4. *Formal programs are guides to shape the culture, not vice versa.* People who are inclined to follow the rules appreciate the rules as a guide to behavior. Formal program elements need to reflect the culture in which they are deployed if they are going to be most effective in driving the company to the desired outcomes.

Culture may be new on the radar screen, but it isn't outside the scope or skills of forward-thinking finance managers and compliance professionals. Culture can be measured, and finance managers can play a leadership role in developing systematic approaches to move companies in the right direction.

Critical Thinking

1. Whose values should guide an organization? Senior management? Middle management? "Workers"? Investors?

2. What might happen in an organization that switched "resilience to withstand integrity challenges" and "pursuit of profit and stability" on the right hand side of the seven levels of an ethical organization, while leaving the left hand side as is?

Internet References

AZ Central
http://yourbusiness.azcentral.com/ethical-behavior-culture-14949.html

Corporate Compliance Insights
http://www.corporatecomplianceinsights.com/guarding-the-slippery-slope-what-can-hr-do-to-create-an-ethical-culture/

Houston Chronicle
http://smallbusiness.chron.com/create-ethical-workplace-10543.html

DAVID GEBLER, JD, is president of Working Values, Ltd., a business ethics training and consulting firm specializing in developing behaviorbased change to support compliance objectives. You can reach him at dgebler@workingvalues.com.

Article   Prepared by: Eric Teoro, *Lincoln Christian University*

Designing Honesty into Your Organization

CHRISTIAN MASTILAK ET AL.

Learning Outcomes

After reading this article, you will be able to:

- Understand how perceptions of fairness impact dishonest behavior in organizations.

- Understand how the framing of organizational processes can lead to dishonest behavior.

- Take concrete, actionable steps to facilitate honest behavior on the part of employees.

The past decade has provided ample evidence that some people don't behave honestly at work. While it's easy to blame individual factors, such as greed or lack of an ethical compass, recent academic research paints a different picture. As a leader in your organization, you may have more influence than you realize about whether your employees act honestly or not. You can design honest behavior into an organization by using fair and properly aligned reward systems and simple communication strategies.

We know dishonesty is costly, and it may be on the rise. The Ethics Resource Center reports that the following percentages of employees surveyed in 2009 had observed these behaviors in the previous year: company resource abuse (23 percent), lying to employees (19 percent), lying to outside stakeholders (12 percent), falsifying time or expenses (10 percent), and stealing (9 percent). The Association of Certified Fraud Examiners suggests United States organizations may have lost as much as $994 billion to occupational fraud in 2008, and a PricewaterhouseCoopers global survey in 2009 suggests that recent economic pressures have increased the likelihood of fraud taking place. But how can this common problem be reduced?

Research suggests that integrity testing goes only so far in predicting honesty in the workplace. It turns out that most employees are neither consistent truthtellers who can be completely trusted in the absence of controls nor consistent liars who can never be trusted. This means preventing dishonesty isn't just a matter of finding the right people. Some factors can motivate employees to be closer to the truthtelling end of the scale. Specifically, research shows that honest behavior is influenced by employees' beliefs about whether they are being treated fairly, whether expectations of honest behavior have been made explicit, and whether organizational control systems reward dishonest behavior. This suggests that honest behavior can be designed into—or out of—an organization. In this article, we first discuss some of the research findings, then draw on them to develop practical suggestions for how managers can create an environment that both discourages dishonest behavior and enables honest behavior.

Why Do Employees Behave Dishonestly?

We broadly define dishonest behavior as making a report known to contain lies or taking an action known to be unauthorized for personal gain. This excludes accidental errors but includes a variety of behaviors common to accounting and finance functions. Most research in accounting has focused primarily on budgeting behavior, such as padding requests in order to keep the extra funds. But research on more direct forms of theft, such as stealing company property, has led to similar conclusions about why employees steal.

Admittedly, the reasons for dishonest behavior are many and varied. Much has been written about the fraud triangle and how the presence of pressure, opportunity, and rationalization increases the chance of fraud. We can't do justice to the entire topic here, but we can discuss some organizational design and control choices that affect people's behavior. Two common themes that surface are *fairness* and *frame*.

Fairness

For years, economic theory has rested on the assumption that two important desires drive people's behavior: leisure and wealth. Business schools teach future managers to assume that employees will avoid working hard and will lie to increase their wealth. These assumptions then show up in practice as internal control systems are developed to help prevent and detect lack of effort and dishonesty.

Recent academic research has identified two other desires that influence behavior: honesty and fairness. So it isn't simply that people want to be as rich and put forth as little effort as possible; rather, most people also care about being honest and want to ensure that their treatment and outcomes are reasonable compared to the treatment and outcomes of others. More importantly, these desires affect honesty in the workplace.

When employees believe they haven't received what they are due, they will look for ways to recover what they believe they're owed.

Several studies provide examples of how tradeoffs among desires for wealth, honesty, and fairness play out in organizational settings. Coauthor Linda Matuszewski conducted one such study with funding from the IMA® Foundation for Applied Research (now called IMA Research Foundation). Appearing in the 2010 issue (Volume 22) of the *Journal of Management Accounting Research*, "Honesty in Managerial Reporting: Is It Affected by Perceptions of Horizontal Equity?" is one of several studies in accounting in which student participants played the role of managers reporting to their employer. Participants knew the amount of actual costs that would be incurred on a project and were asked to submit a budget request. The employer would never know the actual costs. If the participant lied and the budget request exceeded actual costs, the participants kept the difference. This difference was personal gain for participants—at the expense of their employers. That is, the greater the lie, the more money the participants received.

Overall, Matuszewski's results are consistent with "Honesty in Managerial Reporitng," a study by John Evans, Lynn Hannan, Ranjani Krishnan, and Donald Moser in the October

2001 issue of *The Accounting Review*. Matuszewski's study shows that only a small proportion of people (15 percent) lied to maximize their wealth. A similar proportion of people were at the other end of the spectrum, with 19 percent behaving completely honestly. This left the vast majority (66 percent) in the middle—lying some and trading their desire to be honest against their desire for wealth.

At the two extremes, managers could assume the worst and develop expensive management controls to prevent and detect dishonesty, or they could assume the best and not develop any controls. Since most employees don't fall into either extreme, neither of these solutions is likely to be the most cost effective. Managers are left with the challenge of designing control systems for the majority of employees—those who have some desire to be honest but are also willing to lie to some extent. This is where the results of several other studies can be helpful, as they shed some light on factors within a company's control that influence whether an employee's behavior is closer to the honest or the dishonest end of the scale.

One factor is *vertical* fairness. This represents the relationship between employees and their organizations. In "Stealing in the Name of Justice: Informational and Interpersonal Moderators of Theft Reactions to Underpayment Inequity," Jerald Greenberg describes a study in which he promised two groups of research participants a certain level of pay for performing a low-skilled task (*Organizational Behavior and Human Decision Processes*, Volume 54, Issue 1, February 1993). Participants who were treated unfairly by being paid less than they were originally promised "stole" from the researcher, likely rationalizing that they were due the stolen amount. Participants who were given a reasonable explanation for why their pay was less than promised and received an apology from the researcher, however, stole less. Greenberg's work shows that an explanation and empathy can go a long way toward soothing hurt feelings—and reducing retaliation in firms.

Vertical fairness is critical—but it isn't the only element that matters. Look no further than *Strategic Finance's* Annual Salary Survey each June to know that horizontal fairness—how fairly people are treated compared to their peers—is also important. This was the main focus of Matuszewski's study, which demonstrated that participants' beliefs about changes in the *horizontal* fairness of their pay changed the honesty in their budgeting behavior. Participants in the study were paid a salary and received information about the salaries of other participants. When the horizontal fairness of pay declined, the change in honesty was the same, whether it occurred because of a decrease in the participant's own pay or an increase in others' pay. To make matters worse, this dishonest behavior is hard to undo. In Matuszewski's study, improvements in horizontal fairness resulting from decreases in others' pay didn't result in more honest behavior. Thus, being treated fairly right from the beginning is extremely important.

We aren't trying to minimize employees' personal responsibility for their actions. But research shows that when employees believe they haven't received what they are due, they will look for ways to recover what they believe they're owed. Accordingly, we believe that if top management designs fairness into its dealings with employees, it will eliminate this possible rationalization and cause employees to pursue honest behavior more frequently.

Frame

Another way to design honest behavior into organizations is to ensure that an organization clearly communicates that honesty is expected. When would an employee think that honest behavior isn't expected? Think of it this way: Imagine you're playing basketball. Is a head fake unethical? No, it's completely normal behavior because basketball is a competition, and misleading your opponent is expected. Imagine Kobe Bryant complaining that LeBron James cheated because he made a no-look pass. "Not fair! He looked the other way!" That isn't going to happen because Kobe understands they're competing against each other.

How is this relevant? Well, how often do your budgeting processes become framed as strategic competitions among employees and management rather than decisions with ethical implications? You're more likely to find dishonest behavior if employees believe that the budgeting process is expected to be competitive rather than collaborative, strategic rather than honest. That's what Frederick Rankin, Steven Schwartz, and Richard Young found in "The Effect of Honesty and Superior Authority on Budget Proposals" (*The Accounting Review,* July 2008). Participants completed a budgeting task similar to the task in Matuszewski's study. Those who were asked to honestly share their information about actual costs were more honest than those who were simply asked what portion of the profits should be returned to the company. This study suggests that, in the absence of formal controls, people will be more honest if you simply ask them to be!

Rankin, Schwartz, and Young's finding is particularly important given recent research about the costs and benefits of formal controls. In "When Formal Controls Undermine Trust and Cooperation," Margaret Christ, Karen Sedatole, Kristy Towry, and Myra Thomas suggest that employees sometimes view formal controls as a sign that employers question their competence and integrity, and this may undermine trust and cooperation (*Strategic Finance,* January 2008). To be clear, we aren't advocating doing away with all explicit formal controls. In circumstances in which formal controls aren't present or are too costly, Rankin, Schwartz, and Young show that some of the

same benefits can be achieved by describing a task as an ethical dilemma, rather than a strategic competition, and asking for honesty.

Another effect that framing has in determining whether honest behavior is expected showed up in the large-scale fraud at Enron. Bennett Stewart suggests in "The Real Reasons Enron Failed" that Enron's managers were, in fact, paid to do dishonest things (*Journal of Applied Corporate Finance,* Volume 18, Issue, 2, Spring 2006). Stewart documents that performance at Enron was framed as an accounting game rather than as increasing the company's true economic value. In part, this involved manipulating internal performance measures to exclude any costs of capital. Stewart documents the use of EBITDA—the least accountable, most misleading indicator of corporate performance ever devised—by Enron executives who clearly knew better.

Why did they use this measure? Simple: Enron's performance measurement and compensation system, which included stock-based compensation, paid them to do so. Increases in Enron's stock price were driven in large part by—you guessed it—accounting performance. And we shouldn't be surprised when people do what firms pay them to do.

The greatest problem with poorly framed control systems is that, even when employees intend to be honest, a bad control system may discourage that employee from acting on that honest urge and *disable* that honesty. The challenge is for top managers to design control systems that *enable* honesty.

The Designed Honesty Model

Putting these research results together, we present the designed honesty model of organizational behavior (see Figure 1). The model shows that both fairness and frame contribute to designed honesty. Where should top management look to understand why employees aren't behaving honestly? That depends. If employees are grumbling about their working conditions or their pay—especially their pay relative to others within the organization—then they probably believe they aren't being treated fairly and may well be working the system to get what they believe is due them. On the other hand, if employees report conflicts between what they believe they should do and what they believe they're being asked and paid to do, then the culture and control system frame are probably the culprits, leading otherwise honest employees to feel like they are being encouraged to behave dishonestly.

The designed honesty model isn't intended to be complete—the factors that influence honesty and dishonesty are many and varied. As the research shows, most employees value honesty and fairness in addition to wealth and leisure and are influenced by all of these values when deciding whether to behave honestly. Since fairness and frame are within an organization's

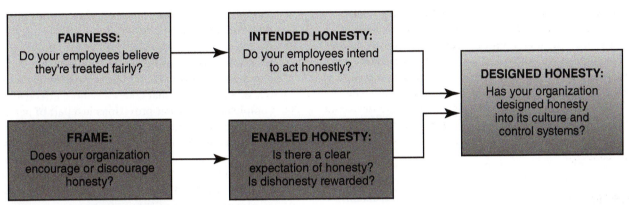

Figure 1   The designed honesty model

Table 1   Six Key Steps toward Designing Honesty into Your Organization

1. Consider vertical and horizontal fairness when making compensation decisions
2. Fully explain compensation policies and procedures
3. Determine whether employees believe they are being paid fairly
4. Show (and feel!) empathy when tough compensation choices need to be implemented
5. Ask employees to be honest, and describe routine decisions as ethical dilemmas rather than strategic competitions
6. Review incentive plans to ensure they reward honest reporting of economic results

control to some extent, it's important for management to understand how these factors can contribute to honest behavior.

Therefore, in addition to attempting to hire the right people, we recommend that companies take the following steps to encourage employees to act on their intentions to be honest (see Table 1):

1. ***Consider vertical and horizontal fairness when making compensation decisions.***

    Employees consider the fairness of their compensation from two perspectives—relative to their exchange with the company (vertical) and relative to the compensation of their peers (horizontal). Managers may be able to get a sense of the perceptions about the vertical fairness of compensation by considering employees' alternative employment opportunities. In today's culture of high turnover, it's reasonable to assume that employees are keeping their eye on the job market and asking "What could I make elsewhere?" But how often do managers consider their subordinates' opportunities when making compensation decisions? Incorporating this practice into the firm's periodic performance review system could help avoid the costs of dishonesty motivated by perceptions of vertical unfairness.

    From the horizontal perspective, although firms often have policies that discourage peers from sharing information about pay, we believe managers should assume that employees know how much money their peers are making so should make an effort to compensate employees fairly compared to their peers.

2. ***Fully explain compensation policies and procedures.***

    Fair doesn't necessarily imply equal. In cases where compensation isn't equal to an alternative employment opportunity or the pay a peer is receiving, detailed explanations may be especially important in helping employees evaluate whether their pay is fair. Communication strategies that help employees understand the justification for compensation policies can be extremely valuable. For instance, employees may be more likely to consider their compensation fair if managers explain the connection between the resources of their division and employee compensation.

3. ***Determine whether employees believe they are being paid fairly.***

    Most large companies have periodic performance review systems in place, and it's through these systems that compensation decisions get communicated. Yet how many of these systems are two-way communication devices designed to determine whether employees believe they are being paid fairly? This data may be challenging to get, especially if employees fear retaliation if they admit they don't believe they are being paid fairly. Managers may need to put themselves in their employees' shoes and pursue indirect methods for answering this question, such as anonymous surveys or hotline methods.

4. *Show (and feel!) empathy when tough compensation choices need to be implemented.*

Of course, managers won't always have the resources to give employees the compensation they want and feel they deserve. But empathy can have an impact on honesty, even when employees face an outcome they believe is unfair.

5. *Ask employees to be honest, and describe routine decisions as ethical dilemmas rather than strategic competitions.*

A logical first step in making it clear that you expect employees to be honest is the establishment of a corporate code of ethics, but even the best code won't be effective unless employees can see the connection between the code and their everyday activities. Think of it this way: Corporate planning doesn't stop with the development of a vision statement. Firms work toward the vision by identifying core competencies, developing organizational strategies, and translating these strategies into operating plans. In the same way, a company must develop strategies for ensuring honest behavior. The research suggests that one successful strategy would be to identify tasks that provide employees with opportunities to benefit from dishonesty and describe these tasks as ethical dilemmas rather than strategic competitions.

This suggestion is consistent with the findings in two 2011 studies published in the *Journal of Business Ethics* that identify factors that contribute to the effectiveness of corporate codes of ethics. Muel Kaptein found in "Toward Effective Codes: Testing the Relationship with Unethical Behavior" (Volume 99, No. 2, March 2011) that the quality of communication regarding a corporate code of ethics has a greater impact on reducing unethical behavior than the quantity of communication about the code. Put simply, it isn't enough to establish a code and talk about it a lot. The code must be accessible, clear, easy to understand, and useful for decision making. In the other study, "Determinants of the Effectiveness of Corporate Codes of Ethics: An Empirical Study" (Volume 101, No. 3, July 2011), Jang Singh found that a code's impact on behavior is determined in part by whether the code guides strategic planning and is useful in resolving ethical dilemmas in the marketplace.

6. *Review incentive plans to ensure they reward honest reporting of economic results.*

Both Kaptein's and Singh's studies also provide insight into the steps managers should take to ensure that their incentive plans promote honesty in the workplace. Singh found that codes are more effective when compliance with their provisions is a part of performance reviews and when there are real consequences for violations. Kaptein found that the most important factor in reducing unethical behavior was senior and local management's embedding of the corporate code of ethics within an organization. More specifically, employees are more likely to be honest when their managers are approachable positive role models who set reasonable performance targets that promote, rather than undermine, compliance with the corporate code of ethics. In addition, it's important that managers don't authorize violations of the code to meet business goals, are aware of the extent to which employees comply with (or violate) the code, and respond to violations appropriately.

To prevent the kind of financial reporting dishonesty that occurred at Enron and many other companies, we suggest that managers should also consider whether performance targets based on economic results are using measures less subject to manipulation than traditional financial accounting measures may be.

Steps Will Go a Long Way

While we can't guarantee that these steps will eliminate all dishonesty in the workplace, we believe that paying attention to the fairness of employees' compensation and highlighting the ethical dimension of certain decisions will go a long way toward designing honesty into your organization.

Critical Thinking

1. Why do some people behave dishonestly at work?
2. Using the Designed Honesty Model presented in the article, develop your own model and explain its strengths and weaknesses compared to the model presented in the article.
3. Pick out one of the "six key steps" toward designing honesty in an organization. Build arguments for and against the key step.
4. If you are a student in a class, engage in a debate for/against with another student concerning the key step you selected.

Internet References

Forbes

http://www.forbes.com/sites/joefolkman/2013/11/18/how-to-make-your-organization-more-honest/

Houston Chronicle: Small Business

http://smallbusiness.chron.com/managerial-ethics-36425.html

Switch and Shift

http://switchandshift.com/honesty-the-secret-to-successful-organizations

CHRISTIAN MASTILAK, PhD, is an assistant professor of accountancy and business law in the Williams College of Business at Xavier University and a member of the North Cincinnati Chapter of IMA. You can reach Christian at (513) 745-3290 or mastilakc@xavier.edu. LINDA MATUSZEWSKI, PhD, is an assistant professor of accountancy in the College of Business at Northern Illinois University and a member of the Rockford Chapter of IMA. You can reach Linda at (815) 753-6379 or lmatus@niu.edu. FABIENNE MILLER, PhD, is an assistant professor of accounting in the School of Business at Worcester Polytechnic Institute and a member of the Worcester Chapter of IMA. You can reach Fabienne at (508) 831-6128 or fabienne@wpi.edu. ALEXANDER WOODS, PhD, is an assistant professor of accounting in the Mason School of Business at The College of William & Mary. You can reach Alex at (757) 221-2967 or alex.woods@mason.wm.edu.

Article   Prepared by: Eric Teoro, *Lincoln Christian University*

Enhancing the Effectiveness of the Ethics Function

Learning Outcomes

After reading this article, you will be able to:

- Understand the nature, requirements, and outcomes or benefits of the ethics function within organizations.
- Understand how to improve the ethics function with organizations.

This IBE Briefing provides insight into the governance of the ethics function and gives examples of common practices, which organizations have adopted to ensure its effectiveness.[1] It is a distillation of IBE research, experience, and conversations with our network of subscribers.

Over the last 30 years, it has become the norm for organizations to encourage their staff to maintain high ethical standards of business practice. This stems from a growing consensus that firms must serve a social benefit if they are to earn a license to operate. The challenge, however, is how to best support employees in living up to the organization's ethical values in their day-to-day business activity.

The Role of an Ethics Function

It is difficult to provide a general definition of the role and scope of the ethics function that would be applicable to all organizations. The operation of each organization's ethics function differs according to its internal structure and the sector in which it operates. Therefore, when considering the effective management of an ethics function, the foremost priority is to define a clear mandate, spelling out the function's key responsibilities specific to a particular organization. This is important as there is no one-size-fits-all approach to business ethics.

It is imperative to set the mandate of this function to go beyond compliance. By definition, business ethics begins where the law ends. It involves discretionary decision-making and relies mainly on individual responsibility and voluntary commitment. Establishing a dedicated function for dealing with ethics will reinforce the company's commitment. In particular, it communicates the idea that a compliance-based approach to rules and regulations is important but insufficient for empowering each employee and ensuring they feel responsible for promoting an ethical culture within their company. A question to ask: Is compliance the ceiling you are aiming for, or the foundation which you are building on?

Generally, it is recognized that the ethics function holds a vital role in ensuring that ethics is part of all business operations and that the core values are embedded and reflected in the organization's culture. Its duty is to guide the implementation of the ethics program, which is often seen as a point of reference for employees wanting to raise concerns or ask questions when faced with an ethical dilemma. This oversight will frequently require the ethics function to translate the organization's ethical values into expectations. There are a number of recurrent elements that provide organizations with an effective way to tackle corporate ethics. These are outlined in the IBE Business Ethics Framework, which is based on its definition of business ethics: "the application of ethical values to business behavior" (see Figure 1).

The responsibilities of the ethics function are commonly grouped into three broad areas of responsibility: general responsibilities, code and policy responsibilities, and management responsibilities (see Figure 2).

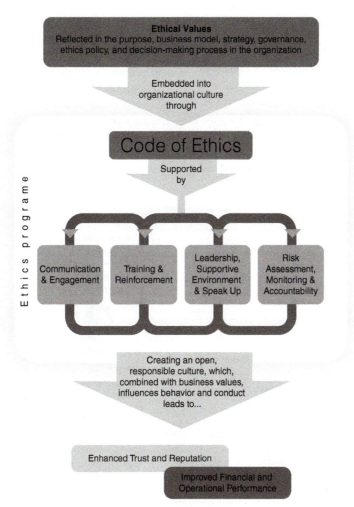

Figure 1   IBE Business ethics framework

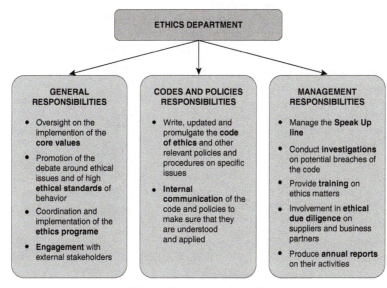

Figure 2   Responsibilities of the ethics function

Benefits of an Ethics Function

An effectively managed ethics function has an important role to play in helping to safeguard an organization's reputation, providing guidance to staff, and creating a shared and consistent corporate culture.[2] According to IBE research, these are the three most common purposes of a company's ethics programe.[3]

Organizations that offer support to their employees on ethical matters are able to influence their behavior positively and, as a consequence, the ethical culture of their organization. The results of the IBE Ethics at Work 2015 survey shows that employee awareness of corporate ethics programs increases both their ethical awareness and their perception of ethical culture.

Employees who indicated that their organization provided all four common elements of an ethics program (code, speak up line, advice line, and ethics training) were more likely to agree with each of the measured indicators of an ethical culture; they further had a more positive perception of the behavior observed in their organization (see Figure 3).[4]

Britain	Response rate:	
	Employer provides "all" elements of an ethics programe	All British respondents
(Q3) Honesty practised ("always or frequently")	85%	81%
(Q4a) Awareness of misconduct ("no")	84%	79%
(Q7a) Pressure to compromise organization's ethical standards ("no")	95%	92%
(Q6) Indicators of an ethical culture ("agree")		
Management behavior		
overall, my line manager sets a good example of ethical business behavior	82%	71%
My line manager supports me in following my organization's standards of ethical behaviour	83%	69%
Communication of ethical standards		
My line manager explains the importance oh honesty and ethics in the work we do	81%	69%
Issues of right and wrong are discussed in staff meetings	76%	65%
Responsible business conduct		
My organization acts responsibly in all its business dealings (with customers, clients suppliers etc.)	86%	78%
My organization lives up to its stated policy of social responsibility	87%	76%
Enforcement of ethical standards		
My organization disciplines employees who violate my organization's ethical standards	83%	72%
base (employer provides, "all," all British respondents) = 436,674		

Figure 3   Benefits of an ethics program

Toward a More Useful Ethics Function

An organization's ethics function is often afforded limited resource both in terms of budget and the number of staff. Although some would describe their functions as lean, there are a number of ways in which the ethics function can make best use of its resources and maximize its impact.

Direct Access to the Board of Directors

Ensuring access to the very top of the organization is vital for building traction of the ethics function. This works in two ways: first, by having the buy in of senior leadership—at both executive and board level—the tone is set by those at the top, cascading down through the organization and played out at different levels. This is widely cited as the greatest enabler of the ethics function.[5]

Second, getting ethics messages heard in the boardroom is of utmost importance. Many organizations we have been in contract with suggest that being able to report directly to the board, in the absence of executive management, allows for an unfiltered upward flow of information capable of informing decision-making at the highest level.

For some companies, one way to ensure this communication is through dedicated board-level committees. IBE analysis of the Terms of Reference of the 55 companies in the FTSE 350 with board-level committees covering corporate responsibility, sustainability, and ethics found that they tend to serve a number of different purposes. However, common themes include the oversight of environmental, social, and governance issues. According to the Terms of Reference of a FTSE 100 Bank, *"The Committee's role will cover: brand positioning, culture and values, reputational risk management and all aspects falling within the Group's sustainability agenda."*[6]

A substantial majority of these committees (69 percent) are found to be chaired by an independent Non-Executive Director. The research also revealed that the most common minimum frequency of committee meetings is between two and four times a year.[7]

Collaborating with Other Functions

Particularly, in organizations where the number of employees dedicated to ethics is limited, many choose to approach the function's responsibilities in a collaborative manner, utilizing the skills, experiences, and resources of other departments. This may require close collaboration with subject matter experts or responsible individuals appointed from elsewhere in the business—across both business units and geographic locations.

Helpful relationships can be forged with a number of different functions, depending on needs. These include internal audit, corporate responsibility, legal, internal communications, compliance, and human resources.[8] This approach is best summarized by one ethics function head who described the relationship with other functions as "independent but collaborative."

Adopting an Oversight Role

Another way of managing the limited resources of an ethics function, while also successfully encouraging individual ethical decision-making, can be to adopt an oversight role, delegating responsibility for the day-to-day management of ethical issues throughout the business. This can be achieved through empowering managers, supervisors, and leaders—thereby delivering the tools to deal with issues locally. In such situations, the ethics function plays the role of resourcing management, providing the capabilities for ethical decision-making. Resources may include management toolkits, training guides, and/or decision-making models.[8] The ethics function may provide an advice line (or equivalent) where managers, and employees more broadly, can ask questions or raise concerns when faced with uncertainty. This could supplement the organization's speak up arrangements.[10]

Another approach found to be beneficial is the appointment of ethics ambassadors (or equivalent) throughout the business. This position may be full time but is typically taken on in addition to an employee's existing day-to-day responsibilities. They can act as the "eyes and ears" of the ethics function, serving as local point of contact for employees and providing a physical presence or "face" for ethics throughout the organization.[11]

Communicate Clearly

Many organizations are more used to informing rather than communicating, which can pose a challenge for an ethics function. Communications from the ethics function should not be as simple as informing employees about facts, figures, and procedures and checking that they are compliant. Instead, the use of true experience is found to be an effective way of getting messages across.

Employees will communicate informal messages about ethics in the organization regardless of the internal communications strategy, whether they realize they are doing so or not. When defining the key messages to come from the ethics function, it is important to be clear, inclusive, and accessible. Common messages from ethics functions will include a call to action, whether to speak up, read the code, or live the values. However, a common mistake is to communicate in one direction, in a way which is commanding or negative, rather than engaging employees in a constructive discussion.

Poster campaigns, special events (such as ethics days), banners on the company Intranet site, internal social media platforms, and videos are all common ways in which positive, engaging messages can be shared.[12]

Monitor and Measure Performance

To maximize the function's effectiveness, a robust reporting framework should demonstrate how the ethics function contributes to the organization's overarching objectives. Defining clear measures of success by making use of metrics will help to build support within the organization. It will also help to identify the parts of the program that require more attention. Such metrics can also provide assurances to the board.

However, deciphering meaningful metrics remains a challenge. Reporting on contacts and cases raised through the organization's speak up, (whistleblowing) systems can provide valuable insights. This is particularly true of information relevant to investigations into misconduct.

Other data sources that can be reported on include feedback from employee surveys or ethics-focused training courses; information gathered in due diligence of potential suppliers or by the internal audit function as part of its assurance program; numbers of breaches of the code; employee turnover figures; exit interview data; main achievements and improvements introduced, as well as steps taken to mitigate the most prominent ethical risks—even cases where suggested action has been absent.[13]

As discussed above, there are numerous internal communication channels through which these can be disseminated to different internal stakeholder groups. The ethics function may also wish to share some of this information externally. The scope of narrative reporting is continuously increasing. It presents an opportunity for the annual report and/or the corporate responsibility report to raise awareness throughout the organization of how seriously the board takes ethical issues and the effectiveness of the ethics function.[14] This notion is supported by Section 172 of the Companies Act, which sets out a duty to promote the success of the company, enjoining directors to report on stakeholder interests with a long-term outlook.[15]

Conclusion

The culture of an organization is shaped by its values and their reflection in employees' behavior. It is important, therefore, that every employee appreciates his/her individual responsibility for promoting high ethical standards through living up to the organization's values. The UK Corporate Governance Code16 asserts a crucial role for the board of directors—it is essential that they set the tone and actively assure themselves that the organization's values are embedded effectively.

Foremost, the presence of a dedicated ethics function or department serves to support these responsibilities, ensuring

their practical impact. Second, where gaps are identified, a dedicated team already exists to assist in overcoming such lapses.

An effectively managed ethics function provides a coherent structure capable of productive implementation and coordination of all the elements of the ethics program across the organization. Key elements include the content of the code of ethics and related policies, the provision of training on ethical matters, and the monitoring of reporting systems, including the oversight of investigative procedures.

It is important to remember that there is no one-size-fits-all approach to business ethics. Each organization needs to identify procedures that are most suited to its culture, needs, and resources. The box below provides a summary of how the effectiveness of the ethics function can be maximized (see Box 1).

> ## Box 1 Ideas for ensuring the effectiveness of the ethics function
>
> IBE research has highlighted some elements that ethics practitioners regard as important to enhancing the effectiveness of the ethics function.
> These include:
> 1. Defining a clear mandate, spelling out its key responsibilities.
> 2. Going beyond compliance.
> 3. Ensuring access to the board of directors.
> 4. Collaborating with other departments.
> 5. Adopting an oversight role.
> 6. Communicating clearly.
> 7. Monitoring, measuring, and reporting on performance.

Notes

1. For the purpose of this Briefing, the shorthand "ethics function" is used to cover a variety of terms given to functions within organizations who are tasked with (among other priorities) embedding the organization's values to reflect its culture and behaviors.
2. IBE Report (2014) *The Role and Effectiveness of Ethics and Compliance Practitioners*—the research uncovered three distinct "domains of activity"—custodianship, advocacy, and innovation—representing different interpretations of the E&C role.
3. IBE Survey (2013) Corporate Ethics Policies and Programs.
4. IBE Survey (2015) *Ethics at Work 2015: Survey of Employees—Main Findings and Themes.*
5. IBE Core Series (2005) *Setting the Tone: Ethical Business Leadership.*

6. IBE Survey (2016) *Culture by Committee: the Pros and Cons.*

7. Ibid.

8. The IBE has considered the interaction between the ethics function and other departments in the following publications: IBE Briefing (2014) Collaboration Between the Ethics Function and HR, IBE Board Briefing (2015) *Checking Culture: A New Role for Internal Audit* and IBE Good Practice Guide (2015): *Communicating Ethical Values Internally.*

9. See IBE Good Practice Guide (2011): *Ethics in Decision-making.*

10. See IBE Good Practice Guide (2007): Speak Up Procedures.

11. See IBE Good Practice Guide (2010): *Ethics Ambassadors.*

12. IBE Good Practice Guide (2015): *Communicating Ethical Values Internally.*

13. IBE Core Series (2006) *Living up to Our Values: Developing Ethical Assurance.*

14. IBE Briefing (2014) *Business Ethics in Corporate Reporting.*

15. Companies Act 2006 Section 172.

16. Financial Reporting Council (2016) *The UK Corporate Governance Code.*

Critical Thinking

1. Describe the IBE Business Ethics Framework. What are its strengths?

2. Describe the responsibilities of an ethics department.

3. Describe how your, or another, organization rates measure up, with respect to the proposed ethics function. What does the organization do well? What does the organization do poorly?

4. Describe specific steps an organization can make to improve it ethics function? What behaviors would be required for, and result from, such improvements?

Internet References

AccountingWEB
https://www.accountingweb.com/practice/practice-excellence/nine-steps-to-make-your-companys-ethics-training-program-stick

Edge Training Systems
https://connect.edgetrainingsystems.com/blog/5-workplace-ethics-training-activities-for-a-perfect-workplace

Graziado Business Review
https://gbr.pepperdine.edu/2012/08/the-ethics-of-ethics-programs/

Article   Prepared by: Eric Teoro, *Lincoln Christian University*

Using Behavioural Ethics to Improve Your Ethics Programme

Judith Houston

Learning Outcomes

After reading this article, you will be able to:

- Understand challenges regarding ethical behaviour and decision-making in organizations.

- How to improve ethical behaviour and decision-making in organizations.

Behavioural ethics is a field of study that seeks to understand how people behave when confronted with ethical dilemmas. Drawing on behavioural economics, psychology, and other behavioural sciences, this Briefing illustrates how companies can use insights from the theory in order to strengthen their ethics program and help their employees to do the right thing.

This Briefing focuses on how people make decisions and what can influence them. Understanding this is important for organizations of all sizes in order to ensure the measures they have in place to promote ethical behaviour are appropriate and that the incentives that they provide do not have unintended—and sometimes counterproductive—consequences.

The Challenges for an Ethics Program

Companies are increasingly investing resources in the development of an ethics program that brings their ethical values to life and provides guidance to their staff on how to tackle ethical dilemmas.[1] However, even companies with a mature ethics program that seems to "tick all the boxes" are not immune from lapses or, in some cases, even major ethical scandals that pose clear questions about the effectiveness of these programs.

There are many factors that can come into play in these situations. Behavioural ethics identifies some key signs (e.g., *ethical blindness* and *moral disengagement*) that might impair the effectiveness of the organization's ethics program and thus increasing ethical risks.

Box 1   Predictors of ethical risks

Ethical blindness, also known as "ethical fading" or "moral myopia," is a temporary and subconscious state in which a person is unable to see the ethical dimension of the decision they are making.[2] Many unethical decisions are not deliberate acts by "bad" people, rather they occur where a well-intentioned person has become ethically blind as a result of any number of individual, organizational, or societal pressures. Such was found to be the case among the NASA engineers who voted for the Challenger space shuttle to take off despite their concerns for its safety. The NASA organizational culture and the imperative to maintain a lead in the space race were found to have narrowed the frame of reference in which the engineers made their decision to allow the shuttle to take off overriding safety concerns.[3] Recognizing different contributory influences and averting ethical blindness is crucial to preventing unethical behaviour.

Moral disengagement is where an individual is aware of the ethical aspects of a decision and actively choses to disengage from these and behave unethically.[4] Often they justify their decision with rationalizations that minimize or neutralize feelings of guilt or shame. As an example, Professor Celia Moore suggests to imagine a situation where Sam, an individual who strongly holds the opinion that theft is wrong, takes a newspaper without paying for it from Starbucks. *"Moral disengagement mechanisms help Sam construe taking the newspaper as no big deal (distortion of consequences), believe that everyone takes small things like a paper sometimes (diffusion of responsibility), that taking the paper is tiny compared to others' violations (advantageous comparison), or that he's seen Starbucks employees take copies of the paper, so why shouldn't he (displacement of responsibility)? He could think that in the grand scheme of things, being an informed citizen is more important than paying for the paper (moral justification). He could even plan on leaving the paper in the café when he was finished with it, so really he was just 'borrowing' it (euphemistic labelling). He could think that Starbucks is a large heartless corporation that won't notice the missing paper (dehumanization), or even deserves having the paper taken from it because it charges so much for coffee (attribution of blame). These mechanisms facilitate understanding his behaviour as unrelated to his internal standard against theft. Thus, he can leave the store, paper under arm, confident in the belief that he's done nothing wrong."*[5] Corporate culture of an organization can influence whether employees are able to disengage from the morality of a decision.

Research shows that ethical blindness and moral disengagement can be common in certain situations. However, identifying them can be challenging. Academics Muel Kaptein and Martien van Helvoort have conducted extensive research in this area. They have identified 60 "neutralizations," which they group into two broad categories: denying unethical behaviour ("It is not unethical") and denying responsibility (I am not responsible for it).[6] Table 1 provides some examples of "neutralization techniques" that are quite common in business.

Why Is Behavioural Ethics Relevant to an Ethics Program?

The awareness of how people make decisions is important to improve the ethics program. A first important lesson that can be learned from behavioural ethics stems from the idea that perfect rationality, which forms the basis of many classical economic theories, is not an accurate description of how people make their decisions. The concept assumes that people always make consistent decisions, based on strict logic, and are narrowly self-interested (*homo economicus*). On one hand, this simplification is necessary in order to design economic models that represent general trends within a population. However, it proves inadequate to describe and predict the complexity of human behaviour at the individual level. Relatively recent theories that focus on behavioural economics have challenged this approach, highlighting the role played by emotions and intuition.

Bounded Rationality

The Theory of "bounded rationally"[8] proposes the idea that, in decision-making, our rationality is restricted by the limited information we have, the cognitive limitations of human mind to process information, and limited amount of time in which to make a decision. These limits—or bounds—mean that we are forced to find ways to simplify reality through mental shortcuts (*heuristics*) and often rely on our intuition or gut feel in complex situations. However, relying on these shortcuts can lead to deviations from perfect rationality, leading us to a decision that is less than ideal or to a judgment error (cognitive bias).

Cognitive biases are mistakes in reasoning and cognitive processing as a result of subjective beliefs regardless of contrary rational information. There are numerous types of cognitive biases and Box 2 provides some examples. The awareness of heuristics and the influence of bounded rationality need to be taken into account to make sure that an ethics program is effective in promoting competent decision-making.

Table 1   Rationalizations or Neutralizations for Unethical Behaviour[7]

Ethical Blindness	Moral Disengagement
"If it isn't illegal, it's ethical"	"Just this once!"
"No one was really harmed"	"They're just as bad"
"There are worse things" "It's for their own good"	"They deserve it"
	"If I don't do it, somebody else will"
"It's a stupid rule anyway"	"What they don't know won't hurt them"
"Everybody does it"	"We've earned the right"
"It's just business"	"I deserve this—I work overtime and the company doesn't appreciate me"
"I'm just giving them what they want"	
"They would want it to be done this way"	"What can I do? My arm is being twisted"

Box 2   Examples of cognitive biases

Confirmation Bias: It leads us to look for information that supports our existing opinion and ignore inconsistent information. During an electoral campaign, for example, people tend to seek out positive information that paints their favorite candidate in a good light while looking for information that casts the opposing candidate in a negative light. As a consequence, people often miss important information in a way that might have otherwise influenced their decision on which candidate to support.

Ambiguity Effect: When two options are available, people tend to choose the option for which the probability of the different outcomes is known. Individuals tend to avoid options for which missing information makes the probability of the possible outcomes unknown. When buying a house, many people choose a fixed rate mortgage, where the interest rate is set, over a variable rate mortgage, where the interest rate fluctuates with the market. This is the case even when a variable rate mortgage has statistically been shown to save money.

Anchoring: It refers to the tendency to rely too heavily, or "anchor," on one trait or piece of information when making decisions, which usually is the first piece of information acquired on that subject. For example, the initial price offered for a second-hand car sets the standard for the rest of the negotiations, so that prices lower than the initial price seem more reasonable even if they are still higher than what the car is really worth.

Supporting Individual Decision-making

There are many ways in which behavioural economics can be used to strengthen an organization's ethics program. Some of the most relevant are illustrated below.

Doing the Right Thing Needs to Become Our Instinctive Reaction

Daniel Kahneman, professor of psychology at Princeton University, proposes that most human decision-making is done intuitively and subconsciously (System 1) before the cognitive part of the brain engages (System 2).[9] In many circumstances, even when people feel they are making a rational decision, their cognitive System 2 is simply rationalizing a decision that their intuitive System 1 has already made. Sometimes this results in a seemingly irrational decision that might increase ethical risk. Embedding ethical values into everything the organization does can help them become part of an employee's "System 1."

People Are Likely to Put Aside Their Personal Moral Standards at Work if They Think This Is What Is Expected from Their Role

How people judge the morality of an action can depend upon the role they perceive that they have while making the decision. Roles come with expectations and these expectations can translate into pressure to compromise one's ethical standards, as the incident in Box 3 illustrates. Putting in place measures to prevent this is crucial. Instead, it is everyone's role within a company to make ethics a priority. Many organizations make explicit in their code of ethics that all employees, and managers in particular, have the responsibility to be a role model for ethics in the organization. It is important that this message is also reinforced through the communications strategy and through training for managers.

Box 3   It's just my job!

In an article published in 2014, Cohn, Fehr, and Maréchal tried to understand whether the numerous scandals involving fraud in the financial industry should be attributed to the financial sector's business culture. Their approach was inspired by the economic theory of identity, which proposes that individuals have multiple social identities based on, for example, gender, ethnicity, or profession. Identities are associated with specific social norms of behaviours. In a given situation, people will apply those norms of behaviour that are associated with the more prominent identity. Thus, if an individual believes that the banking culture favors dishonest behaviours, the authors argue that it should be possible to trigger dishonesty in bank employees by rendering their professional identity prominent.

Employees of a large, international bank were asked to take part in an experiment where they randomly assigned either to a version of the exercise that increased the prominence of their professional identity or to a control one in which their professional identity was not made relevant. The authors report that bank employees were more likely to cheat when their professional identity is rendered salient compared to the control condition. The authors explain that this effect is specific to bank employees because control experiments with employees from other industries and with students show that they do not become more dishonest when their professional identity or bank-related items are rendered salient. Thus, these results suggest that individuals believe that the expectations placed on them in their professional role require them to put aside their ethical values.[10]

Ethics Needs to Become Part of the Reward, Recognition and Promotion System

The availability bias[11] refers to the human tendency to judge an event by the ease with which examples of the event can be retrieved from your memory. The availability bias leads people to overestimate the likelihood of something happening because a similar event has either happened recently or because they feel emotional about a previous similar event.

This has a significant impact on the ability of organizations to promote ethics. If employees can recall a case where a person has been promoted or rewarded for the commercial results they achieved even when it is widely known that how they achieved them was ethically questionable, they will think that this is the norm in the organization—even if it was just a one-off event. On the other hand, publicly recognizing and rewarding people that distinguish themselves for living up to the organization's ethical values or communicating positive stories internally can be a quick and effective way to send employees the message that ethics is important in the organization.

Time Pressure Can Have a Negative Impact on Organizational Culture and the Ability to Consider the Ethical Implications of a Decision

The Good Samaritan Study by Darley and Batson illustrates this clearly.[12] They replicated the Biblical parable of the Good Samaritan with a group of seminary students. The students were asked to begin the experiment in one building, before being told to go to a second building where they had to either prepare a talk on the Good Samaritan or on seminary jobs. Before leaving for the second building, the researchers told participants that they should hurry, varying the amount of urgency between students. Unbeknownst to the students, an actor was situated in an alleyway between the two buildings posing as a sick man. The researchers observed how many students stopped to help the man. The results showed time pressure had a significant impact on the student's willingness to stop and help: in low hurry situations, 63 percent helped, medium hurry, 45 percent, and high hurry, only 10 percent. Even when they were on their way to prepare a talk on the Good Samaritan! Box 4 highlights how GlaxoSmithKline (GSK) are using the principles of this experiment in scenarios for their ethics training.

Internal communications and the language used within an organization can have a significant impact on the ethical culture.

The framing effect[13] is a cognitive bias according to which individuals respond differently to the same problem depending on how it is presented. Choices can be worded in a way that

Box 4   GSK and the Good Samaritan

GSK have been using the principles of behavioural ethics to inform their "Living Our Values" discussion guides. The guides, designed to help managers lead team discussions on ethics, contain 20 scenarios. Scenarios are based on real-life challenges that employees might face. For example, employee surveys showed that maintaining a healthy work–life balance and working effectively under time pressure were areas of concern for some staff. Behavioural ethics research shows that an increase in time pressure negatively impacts on a person's ability to make an ethical decision; this is clearly demonstrated in the Good Samaritan experiment discussed above. GSK used this research as a basis for developing their own scenario that addresses the topic of work–home balance and time pressure. This has enabled employees to discuss the issue openly and increased awareness of the role that time pressure can have on our decision-making abilities.

highlights the positive or negative aspects of the same decision, leading to changes in their relative attractiveness (see Box 5).

The implications for business ethics of these insights are significant and lead to further considerations around the way desired behaviours are encouraged within an organization.

The choice of words and formulation of a statement can manipulate perception and how a situation is interpreted or framed. For example, using the phrase "creative accounting" doesn't sound as serious as "accounting fraud." This makes it easier for employees to rationalize their behaviour. The use of aggressive language, for example, when managers speak

Box 5   Using a positive frame

Another field where the framing effect is particularly used is advertising, as the following examples illustrate.

Presenting a Positive Spin: A sign that says 10 percent of customers are not fully satisfied implies a negative connotation, while "9/10 of our customers are fully satisfied" is a much more positive spin.

Presenting Price in Most Cost-effective Way: Stating the cost of gym membership is £500 a year may deter customers. However, stating it costs just £1.37 a day—less than a cup of coffee!—sounds more appealing.[14]

as if they were at war with their competitors, promotes rigid framing, which can, in turn, drive ethical blindness. On the other hand, using positive language that is consistent with the organization's values can be a driver of change. The global management, engineering, and development consultancy Mott MacDonald recognized this when they changed the name of their reporting line from "whistleblowing facility" to adopt a more positive name—Speak Up Line. As a result, they noticed a significant increase in the number of concerns raised.

In Some Circumstances, "Nudging" Ethics Can Be More Effective Than Enforcing Compliance

The Nudge Theory was developed by the 2017 Nobel laureate Richard Thaler and it suggests that a positive reinforcement and indirect suggestions can be more effective to produce the desired behaviour than direct instructions, legislation, and enforcement. Thaler and Sunstein define a nudge as follows: *"A nudge, as we will use the term, is any aspect of the choice architecture that alters people's behaviour in a predictable way without forbidding any options or significantly changing their economic incentives. To count as a mere nudge, the intervention must be easy and cheap to avoid. Nudges are not mandates. Putting fruit at eye level counts as a nudge. Banning junk food does not."*[15]

This concept has seen many applications in the public policy space.[16] However, it can also find application within an organization to promote an ethical culture and behaviours in line with the core values. In particular, it suggests that an approach that focuses on ethics—communicating the ethical values, explaining how and why an organization does its business, encouraging individual judgment based on ethical values—is at least as important as having clear rules of conduct that employees must follow and the related sanctions.

Individual Responsibility for Values and Associated behaviours Needs to be Encouraged

One of the most researched behaviour patterns refers to the willingness of people to put aside their own moral standards and give up responsibility for their action if they are following the instructions of a person in position of authority. One of the most well-known studies of obedience to authority was carried out by Yale University psychologist, Stanley Milgram, in 1963 (see Box 6). Milgram was particularly interested in seeing how far people would go in obeying an instruction from an authority figure if it involved harming another person. The experiment showed that people are likely to follow orders given by authority figures (e.g., managers, teachers, and police officers, even

---

Box 6   The Milgram experiment[17]

The "learner" (an actor) was strapped into a chair with electrodes. After he learned a list of word pairs, participants who took on the role of "teacher" tested the learner on their recall of the word pairs. The teacher was located in a separate room and instructed by an "experimenter" (an actor). The experimenter wore a lab coat and instructed the teacher to administer an electric shock every time the learner made a mistake and to increase the strength of the shock each time. The electric shock wasn't actually delivered, but the "learner" reacted to it as if it was real and the "teacher" thought they were administering a real shock, which could, in some cases, prove lethal. The "learner" gave mainly wrong answers on purpose. If the "teacher" refused to increase the shock to the learner, the experimenter emphasized their instructions to continue. The results showed that 65 percent of the participants delivered the highest level of electric shock to the "learner."

---

if it means inflicting harm on another human being). Milgram conducted many variations of the experiment and concluded that the behaviour of participants could be explained by suggesting that we have two "states" of behaviour:

The autonomous state: When people direct their own actions and take responsibility for the results of those actions.

The agentic state: When people allow others to direct their actions and then pass off the responsibility for the consequences to the person giving the orders (i.e., they act as an agent for another person).

To prevent this situation, it is important that companies encourage employees to apply critical thinking and learn how to take initiative, rather than just following orders. Promoting an open culture where employees feel empowered to challenge decisions they feel might violate the organization's ethical standards, even when they receive instruction from a superior, is paramount.

People Determine the Appropriate Behaviour by Looking Around

Research presents significant evidence that social pressure from a majority group can cause a person to conform to a certain behaviour. The Asch experiment on conformity is a classic example.[18] More recently, Francesca Gino, Shahar Ayal, and Dan Ariely undertook some research to understand whether exposure to other people's unethical behaviour can increase or decrease an individual's dishonesty (see Box 7).[19]

Box 7   Conformity to the group

The experiments that Gino, Ayal, and Ariely conducted involved a group of students that had to do a test, one of them was an actor. In the first experiment, the actor cheated in an obvious way by finishing a task impossibly quickly and leaving the room with the maximum reward. The other participants' level of unethical behaviour increased when the actor was seen as an in-group member (from the same university), but decreased when the actor was an out-group member (from another university).

In the second experiment, the actor asked a question about cheating which strengthened the prominence of the possibility. Results showed that this decreased the level of unethical behaviour among the other group members, showing that bringing the focus on ethics in a group can have a positive impact on people's behaviour. These results illustrated that the decision to behave ethically or not depends significantly on the social norms produced by the behaviours of those that are part of "our group" and also on the prominence of conversations about ethical issues.

The results obtained suggest that training staff on ethical matters is important to create a shared systems of beliefs and to keep these issues prominent in people's minds when they face a difficult decision. Leadership engagement and the right "tone at the top" are also important in this context. Employees will be more likely to behave unethically if they perceive that their senior leaders and managers do so, as they might think that "this is the way things are done."

Using Behavioural Ethics in Your Ethics Program

There are many ways in which behavioural ethics can help improve the efficacy of an ethics program. In particular, there are some questions that might be worth considering to assess whether any of the elements of the ethics program can be strengthened. The questions below are grouped according to the IBE's framework for an ethics program.

Code of Ethics

- What impact does the language in your Code have? Does it empower employees to do the right thing or is it dictatorial or legalistic? Is it framed in the positive or in the negative? Have you considered the tone? Does it use creative terms to "sugar coat" unethical acts?

- Is the language used in the Code reflected in other departmental policies or do they contradict each other? Ensuring consistency in the language and messaging is essential.

Communication and Awareness

- Communication and awareness raising tools, such as promotional goods or campaigns, can create positive saliency bias, whereby ethics is at the forefront of people's mind, and nudge employees into factoring ethics into their decision-making.

Training and Reinforcement

- Running face-to-face ethics training with groups comprised of varying seniority levels, departments, and cultures provides employees with exposure to differing perspectives, building their moral imagination, preventing moral disengagement, and increasing the prominence of ethics for employees.

- Broadening the scope of ethics training to include awareness of how we make decisions, the impact of organizational context and the signs of ethical blindness and moral disengagement (e.g., through use of rationalizations) can help employees to make better decisions. Supporting decision-making at all levels, from senior leaders to all members of staff, will help to prevent unethical behaviour. Useful tools for this include the Ladder of Inference[20] and the Neutralizations Alarm Clock.[21]

Supporting Context and Culture

- Ensure leaders are aware of the impact that their language has on employees. Are they creating a culture of fear and authoritarianism with their words?

- Are employees treated with respect? When employees are treated as trustworthy, capable members of a team, they're more likely to act accordingly. This is known as the Pygmalion effect and refers to the tendency people have to act the way that other people treat them.[22]

- Celebrate those that speak up. If they are treated badly, others will see this and be unlikely to speak out for fear of being ostracized by the group.

- Involve employees in their own goal setting and gather feedback on targets and incentive structures—are they realistic or are they encouraging employees to cut corners due to the pressure?

- Review industry practices if possible. Are there ethical challenges that need to be addressed? Acknowledge these and discuss with employees who are likely to be engaging with people in the wider industry.

Monitoring and Accountability

- Promote transparent decision-making and individual accountability. It is easier for an employee to make an unethical decision when they are acting as an "agent" with no accountability or visibility of their actions.
- Include questions in staff surveys to help identify ethical blindness and moral disengagement, framing them in such a way that employees will understand (e.g., have they ever heard rationalizations used in the workplace, do they feel under significant time pressure, etc.).

Notes

1. See IBE (2015) Ethics at Work: Survey of employees.
2. See A. E. Tenbrunsel and D. M. Messick, Ethical Fading: The Role of Self-Deception in Unethical Behaviour, Social Justice Research, June 2004, Volume 17 and M. E. Drumwright and P. E. Murphy, How Advertising Practitioners View Ethics: Moral Muteness, Moral Myopia, and Moral Imagination, Journal of Advertising, 2004, Volume 33.
3. See http://www.values.com.au/volkswagens-ethical-blindness-is-more-common-than-we-think/.
4. See Albert Bandura, Moral Disengagement: How People Do Harm and Live with Themselves, Worth (2015).
5. http://www.celiamoore.com/uploads/9/3/2/1/9321973/moore_-_current_opinion_in_psychology_-_2015_-_moral_disengagement.pdf.
6. Muel Kaptein and Martien van Helvoort, The Neutralisations Alarm Clock: A Model of Existing Neutralization Techniques Sept 2017, ResearchGate.
7. Ethics Alarms: Unethical Rationalizations and Misconceptions.
8. Bounded rationality is a term coined by US Nobel Prize laureate economist Herbert Simon. Cognitive biases was introduced by Amos Tversky and Daniel Kahneman in 1972.
9. Daniel Kahneman (2011) Thinking Fast and Slow.
10. Cohn A, Fehr E, Maréchal MA (2014) *Business culture and dishonesty in the banking industry*, Nature.
11. Kahneman, D., & Tvesrky, A. (1973). Availability: A hesuristic for judging frequency and probability.
12. The Good Samaritan Experiment: http://faculty.babson.edu/krollag/org_site/soc_psych/darley_samarit.html.

13. Kahneman, D., & Tversky, A. (1979). Prospect theory: An analysis of decision under risk. Econometrica, 47, 263–291.
14. 14. https://www.economicshelp.org/blog/glossary/framing-effect/.
15. Thaler R., & Sunstein C. (2008). Nudge—Improving decisions about health, wealth and happiness, p. 6.
16. The Economist (24/03/2012) Nudge nudge, think think
17. The Milgram Experiment: https://www.simplypsychology.org/milgram.html 18.
18. https://www.youtube.com/watch?v=NyDDyT1lDhA.
19. http://citeseerx.ist.psu.edu/viewdoc/download?doi=10.1.1.387.1342&rep=rep1&type=pdf.
20. Ladder of Inference: https://www.mindtools.com/pages/article/newTMC_91.htm.
21. Muel Kaptein and Martien van Helvoort, The Neutralisations Alarm Clock: A Model of Existing Neutralization Techniques Sept 2017, ResearchGate: https://www.researchgate.net/publication/320101243_THE_NEUTRALIZATIONS_ALARM_CLOCK_A_MODEL_OF_EXISTING_NEUTRALIZATION_TECHNIQUES.
22. The Pygmalion effect, Wikipedia: https://en.wikipedia.org/wiki/Pygmalion_effect.

Critical Thinking

1. Describe instances of cognitive bias that you have witnessed or committed?
2. What challenges have you faced with respect to ethical behaviour in the workplace? How did you resolve or overcome these challenges? When and why did you fail at these challenges?
3. Develop a code for your personal ethics. Develop a code of ethics for your organization. Describe how the two codes relate to and reinforce each other.

Internet References

Ethics Unwrapped: McCombs School of Business
https://ethicsunwrapped.utexas.edu/subject-area/behavioral-ethics

Scholarship @ Georgetown Law
https://scholarship.law.georgetown.edu/cgi/viewcontent.cgi?article=2519&context=facpub

Working Knowledge: Harvard Business School
https://hbswk.hbs.edu/item/behavioral-ethics-toward-a-deeper-understanding-of-moral-judgment-and-dishonesty

Article

Prepared by: Eric Teoro, *Lincoln Christian University*

Hiring Character

In their new book, **Integrity Works,** authors Dana Telford and Adrian Gostick outline the strategies necessary for becoming a respected and admired leader. In the edited excerpt that follows, the authors present a look at business leader Warren Buffett's practice of hiring people based on their integrity. For sales and marketing executives, it's a practice worth considering, especially when your company's reputation with customers—built through your salespeople—is so critical.

DANA TELFORD AND ADRIAN GOSTICK

Learning Outcomes

After reading this article, you will be able to:

- Describe the ethicality of Warren Buffet.

- Determine if résumés are accurate.

- Ask ethics-based questions during hiring interviews.

This chapter was the hardest for us to write. The problem was, we couldn't agree on whom to write about. We had a number of great options we were mulling over. Herb Brooks of the Miracle on Ice 1980 US hockey team certainly put together a collection of players whose character outshined their talent. And the results were extraordinary. We decided to leave him out because we had enough sports figures in the book already. No, we wanted a business leader. So we asked, "Who hires integrity over ability?"

The person suggested to us over and over as we bandied this idea among our colleagues was Warren Buffett, chairman of Berkshire Hathaway Inc.

Sure enough, as we began our research we found we had not even begun to tell Buffett's story. But we were reluctant to repeat his story. Buffett had played an important part in our first book. And yet, his name kept coming up. So often, in fact, that we finally decided to not ignore the obvious.

Perhaps more than anyone in business today, Warren Buffett hires people based on their integrity. Buffett commented, "Berkshire's collection of managers is unusual in several ways. As one example, a very high percentage of these men and women are independently wealthy, having made fortunes in the businesses that they run. They work neither because they need the money nor because they are contractually obligated to—we have no contracts at Berkshire. Rather, they work long and hard because they love their businesses."

The unusual thing about Warren Buffett is that he and his longtime partner, Charlie Munger, hire people they trust—and then treat them as they would wish to be treated if their positions were reversed. Buffett says the one reason he has kept working so long is that he loves the opportunity to interact with people he likes and, most importantly, trusts.

Buffett loves the opportunity to interact daily with people he likes and, most importantly, trusts.

Consider the following remarkable story from a few years ago at Berkshire Hathaway. It's about R.C. Willey, the dominant home furnishings business in Utah. Berkshire purchased the company from Bill Child and his family in 1995. Child and most of his managers are members of the Church of Jesus Christ of Latter-day Saints, also called Mormons, and for this reason R.C. Willey's stores have never been open on Sunday.

Now, anyone who has worked in retail realizes the seeming folly of this notion: Sunday is the favorite shopping day for many customers—even in Utah. Over the years, though, Child had stuck to his principle—and wasn't ready to rejigger the formula just because Warren Buffett came along. And the formula was working. R.C.'s sales were $250,000 in 1954 when Child took over. By 1999, they had grown to $342 million. Child's determination to stick to his convictions was what attracted Buffett to him and his management team. This was a group with values and a successful brand.

Arnie Ferrin, longtime friend of Child, said, "I believe that [Child] is a man of extreme integrity, and I believe that Warren Buffett was looking to buy his business because he likes to do business with people like that, that don't have any shadows in their lives, and they're straightforward and deal above-board."

This isn't to say Child and Buffett have always agreed on the direction of the furniture store.

"I was highly skeptical about taking a no-Sunday policy into a new territory, where we would be up against entrenched rivals open seven days a week," Buffett said. "Nevertheless, this was Bill's business to run. So, despite my reservations, I told him to follow both his business judgment and his religious convictions."

Proving once again that he believed in his convictions, Child insisted on a truly extraordinary proposition: He would personally buy the land and build the store in Boise, Idaho—for about $11 million as it turned out—and would sell it to Berkshire at his cost if—and only if—the store proved to be successful. On the other hand, if sales fell short of his expectations, Berkshire could exit the business without paying Child a cent. This, of course, would leave him with a huge investment in an empty building.

You're probably guessing there's a happy ending to the story. And there is. The store opened in August of 1998 and immediately became a huge success, making Berkshire a considerable margin. Today, the store is the largest home furnishings store in Idaho.

Child, good to his word, turned the property over to Berkshire—including some extra land that had appreciated significantly. And he wanted nothing more than the original cost of his investment. In response, Buffett said, "And get this: Bill refused to take a dime of interest on the capital he had tied up over the two years."

And there's more. Shortly after the Boise opening, Child went back to Buffett, suggesting they try Las Vegas next. This time, Buffett was even more skeptical. How could they do business in a metropolis of that size and remain closed on Sundays, a day that all of their competitors would be exploiting?

But Buffett trusts his managers because he knows their character. So he gave it a shot. The store was built in Henderson, a mushrooming city adjacent to Las Vegas. The result? This store outsells all others in the R.C. Willey chain, doing a volume of business that far exceeds any competitor in the area. The revenue is twice what Buffett had anticipated.

As this book went to print, R.C. Willey was preparing to open its third store in the Las Vegas area, as well as stores in Reno, Nevada, and Sacramento, California. Sales have grown to more than $600 million, and the target is $1 billion in coming years. "You can understand why the opportunity to partner with people like Bill Child causes me to tap dance to work every morning," Buffett said.

Here's another example of Buffett's adeptness at hiring character. He agreed to purchase Ben Bridge Jeweler over the phone, prior to any face-to-face meeting with the management.

Ed Bridge manages this 65-store West Coast retailer with his cousin, Jon. Both are fourth-generation owner-managers of a business started 89 years ago in Seattle. And over the years, the business and the family have enjoyed extraordinary character reputations.

Buffett knows that he must give complete autonomy to his managers. "I told Ed and Jon that they would be in charge, and they knew I could be believed: After all, it's obvious that [I] would be a disaster at actually running a store or selling jewelry, though there are members of [my] family who have earned black brits as purchasers."

Talk about hiring integrity! Without any provocation from Buffett, the Bridges allocated a substantial portion of the proceeds from their sale to the hundreds of coworkers who had helped the company achieve its success.

Overall, Berkshire has made many such acquisitions—hiring for character first, and talent second—and then asking these CEOs to manage for maximum long-term value, rather than for next quarter's earnings. While they certainly don't ignore the current profitability of their business, Buffett never wants profits to be achieved at the expense of developing ever-greater competitive strengths, including integrity.

It's an approach he learned early in his career.

Warren Edward Buffett was born on August 30, 1930. His father, Howard, was a stockbroker-turned-congressman. The only boy, Warren was the second of three children. He displayed an amazing aptitude for both money and business at a very early age. Acquaintances recount his uncanny ability to calculate columns of numbers off the top of his head—a feat Buffett still amazes business colleagues with today.

At only 6 years old, Buffett purchased six-packs of Coca-Cola from his grandfather's grocery store for 25 cents and resold each of the bottles for a nickel—making a nice five-cent profit. While other children his age were playing hopscotch and jacks, Buffett was already generating cash flow.

Buffett stayed just 2 years in the undergraduate program at Wharton Business School at the University of Pennsylvania. He left disappointed, complaining that he knew more than his professors. Eventually, he transferred to the University of Nebraska–Lincoln. He managed to graduate in only 3 years despite working full time.

Then he finally applied to Harvard Business School. In what was undoubtedly one of the worst admission decisions in history, the school rejected him as "too young." Slighted, Buffett applied to Columbia where famed investment professor Ben Graham taught.

Professor Graham shaped young Buffett's opinions on investing. And the student influenced his mentor as well. Graham bestowed on Buffett the only A+ he ever awarded in decades of teaching.

While Buffett tried working for Graham for a while, he finally struck out on his own with a revolutionary philosophy: He would research the internal workings of extraordinary companies. He could discover what really made them tick and why they held a competitive edge in their markets. And then he would invest in great companies that were trading at substantially less than their market values.

Ten years after its founding, the Buffett Partnership assets were up more than 1,156 percent [compared to the Dow's 122.9 percent], and Buffett was firmly on his way to becoming an investing legend.

In 2004, Warren Buffett was listed by Forbes as the world's second-richest person (right behind Bill Gates), with $42.9 billion in personal wealth. Despite starting with just $300,000 in holdings, Berkshire's holdings now exceed $116 billion. And Buffett and his employees can confidently say they have made thousands of people wealthy.

We often ask business leaders one simple question: Which is more dangerous to your firm—the incompetent new hire or the dishonest new hire? It's the part of our presentation where attendees sit up straight and start thinking.

We always follow the question with an exercise on identifying and hiring integrity. Though it becomes obvious that many of the executives and managers haven't given employee integrity much thought, most of the CEOs in the audiences are increasingly concerned about hiring employees with character.

So, how do you hire workers with integrity? It's possible, but not easy. It is important to spend more time choosing a new employee than you do picking out a new coffee machine. Here are a few simple areas to focus on:

It is important to spend more time choosing a new employee than you do picking out a new coffee machine.

First, ensure educational credentials match the resume. Education is the most misrepresented area on a resume. Notre Dame football coach George O'Leary was fired because the master's degree he said he had earned did not exist, the CEO of software giant Lotus exaggerated his education and military service, and the CEO of Bausch & Lomb forfeited a bonus of more than $1 million because he claimed a fictional MBA.

Job candidates also often claim credit for responsibilities that they never had. Here's a typical scenario:

Job candidate: "I led that project. Saved the company $10 million." Through diligent fact checking, you find an employee at a previous employer who can give you information about the candidate:

Coworker: "Hmm. Actually, Steve was a member of the team, but not the lead. And while it was a great project, we still haven't taken a tally of the cost savings. But $10 million seems really high."

How do you find those things out? Confer with companies where the applicant has worked—especially those firms the person isn't listing as a reference. Talk to people inside the organization, going at least two levels deep (which means you ask each reference for a couple more references). Talk to the nonprofit organizations where the person volunteers. Tap into alumni networks and professional associations. Get on the phone with others in the industry to learn about the person's reputation. Check public records for bankruptcy, civil, and criminal litigation (with the candidate's knowledge). In other words, check candidates' backgrounds carefully (but legally, of course).

We find that most hiring managers spend 90 percent of their time on capability-related questions, and next to no time on character-based questions. In your rush to get someone in the chair, don't forget to check backgrounds and be rigorous in your interviewing for character. Hiring the wrong person can destroy two careers: your employee's—and your own.

Ask ethics-based questions to get to the character issue. We asked a group of executives at a storage company to brainstorm a list of questions they might ask candidates to learn more about their character. Their list included the following questions:

- Who has had the greatest influence on you and why?
- Who is the best CEO you've worked for and why?
- Tell me about your worst boss.
- Who are your role models and why?

- How do you feet about your last manager?
- Tell me about a time you had to explain bad news to your manager.
- What would you do if your best friend did something illegal?
- What would your past manager say about you?
- What does integrity mean to you?
- If you were the CEO of your previous company, what would you change?
- What values did your parents teach you?
- Tell me a few of your faults.
- Why should I trust you?
- How have you dealt with adversity in the past?
- What are your three core values?
- Tell me about a time when you let someone down.
- What is your greatest accomplishment, personal or professional?
- What are your goals and why?
- Tell me about a mistake you made in business and what you learned from it.
- Tell me about a time when you were asked to compromise your integrity.

It's relatively easy to teach a candidate your business. The harder task is trying to instill integrity in someone who doesn't already have it.

Of course, we don't want to imply that it's impossible. Sometimes people will adapt to a positive environment and shine. Men's Wearhouse has certainly had tremendous success hiring former prison inmates, demonstrating everyone should have a second chance.

But integrity is a journey that is very personal, very individual. An outside force, such as an employer, typically can't prescribe it. It's certainly not something that happens overnight. That's one reason many of the CEOs we have talked with prefer promoting people from inside their organizations when possible.

Don Graham, chairman and CEO of the Washington Post Company, said, "There's a very good reason for concentrating your hires and promotions on people who already work in your organization. The best way to predict what someone's going to do in the future is to know what they've done in the past—watch how people address difficult business issues, how they deal with the people who work for them, how they deal with the people for whom they work. You may be able to put on a certain face for a day or even a week, but you're not going to be able to hide the person you are for five or ten years."

Graham tells a story about Frank Batten, who for years ran Landmark Communications and founded The Weather Channel. "Frank is a person of total integrity," Graham says. "Frank once said, 'When you go outside for hire you always get a surprise. Sometimes it's a good surprise. But you never hire quite the person you thought you were hiring.'"

What do you look for in a job applicant? Years of experience? College degree? Specific skill sets? Or do you look for character? If so, you're in good company.

Years ago, Warren Buffett was asked to help choose the next CEO for Salomon Brothers. "What do you think [Warren] was looking for?" Graham asks. "Character and integrity—more than even a particular background. When the reputation of the firm is on the line every day, character counts."

Don't like surprises? Then hire people who have integrity. Want to ensure a good fit with the people you hire? Then hire people who have integrity. Want to ensure your reputation with customers? Then hire people who have integrity.

Are we saying that nothing else matters? No. But we are saying that nothing matters more.

Critical Thinking

1. Describe Warren Buffett's hiring practices that assure he is hiring integrity.
2. What are the top three characteristics that an ethical leader must exhibit (from your perspective)?
3. What area in your life do you need to work on to become an ethical job candidate? What steps can you take to develop ethically in that area?

Internet References

Entrepreneur
   http://www.entrepreneur.com/article/235101

Montana State University Billings
   http://www.msubillings.edu/BusinessFaculty/larsen/MGMT452/HR%20Articles/Can%20You%20Interview%20for%20Integrity%20-%20Across%20the%20Board%20%28MarApr%202007%29.pdf

Recruiterbox
   http://recruiterbox.com/blog/what-warren-buffett-wants-to-know-before-he-hires-you/

From *Integrity Works: Strategies for Becoming a Trusted, Respected and Admired Leader* by **Dana Telford** and **Adrian Gostick.**

Article   Prepared by: Eric Teoro, *Lincoln Christian University*

Diversity and Inclusion, Past, Present, and Future

LAURA WISE

Learning Outcomes

After reading this article, you will be able to:

- Understand the changing nature of diversity and inclusion.

- Understand key issues with respect to diversity and inclusion.

As social movements across the country continue to shape global conversations around equity, the spotlight and opportunity have been thrust onto the business sector to reflect the values society cares about most. For the first time ever, this generation of the U.S. workforce is demanding a more genuine commitment to diversity and inclusion, one that represents the spectrum of our population and the various social movements happening in and across the communities they serve.

The Civil Rights era, the fight for Women's Rights, and countless other movements have laid the groundwork for how the business community engages in D&I today. In 1948, President Truman desegregated the armed forces with EO 9981, making discrimination based on race, color, religion, or natural origin illegal for all members of the armed services. Nearly two decades later, The Civil Rights Act of 1964 made it illegal for any business to practice discriminatory hiring, or firing, practices. Fast forward some 48 years to Pao v. Kleiner Perkins: Even though Ellen Pao lost this landmark case, she succeeded in bringing gender discrimination in the workplace to the forefront of public conversation.

Since the advent of the dot.com era, technology, and tech companies as we know it, D&I has experienced a resurgence. The concept of the "whistle blower" was once reserved for issues of national security, that is, Watergate, WikiLeaks, and the Chelsea Manning case. However, in recent years, the concept has been used to expose inequality in the workplace. In February 2017, Susan Fowler published the now viral essay, "Reflecting on one very, very strange year at Uber," calling the company out for their sexist work environment. Google has come under fire in recent years as well when then Google employee James Damore's erratic manifesto on "women's neuroticism" also went viral.

D&I is no longer black and white, it is now a part of a larger dialogue about equity for all who come to the table with diverse perspectives.

D&I is no longer black and white, it is now a part of a larger dialogue about equity for all who come to the table with diverse perspectives. While D&I was once conveniently buried deep within the pages of the annual reports of our top organizations, the public conversation has changed the way that companies across industries engage with the issue.

Earlier this year, Pew Research Center published a report on equity and diversity in the STEM workplace. They found that African Americans who work in science, technology, engineering, and math fields are more likely than other STEM workers from other racial or ethnic backgrounds to say they have faced discrimination on the job. The experiences of women also highlight the glaring inequalities in male-dominated STEM workplaces. Not to mention that women—women of color in particular—have been well-documented for shedding light on the reality that there is a glaring lack of funding for founders of color.

CEO of Marca Studio and Clinical Professor of Marketing for the Bard MBA in Sustainability program, Jorge Fontanez, shared three critical insights on the trends that we're seeing in the D&I space today:

1. **CEO Leadership Is an Opportunity:** Fontanez points out that trust in organizations is at an all-time low, but trust in CEOs, however, is up. This trust provides an opportunity for leaders to speak up and out about equity in the workplace. Fontanez shares a recent example, "CEO of Salesforce, Marc Benioff, was recently in a 60-minute interview speaking to how Salesforce is attempting to create equity in respect to pay. They have invested something like six million dollars or more to make sure that women and men are paid equally in the post that they are in."

2. **Retention:** Representation is no longer enough. Success in D&I in the future will be centered around retention. Fontanez explains, "D&I in its name focuses on inclusion. It's important to recognize that the focus on inclusion is as much about who's at the table as it is to create organizations where employees wanting to stay."

3. **Culture:** It will be the role of companies now and in the future to create more welcoming workplaces. Often times companies recruit diverse talent, but don't think to recreate a culture where diverse talent can thrive. Fontanez explains how retention and culture overlap, "This is a different dynamic, particularly for a generation who has in some ways navigated their careers going from one company to another and gaining experience in a very different way than the baby boomer generation who stuck around for 25 years until retirement; it leads to a lot of institutional knowledge being lost. Culture is what should be addressed as a result and more so over the next 20 years."

More often than not, leaders within the D&I movement say issues of retention are about more than just cultivating a strong pipeline of diverse candidates. D&I should be about creating a company culture that not only brings in young, diverse, talent but also knows how to create avenues for success. Fontanez makes it a point to regularly ask his MBA students the critical question that many in the CR space often wrestle with, "Are corporations responsible for advancing social progress?" Although there's no one-size-fits-all solution, it has been said that social progress is a topic this generation of the American workforce cares about and wants to see reflected in their everyday work environment.

As millennials rise in the ranks of corporate leadership, office cultures will change. Looking ahead, the key to a thriving organization will be one that makes room for diverse ideas, backgrounds, and experiences, and recreates a model of success that redefines and strengthens opportunity for all.

Critical Thinking

1. Describe instances where you have witnessed violations of diversity and inclusion. Why do you consider these to be violations? What should have taken place?

2. Develop a standard for diversion and inclusion in the workplace. What behaviors are associated with, required of, necessary to implement, the standard?

3. What challenges do you, personally, have with respect to diversity and inclusion? How can you address these challenges?

Internet References

Advance Systems
https://advancesystemsinc.com/maintaining-workplace-diversity/

Ethics & Compliance Initiative
https://www.ethics.org/how-to-turn-diversity-into-a-business-imperative/

ResearchGate
https://www.researchgate.net/publication/254842670_Reframing_the_Business_Case_for_Diversity_A_Values_and_Virtues_Perspective

Article   Prepared by: Eric Teoro, *Lincoln Christian University*

The Pernicious Problems of Diversity Training

JAYINEE BASU

Learning Outcomes

After reading this article, you will be able to:

- Understand barriers to effective diversity training.

- Understand steps an organization can take to improve diversity training.

For many of us who work in compliance, the crucial role of training in creating and maintaining diverse workplaces that are free of discrimination is abundantly clear. Since the enactment of Title VII that protects individuals from unfair discrimination in the workplace, the employment landscape of our nation has changed rapidly to more adequately reflect the multitude of identities and ways of being that exist in the national population.

However, we still have a long way to go. 2015 marked the 50th anniversary of the Equal Employment Opportunity Commission (EEOC). Last year, the EEOC filed 142 lawsuits alleging discrimination in the private sector and secured more than $525 million for victims of discrimination in private, state, and local government, and federal workplaces. It's apparent that there are still individuals and organizations who either do not know about or do not prioritize diversity within their work culture, and compliance training is an excellent way to establish a common expectation of behavior.

Or is it? The complexity of human psychology often means that the simplest and most intuitive solutions don't work. Last week, we discussed the importance of diversity in the workplace. This week, we'll look at the barriers to effective compliance training and how to address them in order to foster a diverse community.

Forcing Managers to Take Diversity Training Can Backfire

The terms "diversity training" and "compliance training" are often conflated. Indeed, when diversity education is built into compliance requirements, diversity and compliance training may be one and the same. While this kind of bundling may appear convenient, it may not be the most effective. Without thoughtful implementation of each, neither one is particularly successful, or worse, are counterproductive. As an analysis of data collected from 800 firms over 30 years conducted by two professors of sociology showed:

> [F]irms that put managers through diversity training and give them annual diversity ratings signal to those managers that they are the problem. Formal job tests and performance ratings that are used to stem bias send the message that managers can't be trusted to make personnel decisions. Civil-rights grievance procedures signal that workers have to be protected from managers.

Of course, the solution is not to get rid of civil-rights grievance procedures, which have been crucial in protecting basic freedoms. Nor is it to eliminate compliance training, leaving large swaths of people in the dark about their duties under the law.

What this analysis does suggest, however, is that organizations should use a *program*, instead of a single course, that is designed specifically to take into account the social and psychological context of its audience. An effective training program should identify which kinds of discourse are appropriate for compliance and which kinds of discourse ought to be facilitated under noncompliance contexts. In addition to our current course catalog, LawRoom is in the process of developing a suite of courses that can be mixed and matched to create a program that's right for your organization. Our Learning Management System and reporting allows administrators to assign, track progress, and analyze long-term trends.

Diversity Training Courses Are Often Low Quality

Presumed fair: Ironic effects of organizational diversity structures, a paper published in the Journal of Personality and Social Psychology (Kaiser et al.), explains that the effect of diversity training ironically reducing diversity happens at least partially due to training programs being "developed by human resource managers and self-professed diversity experts who have neither the training in theoretical and empirical issues from science on diversity nor the necessary background to evaluate the effects of these programs." This means that using training built on strong research and instructional excellence is of utmost importance.

Diversity Needs to be Operationalized

One big problem in training on these matters is that not many organizations use an operational definition of diversity. That is, they haven't outlined *what* kind of diversity they want to foster and *why*. There are legal expectations that every organization is nondiscriminatory of protected characteristics like gender or race, but that should generally be the minimum standard for a diverse workforce. Cognitive diversity may be just as important, but harder to operationalize. The Deloitte University Press suggests that hiring managers find the skill gaps in their operations, then hire with the specific goal of filling those gaps instead of picking the most overall qualified applicant. Often, gaps are difficult to define due to interconnected complexities. In such a case, Deloitte suggests hiring and encouraging opinionated employees who can bring fresh thinking to a problem, even if it means an overhaul of how things have generally been done. The potential disruption this may cause could also be viewed as growing pains.

Too Many Diversity Initiatives Talk the Talk but Don't Walk the Walk

A particularly difficult problem in establishing effective diversity structures is that organizations hyping their own commitment to diversity can actually reduce their diversity by instilling a false sense of security in not only its own personnel but even the justice system. Kaiser and colleagues noted that an examination of more than "1,000 federal civil rights legal decisions over a 35-year period" indicated that "over time, judges increasingly showed deference to organizations' diversity management structures." This led to the conclusion that judges tended to assume that "the mere presence of diversity structures was evidence of an organization's compliance with civil rights law, without questioning whether the structure actually provided protection for employees or more fair systems of governance."

The most effective action an organization can take to increase its diversity is to create task forces and actively recruit diverse individuals for supervisory positions. A paper in the American Sociological Review concludes that:

Reforms that engage managers in recruiting and training women and minorities for management posts promote diversity. Those designed to control managerial bias lead to resistance and tend to backfire. Reforms that increase hiring and promotion transparency advance diversity by expanding the applicant pool and eliciting accountability. Accountability to diversity managers or federal regulators, moreover, leads managers to be more attentive to the effects of reforms, rendering discretion-control and transparency reforms more effective.

The implications of poor diversity training are massive. Organizations that use low-quality training that is designed primarily to "check the box" are not only ineffective but actively causing harm. Choosing a training program that is thoughtfully structured and well-researched, operationalizing the definition of diversity, and bolstering training with active recruiting and mentoring initiatives are some solid ways to ensure that your organization is reaping the benefits of a diverse workforce.

LawRoom provides online compliance training on topics like ethics, unconscious bias, and data security to thousands of companies and universities. To learn more, visit us here: LawRoom.com.

Critical Thinking

1. Describe diversity-training programs in which you have participated. What were their strengths and weaknesses?

2. Develop an outline for a diversity-training program. What topics would you cover? Why would you cover those topics?

Internet References

Harvard Business Review
https://hbr.org/2017/07/two-types-of-diversity-training-that-really-work

The Verge
https://www.theverge.com/2017/8/9/16122072/google-diversity-bias-training-james-damore-memo

---

JAYINEE BASU is an instructional writer and part of the creative development team at EverFi. Having earned her BA in Literature/Writing and Political Science at UC San Diego, she is currently finishing a post-bac program at UC Berkeley. She is the author of a book of poems entitled Asuras (Civil Coping Mechanisms 2015).

Article   Prepared by: Eric Teoro, *Lincoln Christian University*

Intel Wants a Less White, Less Male Staff. Good Luck

Recruiting and retaining minority employees in a large company takes years, not months.

Akane Otani

Learning Outcomes

After reading this article, you will be able to:

- Describe the steps Intel is taking to increase workplace diversity.

- Describe the challenges with increasing workplace diversity.

Intel wants to be less male and white. Chief Executive Officer Brian Krzanich pledged on Tuesday to spend $300 million to boost the diversity of the workforce at Intel, which, like many other technology companies, has been criticized for employing woefully few women, blacks, and Hispanics. By 2020, Intel hopes, women and underrepresented minorities will be fully represented in its workforce.

Intel's ambitions are admirable. The company may well be the first tech giant to publicly set aside this much money to tackle workplace diversity, even as others—including Facebook and Microsoft—have paid lip service to the topic in recent months. Yet it would be premature to consider the battle anywhere near won. Making a large company more diverse is harder than most people think.

"Diversity isn't something you can buy quickly. It has to be an investment, and it has to take time," says Marilyn Nagel, CEO of Watermark, a nonprofit working to increase the representation of female leaders in companies.

The first problem is one of mathematics. Intel, according to its 2013 EEO-1 (Equal Employment Opportunity) report, has more than 57,000 employees in the U.S., 57 percent of whom are white and 29 percent of whom are Asian. Just 8 percent of its employees are Hispanic; 4 percent black; 1 percent multiracial; 0.5 percent American Indian; and 0.2 percent native Hawaiian or Pacific Islander. Women are outnumbered 3 to 1 by men. The racial and gender disparities are even more stark at the top of the company, where white men hold 133 of 187 executive and senior management positions and white women hold an additional 23.

Intel hopes to attract more women and minorities to its ranks by funding engineering scholarships and working more closely with computer science departments at historically black colleges and other schools. But realistically, Intel will have to recruit and hire thousands of qualified software engineers and developers before it makes a dent in its percentage of minority and female employees—a venture that will take years, not months, to carry out.

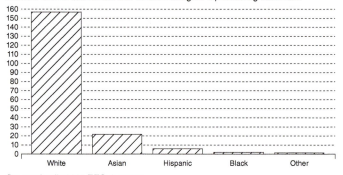

It's Lonely at the Top
Number of Intel executives and senior managers representing each race

Source: Intel's 2013 EEO-1 report

Making things more difficult, it's not just a matter of getting

Making things more difficult, it's not just a matter of getting more employees of different races and genders into the building. Diversity has to stick. Hiring may spike, but if minority employees don't feel like they're welcome, they'll leave. And there's plenty of evidence showing large swaths of minorities and women have felt isolated by peers in the tech industry—whether they've been told not to ask for pay raises; mistaken as a security guard or administrative assistant as a black employee; or assumed, as a female developer attending an industry event, to be the girlfriend of a man.

Where Are the Women in the Tech Industry?
Percentage of male and female employees in different roles at Intel

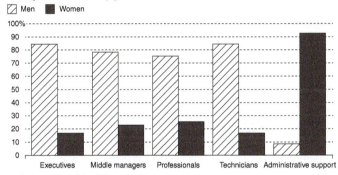

Source: Intel's 2013 EEO-1 report

"People who are being recruited have to be able to say they know Intel is a company that will support people like them at the highest level," Watermark's Nagel says. That takes seeking out diverse candidates for senior roles and "educating the entire organization to make sure there aren't unconscious biases, or even conscious biases, that are keeping the playing field from being level," she says. It requires making sure employees have advocates who can stand up for them in the workplace.

Companies have failed to take diversity seriously for years. Why? Often, employees say, they don't see their workplace putting enough skin in the game. In a *Forbes* survey of 321 executives working at large multinationals, 46 percent said they felt budget issues were holding them back. Another 46 percent said middle managers weren't carrying out diversity initiatives adequately, and 42 percent said people were more concerned with surviving the economy than improving diversity.

Abercrombie & Fitch offers a cautionary tale: After settling a $40 million lawsuit over allegedly putting minority employees in back-of-store jobs, the clothing retailer agreed in 2004 to conduct diversity training for hiring managers and to tie progress on diversity initiatives into managers' compensation. Since then, Abercrombie has been accused of telling an employee her hijab violated the company's dress code, wrongfully dismissing an employee with a prosthetic limb, and discriminating against plus-size consumers.

Making a company more diverse in a meaningful, lasting way requires more than a new policy here, a few polite words there. Intel should keep that in mind as it starts to transform this laudable commitment into a tangible reality.

Because of the company's size and reach, Nagel says, substantial change will be a challenge. "It's going to take a major cultural shift over time."

Critical Thinking

1. Is workplace diversity an ethical issue? Why or why not?
2. How can workplace diversity impact workplace ethics? Defend your position.
3. Should companies look for employees who have diverse ethical viewpoints? Why or why not?

Internet References

Houston Chronicle: Small Business
http://smallbusiness.chron.com/cultural-diversity-business-ethics-26116.html
Sage Journals
http://sgo.sagepub.com/content/2/2/2158244012444615
Texas Tech University
http://sdh.ba.ttu.edu/OrgDyn07%20Ethics.pdf

Article   Prepared by: Eric Teoro, *Lincoln Christian University*

Sexual Harassment Training Doesn't Work. But Some Things Do

Traditional Methods Can Backfire, but Ideas like Teaching Bystanders to Intervene and Promoting More Women Have Proved Effective

CLAIRE CAIN MILLER

Learning Outcomes

After reading this article, you will be able to:

- Understand how harassment training can backfire.
- Understand how to create a workplace culture that effectively works against harassment.

Many people are familiar with typical corporate training to prevent sexual harassment: clicking through a PowerPoint, checking a box that you read the employee handbook, or attending a mandatory seminar at which someone lectures about harassment while attendees glance at their phones.

At best, research has found that type of training succeeds in teaching people basic information, like the definition of harassment and how to report violations. At worst, it can make them uncomfortable, prompting defensive jokes, or reinforce gender stereotypes, potentially making harassment worse. Either way, it usually fails to address the root problem: preventing sexual harassment from happening in the first place.

That's because much of the training exists for a different reason altogether. Two 1998 Supreme Court cases determined that for a company to avoid liability in a sexual harassment case, it had to show that it had trained employees on its anti-harassment policies.

But while training protects companies from lawsuits, it can also backfire by reinforcing gender stereotypes, at least in the short term, according to research by Justine Tinkler, a sociologist at the University of Georgia. That's because it tends to portray men as powerful and sexually insatiable and women as vulnerable. Her research has shown this effect no matter how minimal the training. "It puts women in a difficult position in terms of feeling confident and empowered in the workplace," she said.

Other research found that training that described people in a legal context, as harassers or victims, led those being trained to reject it as a waste of time because they didn't think the labels applied to them, known as an "identity threat reaction," said Shannon Rawski, a professor of business at the University of Wisconsin, Oshkosh. Training was least effective with people who equated masculinity with power. "In other words, the men who were probably more likely to be harassers were the ones who were least likely to benefit," said Eden King, a psychologist at Rice University.

Training is essential but not enough, researchers say. To actually prevent harassment, companies need to create a culture in which women are treated as equals and employees treat one another with respect.

"Organizations often implement training programs in order to reduce their likelihood of being named in harassment suits or to check a box for E.E.O.C. purposes," Ms. King said, referring to the Equal Employment Opportunity Commission. "If we're actually trying to change or reduce the likelihood of sexual harassment, that's a different outcome altogether. That's not a knowledge problem, that's a behavior problem."

Here are evidence-based ideas for how to create a workplace culture that rejects harassment. Researchers say they apply not just to men attacking women but to other types of harassment, too.

Empower the Bystander

This equips everyone in the workplace to stop harassment, instead of offering people two roles no one wants: harasser or victim, Ms. Rawski said. Bystander training is still rare in corporate America but has been effectively used on college campuses, in the military and by nonprofits.

One study found that soldiers who received the training were significantly more likely than those who did not to report having taken action when they saw assault or harassment. Another found that it changed college students' attitudes regarding sexual violence and individuals' ability to stop it, a change measurable both immediately after the training and a year later.

Trainers suggest choices for what to do as a bystander. Most don't advise confronting the harasser in the moment, because it can escalate and put the bystander in jeopardy. If comfortable doing so, they suggest a bystander can say something like, "That joke wasn't funny."

Another option is to disrupt the situation, such as by loudly dropping a book or asking the victim to come to the conference room. (Charles Sonder, referred to as Snackman in a widely shared video, defused a fight on the subway by standing between the combatants, eating chips.)

Observers can talk to the harasser later, by asking questions but not lobbing accusations: "Were you aware of how you came off in that conversation?" Researchers also suggest talking openly about inappropriate behavior, like asking colleagues: "Did you notice that? Am I the only one who sees it this way?"

One crucial element, researchers say, is for bystanders to talk to targets of harassment. They often feel isolated, and observers might not know if they thought the interaction was consensual or amusing. Colleagues could say: "I noticed that happened. Are you O.K. with that?" If not, they could offer to accompany the victim to the human resources department.

"So many victims blame themselves, so a bystander saying, 'This isn't your fault, you didn't do anything wrong,' is really, really important," said Sharyn Potter, a sociologist at the University of New Hampshire who runs a research group there for sexual violence prevention.

Bystanders are unlikely to be present when the most egregious offenses happen, but harassers often test how far they can go by starting with inappropriate comments or touches, said Robert Eckstein, the lead trainer at the research group. A good workplace culture stops them before the offenses get worse.

"Bystander intervention is not about putting on your cape and saving the day," he said. "It's about having a conversation with a friend about the way they talk about women."

Encourage Civility

One problem with traditional training, researchers say, is that it teaches people what not to do—but is silent on what they should do. Civility training aims to fill that gap.

Fran Sepler, who designed new training programs for the E.E.O.C., starts by asking participants to brainstorm a list of respectful behaviors. These often sound trivial, she said, but aren't common enough, like praising work, refraining from interrupting and avoiding multitasking during conversations. A big one is spotlighting contributions by people who are marginalized. A person could say: "She just raised that same idea. Would she like to expand on it?"

Ms. Sepler gives people scripts for how to give and receive constructive feedback about rude behavior, so it can be dealt with in the moment. She teaches supervisors how to listen to complaints without being dismissive.

Train Seriously and Often

The most effective training, researchers say, is at least four hours, in person, interactive, and tailored for the particular workplace—a restaurant's training would differ from a law firm's. It's best if done by the employees' supervisor or an external expert (not an H.R. official with no direct oversight).

It also seems to help if white men are involved in the training. A recent paper found that women and minorities are penalized in performance reviews for supporting diversity, while white men are taken more seriously when they do it. Another found a backlash against training when it was done by a woman but not a man.

Training shouldn't be infrequent, and the topic should come up in conversations about other things, whether strategy or customer service, said KC Wagner, a harassment prevention trainer at Cornell's ILR School.

"We're talking about literally generations of people getting away with abusing power," Mr. Eckstein said. "Thinking you can change that in a one-hour session is absurd. You're not going to just order some bagels and hope it goes away."

Promote More Women

Research has continually shown that companies with more women in management have less sexual harassment. It's partly because harassment flourishes when men are in power and women aren't, and men feel pressure to accept other men's sexualized behavior.

It also helps to reduce gender inequality in other ways, research shows, like paying and promoting men and women equally, and including both sexes on teams.

Encourage Reporting

Most women don't report harassment. Some don't want to take the risk alone; fear retaliation; don't know whom to report it to; or don't think anything will be done. They may not want to end someone's career—they just want to stop the behavior.

The E.E.O.C. has suggested a counterintuitive idea: reward managers if harassment complaints increase, at least initially, in their departments—that means employees have faith in the system. It also recommended giving dozens of people in the organization responsibility for receiving reports, to increase the odds that victims can talk to someone they're comfortable with.

Ian Ayres, a Yale professor of law and management, has written about using so-called information escrows for harassment reporting. Victims submit a time-stamped complaint against an abuser, and can request that it is reported only if another employee files a complaint against the same person.

Researchers also suggested proportional consequences: harassers shouldn't be automatically fired; it should depend on the offense.

"If the penalty is someone's always going to get fired, lots of targets won't come forward," Ms. Rawski said. "But research suggests if you let the small things slide, it opens the door for more severe behaviors to enter the workplace."

Critical Thinking

1. Describe instances of harassment you have witnessed in organizational settings. What were the effects of such harassment?

2. Describe harassment policies with which you are familiar, or research several organizations regarding harassment policies. What are the strengths and weaknesses of the policies?

3. Develop a harassment policy for the organization at which you work. What behaviors would violate the policy? What behaviors would adhere to, uphold, promote the policy?

Internet References

Society for Human Resource Management
https://www.shrm.org/resourcesandtools/hr-topics/employee-relations/pages/workplace-harassment-training.aspx

Software Advice
https://www.softwareadvice.com/resources/ideas-for-sexual-harassment-training/

U.S. Equal Employment Opportunity Commission
https://www.eeoc.gov/eeoc/task_force/harassment/report.cfm#_Toc453686310

CLAIRE CAIN MILLER writes about gender, families, and the future of work for The Upshot. She joined *The Times* in 2008, and previously covered the tech industry for *Business Day*.

Unit 4

UNIT

Prepared by: Eric Teoro, *Lincoln Christian University*

Ethical Issues and Dilemmas in the Workplace

An ethical issue can be defined as a situation in which a person or group of individuals need to choose between alternatives, and the need for those alternatives to be assessed as being either morally right or wrong. Typically, ethical issues focus on the conflict between ethical and unethical behavior. An ethical dilemma, on the other hand, refers to a situation in which an individual or group of individuals need to make a choice between moral requirements. As such, ethical dilemmas pose more complex problems. Regardless of the choice an actor or group of actors make, they risk violating other ethical principles. Both ethical issues and ethical dilemmas occur within organizational settings. It is imperative, therefore, that managers, employees, and students recognize different courses of actions, and determine the ethicality of those courses.

Today's businesses face many ethical issues and dilemmas. Should employees should blow the whistle when they are aware of corporate wrongdoing? How should such employees navigate the competing claims of loyalty to an employer and the common good? What if blowing the whistle hurts innocent people? How can companies overcome the temptation to commit fraud when faced with competing claims? What are the parameters for utilizing technology in market research, and how does a company balance its need for consumer information and consumers' right to privacy? How does a company prohibit employee social media usage at the workplace to prevent loss of productivity while using that same technology to develop an unhealthy addiction in customers to the company's products or services? What ethical concerns arise when marketing to children? Who is primarily responsible for the marketing messages children receive–companies or parents?

Article   Prepared by: Eric Teoro, *Lincoln Christian University*

Overcoming the Fraud Triangle

CURTIS C. VERSCHOOR

Learning Outcomes

After reading this article, you will be able to:

- Describe the three elements that contribute to fraud.
- Describe the role of whistleblowing in combating fraud.

Companies still need to do more to lessen the financial pressures and reduce the rationalizations that lead to fraud.

The Financial Executives Research Foundation (FERF) recently published the results of its surveys of financial executives, managers, and staff. The report, Breaking the Cycle of Fraud, recommends strategies to mitigate wrongdoing in the two areas of the fraud triangle that are most closely connected to ethical matters: financial pressure and rationalization.

The fraud triangle was created by criminology researchers Edwin Sutherland and Donald Cressey to describe the three elements that come together when an individual commits fraud:

- Opportunity (weak internal controls) allows the fraud to occur.
- Financial pressure (motive) is the perceived need for committing the fraud.
- Rationalization (weak ethics) is the mind-set of the fraudster that justifies the crime.

By imposing stronger internal controls and processes, companies can take specific, visible action to reduce the risk of opportunity. But financial pressure and rationalization closely involve individuals' ethical framework and organizational culture, and those are much more difficult to influence overtly and directly.

Financial Pressure

Breaking the Cycle reiterates the widely described importance of a positive tone at the top of the organization in mitigating financial pressure. The report describes numerous historical examples where a pressured corporate culture brought ruin. In these cases, achieving short-term financial performance targets for bonus purposes was given far higher priority by senior executives than was acting ethically and considering the sustainability of the enterprise.

A resulting ethical culture of failure to "walk the talk" permeates the attitudes of lower-level executives and employees who are likely to do almost anything to please their bosses— even if it violates provisions in the organization's code of conduct as well as their own personal ethical standards.

It doesn't seem like companies are expanding performance goals to avoid this trap. On April 29, 2015, the SEC announced a proposed rule to require companies to disclose "the relationship between executive pay and a company's financial performance." The new rule is intended to help shareholders be better informed when electing directors and voting on executive compensation. The metric chosen to represent company performance is total shareholder return (TSR) calculated on an annual basis and compared to the TSR of a peer group of companies. But this rule will only reinforce the existing focus on short-term financial goals and targets. Performance measurements for rewarding senior executives and others should be expanded to include accomplishment of more ethics-based matter.

Rationalization

The FERF report lists a number of important aspects of an effective ethical culture that strengthen efforts to avoid rationalization of improper behavior. These include useful ethics training tailored to the organization, annual surveys of employee attitudes, and effective whistleblowing programs. The training should involve all levels of the organization. It should contain real-world examples of the negative consequences of unethical behavior, be based on the organization's code of ethics, and include true-to-life applications. Other research has shown that in-person training is likely to be most effective.

The annual surveys of employee attitudes and evaluations of the ethical climate recommended by Breaking the Cycle must be professionally designed to avoid leading questions. Surveys must also be administered anonymously to encourage truthful responses that will be helpful in assessing the ethical climate of the organization and the effectiveness of the ethics program. Otherwise, the effort could backfire.

If administered properly, whistleblower or helpline programs are extremely important in detecting and deterring unethical behavior in an organization. The 2014 biannual survey by the Association of Certified Fraud Examiners (ACFE) reports that the most common method through which occupational fraud and abuse is revealed (40 percent) is tips. This is "more than twice the rate of any other detection method. Employees accounted for nearly half of all tips that led to the discovery of fraud," according to the report.

Encourage Whistleblowing

The Anti-Fraud Collaboration reported in 2014 that many employees are hesitant to report wrongdoing internally using their organization's reporting process. The reasons for hesitating are because they have a significant fear of retaliation or because they believe that senior management is involved or won't take any action to stop unethical behavior. There are some legal protections for whistleblowers in some states and some industries. This is why the IMA Statement of Ethical Professional Practice recommends that individuals having an ethical conflict should consult their own attorney—not someone affiliated with their employer—regarding their legal obligations and rights.

Ethics training should include motivation for everyone in the organization, as well as suppliers, to utilize the helpline when warranted. Some of the features of a well-designed whistleblower helpline include wide access with global language capability and adaptation to local customs, if necessary; a single helpline for all ethics-related issues; protocols for handling any

reports professionally, including documented formal processes for timely investigation and procedures for confidential reporting of results; and formal data security and document retention policies.

The IMA Statement requires that all members "shall encourage others within their organization to act in accordance with its overarching principles: Honesty, Fairness, Objectivity, and Responsibility." Have you done your share of encouragement lately?

Critical Thinking

1. Develop concrete steps a company can employ to combat fraud. Defend your recommendations.
2. Describe fraudulent behaviors. How do individuals rationalize them?

Internet References

Business Ethics
   http://business-ethics.com/2014/09/23/1840-business-fraud-culture-is-the-culprit/
EY
   http://www.ey.com/GL/en/Services/Assurance/Fraud-Investigation—Dispute-Services/11th-Global-Fraud-Survey—Driving-ethical-growth—new-markets—new-challenges
Fraud Magazine
   http://www.fraud-magazine.com/article.aspx?id=4294969523

CURTIS C. VERSCHOOR, CMA, CPA, is the Emeritus Ledger & Quill Research Professor, School of Accountancy and MIS, and an honorary Senior Wicklander Research Fellow in the Institute for Business and Professional Ethics, both at DePaul University, Chicago. He also is a Research Scholar in the Center for Business Ethics at Bentley University, Waltham, Mass., and chair of IMA's Ethics Committee. He was selected by Trust Across America-Trust Around the World as one of the Top Thought Leaders in Trustworthy Business–2015. His e-mail address is **curtisverschoor@sbcglobal.net.**

Article   Prepared by: Eric Teoro, *Lincoln Christian University*

Conceptualizing a Framework for Global Business Ethics

WILLIAM J. KEHOE

Learning Outcomes

After reading this article, you will be able to:

- Trace the history of business ethics literature.

- Describe unethical business practices being conducted in a global market.

- Develop a system that promotes global business ethics.

The imperative of globalization arguably is one of the more significant changes experienced by business in the past several decades (Levitt, 1983; Kehoe and Whitten, 1999; Hill, 2001; Cateora and Graham, 2002; Czinkota, Ronkainen, and Moffett, 2002; Keegan, 2002; Griffin and Pustay, 2003; Hill, 2003; Lascu, 2003; Yip, 2003). In pursuing globalization, firms analyze, and debate various entry strategies to host-country markets; carefully consider the appropriateness of sourcing equipment, financing, materials, personnel, and other factors of production across the global arena; argue the merits of operating in a home-country currency versus host-country currencies; and study the cultures of host countries. However, the challenges of implementing an ethical system globally sometimes are addressed only as an afterthought, particularly when an ethical problem occurs.

This manuscript addresses the importance of developing and implementing an ethical framework to facilitate the application of ethics across the expanse of a global firm's operating arena. Prior to presenting the framework, the field of global business ethics is summarized, and the more interesting, wellconceptualized, and significant literature in the field is reviewed. Then, unethical business practices in global business are identified and discussed, so as to present a platform for the development of a framework for global business ethics. The framework is conceptualized and discussed and implementation suggestions for management are presented.

Global Business Ethics as a Field of Study

Almost a decade ago, DeGeorge (1994) opined, "business ethics is still a young field, and its international dimensions have scarcely been raised, much less adequately addressed." While still relatively a young field, the literature base of global business ethics is developing rapidly and has a richness of content.

Literature of 1960s and 1970s

Among the more interesting and well-conceptualized literature in the field during the 1960s and 1970s is the work of such scholars as Baumhart (1961) introducing the concept of ethics in business and exploring the ethics of business practitioners. Raths, Harmin, and Simon (1966) provided important underpinnings on values and teaching for the new field of business ethics; Smith (1966) advanced a theory of moral sentiments; Boulding (1967) provided important underpinnings to business ethics in his scholarly examination of value judgments in economics; and Perlmutter (1969) reflected on the difficult evolution of a multinational corporation. Other notable literature of the period includes work by Kohlberg (1971) conceptualizing stages of moral development, by Bowie (1978) developing an early taxonomy of ethics for multinational corporations, and by Carroll (1979) presenting a model of corporate social performance.

Literature of the 1980s

Moving to the 1980s, significant scholarship included such literature as Engelbourg (1980) in a significant examination of the early history of business ethics and Drucker (1981) examining the concept of business ethics. Nash (1981), enlivening Bowie's (1978) taxonomy, posited 12 questions for managers to ask when considering the ethical aspects of a business decision and offered a taxonomy of shared conditions for successful ethical inquiries.

Berleant (1982) explored problems of ethical consistency in multinational firms, raising questions relevant to this day.

Laczniak (1983) developed one of the first primers in ethics for managers. McCoy (1983), in a classic article, presented a parable that is used to differentiate corporate and individual ethics. Donaldson (1985) reconciled international norms with ethical business decision-making, Kehoe (1985) examined ethics, price fixing, and the management of price strategy, and Laczznik and Murphy (1985) published a book of ethical guidelines for marketing managers. Ferrell and Gresham (1985) conceptualized a contingency framework for understanding ethical decision-making, Hoffman, Lange, and Fedo (1986) examined ethics in multinational corporations, and Murphy (1988) focused on processes for implementing business ethics. The literature period of the 1960s/1970s/1980s closed with a comprehensive work by Donaldson (1989) examining the ethics of international business.

Overall, the literature of the 1960s/1970s/1980s tended to be descriptive in methodology, nature, and tone. Of course, a descriptive nature is to be expected, as business ethics was an embryonic field at that time then. The literature introduced ethical concepts and theories to academics and practitioners in business. It anchored the field of business ethics, conceptualized its early content, developed taxonomies, and established the importance and the validity of the concept of ethics in business with both academics and practitioners.

Literature of the Early 1990s

The period of the early 1990s saw the field of business ethics begin to flourish conceptually, empirically, and operationally. Bowie's (1990) article on business ethics and cultural relativism signaled a movement from the field's descriptive tone toward higher levels of abstraction and inquiry. DeGeorge (1990) authored a book chapter examining international business systems and morality, while Donaldson (1992) presented a classic article on the language of international corporate ethics. Koehn (1992) examined the ethic of exchange, an important article in that the concept of exchange is a central underpinning of business. Velasquez (1992) explored questions of morality and the common good in international business. DeGeorge (1993) addressed the concept of competing with integrity. Green (1993) placed business ethics in a wider global context, while Kehoe (1993) examined theory and application in business ethics.

The Business Ethics Quarterly heralded a defining moment in the scholarship of business ethics by publishing an entire issue (January 1994) devoted to international business ethics. Nicholson (1994) presented a framework for inquiry in organizational ethics, the first such framework in the literature. Fraedrich, Thorne, and Ferrell (1994) assessed the application of cognitive moral development theory to business ethics.

Rossouw (1994) addressed the ethics of business in developing countries, an important article given that many ethical abuses occur in developing countries.

Delener (1995) advanced earlier scholarship on ethical issues in international marketing, Smith (1995) described marketing strategies for an ethics era, while Rogers, Ogbuehi, and Kochunny (1995) raised troubling questions of the ethics of transnational corporations in developing countries. Perhaps fittingly, given the emerging questions about ethics of transnational corporations, the Caux Roundtable's Principles for Business (1995) were published at this time, believed to be the first international code of ethics created through collaboration of business leaders in Europe, Japan, and the United States (Skelly, 1995; Davids, 1999).

Literature of the Later 1990s

Donaldson (1996), perhaps building from the troubling questions about ethics in the early 1990s, examined values in tension when home-country ethics are employed in host-country markets away from a home country. Bowie (1997) posited the moral obligations of multinational corporations, while Johnson (1997) foreshadowed ethics during turbulent times as he examined ethics in brutal markets. Kung (1997) reminded scholars that globalization calls for a global ethic. Becker (1998) applied the philosophy of objectivism to integrity in organizations. Costa (1998) argued that moral business leadership is an ethical imperative, and Dunfee (1998), in an article based on a 1996 speech, explored the marketplace of morality from the focus of a theory of moral choice. Hasnas (1998), in an article subtitled "a guide for the perplexed," attempted to clarify the field of business ethics in an interesting article examining three leading normative theories of business ethics—the stockholder theory, the stakeholder theory, and the social contract theory.

A more scholarly tone in business ethics is found particularly in works by Brock (1998), questioning whether corporations are morally defensible and by Collier (1998), theorizing the ethical organization. Other significant literature includes Ferrell (1998) examining business ethics in a global economy, Bowie (1999) reaffirming the place of a Kantian perspective in business ethics, and Buller and McEvoy (1999) examining how to create and to sustain an ethical capability in a multinational corporation. Lantos (1999) considered how to motivate moral corporate behavior, Mackenzie and Lewis (1999) focused on the case of ethical investing, and Weaver, Trevino, and Cochran (1999) posited corporate ethics programs as control systems.

In each of these articles of the later 1990s, a more scholarly, more theoretical, and less descriptive approach is manifest than in many earlier articles in the field, particularly in the literature of the 1960s, 1970s, and early 1980s.

A New Century's Literature

Continuing the scholarly tone of the later 1990s, Chonko and Hunt (2000) presented an important retrospective analysis and prospective commentary on ethics and marketing management, while Freeman (2000) examined business ethics at the millennium. Robin (2000) developed a hierarchical framework of ethical missions and a model of corporate moral development. Velasquez (2000) considered globalization and the failure of ethics. Werhane (2000) authored a seminal work on global capitalism in the 21st century—a work that foreshadows the level of analysis and depth of scholarship to which business ethics aspires and which it must attain.

A question for consideration is whether business ethics is moving toward a postmodern phase (Carroll, 2000; Gustafson, 2000), in which it is not the rules of ethics but rather the "questions that raise issues of responsibility" that will guide business ethics to its tomorrows beyond. Is the field moving toward an interesting future for scholarship in ethics in which content and issues about ethical issues not envisioned in the early 1980s will emerge for serious reflection and scholarship? Contents and issues such as a cross-cultural comparison of ethical sensitivity (Blodgett, Lu, Rose, and Vitell, 2001); myth and ethics (Geva, 2001); an examination of questions at the intersection of ethics and economics (Hosmer and Chen, 2001); ethics and perceived risk (Cherry, 2002); ethics and privacy (Connolly, 2000; McMaster, 2001); ethics and stakeholder theory (Cragg, 2002; Jensen 2002; Kaufman, 2002; Orts and Strudler, 2002); religiosity and ethical behavior (Weaver and Agle, 2002), and multinationality and corporate ethics (van Tulder and Kolk, 2001; Singer, 2002). All of these emergent areas of reflection and scholarship are areas of inquiry important in a home country, but exponentially more critical for examination as organizations move increasingly to host-country markets throughout the world.

From Literature Emerges Imperatives for Research

As the tomorrows emerge for the field of business ethics, several imperatives flow from an examination of the extant literature. One, the field of business ethics, over the past several decades, has been descriptive in nature and tone. It is imperative that business ethics rises above its descriptive beginning. Second, is the necessity to develop a replication tradition. It is troubling that the field of business ethics is somewhat lacking of a replication tradition, possibly due to being an emergent field of inquiry. There is little replication in the field, even into the 1990s or so it seems. A third imperative, possibly related to the lack of a replication tradition or perhaps causative of a lack of replication, concerns a low heuristic power of much of extant research. It is imperative that scholars in the field replicate research and build from and upon the research of others.

Diversity in Understanding of Ethics

Just as there is diversity in research in business ethics, so, too, is there diversity in the understanding of systems of ethics in the conduct of global business, a diversity of understanding that is a function of a host of economic, political, religious, and social variables that define the differences between peoples, nations, and cultures. As an example, Donaldson and Dunfee (1994), postulated that "Muslim managers may wish to participate in systems of economic ethics compatible with the teachings of the Prophet Muhammad, European and American managers may wish to participate in systems of economic ethics giving due respect to individual liberty, and Japanese managers may prefer systems showing respect for the value of the collective." In each of these situations and in similar situations within the many countries of the world, a given system of ethics, particularly a system of ethics that is home-country specific, may not be accepted, respected, understood, or practiced by host-country nationals.

While the ethics of individuals differ around the world and while a system of ethics from a home country may not be embraced by host-country nationals, managers of global firms nevertheless must raise ethics in the consciousness of their employees regardless of where employees are assigned in the world or whatever their national origins. In raising ethical consciousness, it is insufficient to do so simply by establishing a code of ethics in an organization. Rather, management must develop an ethical culture across an organization (O'Mally, 1995) and put in place an organizational structure or framework for ethics, perhaps a framework such as is advocated in this manuscript.

By advocating an ethical culture as well as having an ethical framework, Paine (1994) argued that the reputation of a firm is enhanced and its relationships with its constituencies are strengthened. Sonnenberg and Goldberg (1992) found that employees feel better about a firm and perform at higher levels when they sense ethics as part of its culture. As a result, it is posited in this research that a firm will realize higher-level results when a concern for ethics pervades the organization and is a part of its culture.

A concern for ethics and ethical values must be developed for a global firm to be holistic, to be greater than the sum of its many parts, whether a firm and its operating units are located in the home country and/or in host countries. Global holism is a necessity for success in global business and requires that "the organization has shared beliefs, attitudes, and values," including a system of ethics, which, when taken together, "creates a consistency in the way the firm treats customers, vendors, other business partners, and each other, wherever business is being done" (Daniels and Daniels, 1994). A concern for ethics in global business is a major responsibility of management, is an integral aspect (Roddick, 1994) of international trade, contributes to global holism, and is an imperative for success in global business (Trevino, Butterfield, and McCabe, 1998).

Unethical Practices in Global Business

There are many ways in which a firm might engage in unethical business practices in the global business arena, hopefully inadvertently rather than deliberately. Unethical corporate behavior may have genesis in a lack of understanding of, or an appreciation for, the culture of a host country in which a firm is operating. Many examples of unethical practices are reported in the literature. Presented below are examples developed by Kehoe (1998) and selected by a panel of executives as being among the most egregious. Since being developed as 12 examples in1998, the research has been updated to include 15 examples reported in the following paragraphs in no particular order of significance.

- The first egregious example is an unethical practice of making of payments, often unrecorded, to officials in a host country in the form of bribes, kickbacks, gifts, and/or other forms of inducement (Landauer, 1979; Kimelman, 1994; Rossouw, 2000; Sidorov, Alexeyeva, and Shklyarik, 2000; Economist Reporter, 2002c; Hanafin, 2002). These payments often are made in spite of prohibitions of the US Foreign Corrupt Practices Act (1977) against such practices.

- A second egregious example is management representing a firm as financially healthier than its actual condition. This allegedly occurred by managers requiring employees to alter forecasts, plans, and budgets in order to mirror market expectations (Fuller and Jensen, 2002), to report sales or business activity at inflated levels (Leopold, 2002), or to inflate pro forma earnings (Roman, 2002). Additionally, some managers allegedly established complex and off-balance-sheet financial structures (Colvin, 2002; Economist Editorial, 2002; Elins, 2002; McLean, 2002; Zellner and Arndt, 2002; Zellner, France, and Weber, 2002) with assets of dubious quality designed to cause an organization to appear financially healthier than was actually its true condition.

- A third egregious example is for an individual to use a position within a firm to advance one's personal

wealth at the expense of others, as is alleged to have occurred in Enron (Colvin, 2002; Elins, 2002; McLean, 2002; Nussbaum, 2002; Schmidt, 2002; Schwartz, 2002; Zellner, Anderson, and Cohn, 2002) and Nortel Networks Corporation (Crenshaw, 2002).

- A fourth egregious example, related to the first, second, and third examples and as equally egregious, and is a situation of management punishing those employees who come forward to report or blow a whistle about an unethical practice or practices (Alford, 2001; Economist Reporter, 2002a, 2002b; Mayer and Joyce, 2002). Posited as perhaps even more egregious is to ignore or to marginalize a whistleblower, alleged to have occurred in the Enron bankruptcy situation (Arndt and Scherreik, 2002; Krugman, 2002; Mayer and Joyce, 2002; Morgenson, 2002; Sloan and Isikoff, 2002; WSJ Editorial, 2002; Zellner, Anderson, and Cohn, 2002).

- A fifth example is the marketing of products abroad that have been removed from a home-country market due to health or environmental concerns. Examples given by Hinds (1982) include chemical, pharmaceutical, and pesticide products, as well as contraceptive devices, which were removed from the US market allegedly for being unsafe to the environment and/or to health, but for which marketing in other countries was continued, and, in some cases, was accelerated.

- Marketing products in host countries that are in questionable need or which are detrimental to the health, welfare, and/or economic well-being of consumers is a sixth egregious unethical practice. An often-cited example (Willatt, 1970; Post, 1985; French and Granrose, 1995; Ferrell, Fraedrich, and Ferrell, 2002) is the marketing of infant formula in developing countries by Nestle S.A. (www.nestle.com). Parents in developing countries are alleged to have been unable to afford the formula, unable to read directions to use the formula appropriately, unable to find sanitary sources of water for preparing the formula, and not to have needed the formula until Nestle convinced them that its use was necessary. Another example (White, 1997; Ferrell, Fraedrich, and Ferrell, 2002) is marketing of cigarettes in developing countries by advertising that implies that most people in the United States smoke and that smoking is "an American thing to do."

- A seventh example is a firm operating in countries that are known to violate human rights and/or failing to be an advocate for human rights in such countries. During the apartheid era in South Africa, US firms were criticized for doing business in the country and for failing to advocate human rights by publicly opposing the discrimination, oppression, and segregation of apartheid (Deresky, 1994; Sethi and Williams, 2001).

- An eight example is a firm moving jobs from a home country to low-wage host countries. When this occurs, workers in the home country are hurt because of loss of jobs (Kehoe, 1995), while workers in a host country are exploited by low wages. For example, Ballinger (1992) argued that Nike's (www.nike.com) profits increased due, in part, to the lower wages paid to workers in Nike-contracted plants outside the United States. Employees in these plants allegedly worked in excess of 10 hours per day, six days a week, for a weekly salary of less than US $50 for their efforts. The Associated Press (1997) reported that employees in Nike-contracted plants in Vietnam were paid US 20 ¢ per hour for working a 12-hour day. Encouragingly, reports in *The New York Times* (Staff Report, 1997), *Time* (Saporito, 1998), and *Fortune* (Boyle, 2002) imply that Nike is correcting the alleged abuses of employees in contracted plants in Vietnam.

- Utilizing child labor (Nichols et.al., 1993) in host countries when the law in a firm's home country prohibits such use is the ninth example of an unethical practice. While the use of child labor in a host country may be a necessity to support a child and her/his family, be preferable to unemployment, and not be of a concern to the host government, is it ethical to use children as laborers? In the past several years, a group of firms, including Nike, Reebok, L.L. Bean, Liz Claiborne, and Toys R Us, committed to a policy of prohibiting the employment of children younger than 15 years of age in factories in host countries (Headden, 1997; Bernstein, 1999; Singer, 2000). Additionally, Toys R Us has requested suppliers to seek SA 8000 certification, an international standard certifying working conditions (Singer, 2000).

- Tenth is a practice of operating in countries whose environmental standards are lax, or, the converse, being lax in respect for a host country's environment. In the Amazon, global corporations are reported (Thomson and Dudley, 1989) to have ignored their own and the host country's environmental guidelines in extracting oil. In Ireland, global firms are suspected (Keohane, 1989) of ignoring environmental regulations and to be illegally dumping hazardous waste throughout the country. In several countries, large agriculture conglomerates are bioengineering and genetically modifying crops, perhaps to the determent of the environment, animals, and people (Comstock, 2000). Finally, an emerging issue under the tenth example is the dumping of waste materials in less-developed host countries, sometimes waste of a hazardous nature that would require special handling in a home country but which is dumped carelessly in host countries (Ferrell, Fraedrich, and Ferrell, 2002).

- Eleventh is operating in a host country with a lower regard for workers' health and well-being than in the home country. Japanese companies are alleged (Itoh, 1991) to have over worked their employees both in Japan and in host countries and to have been indifferent to their health. Union Carbide is alleged (Daniels and Radebaugh, 1993) to have operated a plant in Bhopal, India with lower safety standards than its plants in more developed countries.

- Conducting business in a developing nation in such a manner as to dominate the nation's economy is a 12th example of an unethical practice. Several rubber companies have been accused of dominating the economies of the developing nations in which they operated rubber plantations. Such domination has been called *dependencia* (Turner, 1984), and has been shown to be damaging to a host country's economy, demoralizing to its people, and of questionable ethics.

- A 13th example is intervening in the affairs of a host country through such activities as influence peddling or other efforts to affect local political activity. In Italy, for example (Anonymous, 1993a), an investigation was undertaken into the alleged illegal financing of political parties by Italian business firms, as well as by foreign business entities operating in the country.

- Taking actions abroad that would be unpopular, controversial, unethical, or illegal in the home country is a 14th example. For instance, MacKenzie (1992) raised the controversial issue of whether, given advances in DNA research, a business firm has a right to patent a life form? Officials at the European Parliament in Brussels debated the legal and moral issues of this question. While a conclusion has not been reached, assuming an affirmative conclusion, may a non-European firm, operating in a European market, patent life forms in Europe if such patenting activity is unethical or illegal in the firm's home country?

- A 15th and final example is an egregious practice of a firm reinvesting little of the profit realized in a host country back in that country due to a restrictive covenant in corporate policy requiring that a majority of profit earned in a host country be repatriated back to the home country. This means that a global firm may reinvest very little back in a host country, and the citizens of the country may be exploited as a result.

Conceptualizing a Framework for Global Business Ethics

It is posited in this research that a framework for ethics is needed for firms engaged in global business across the many cultures that are encountered. A framework that points a firm safely along the global road—a code for the road, as in the lyrics of Crosby, Stills and Nash (1970), "you, who are on the road, must have a code that you can live by. . . ." Is it possible to design such a framework and to develop a code by which global businesses might live? Where do managers begin the process?

The framework for global business ethics presented here has eight stages. A firm ideally should progress through all eight stages in designing and implementing a global ethical system. The framework begins with the stage of understanding the orientation of a firm, and concludes with recommendations for promulgating and using a framework of global business ethics.

Step One—Orientation of a Firm

The first step in a framework for global business ethics is to define a firm's orientation in the global business arena. A firm may participate in global business as an exporter, a multinational firm, a multilocal multinational firm, a global firm, or some combination of these methods. Each of these methods of participation moves a firm further from being a domestic firm and gives it an increasing array of experiences in world markets. The orientation of a firm may be ethnocentric—home-country oriented; polycentric—adaptive to host countries; or geocentric—open to using the best resources wherever they are available in the world. Each of these orientation positions has implications for ethics.

As an exporter, the orientation of a firm may be generalized as primarily ethnocentric. The logic-in-use of an exporter may be generalized as being that home-country approaches should be applied wherever in the world the firm may operate. This ethnocentric logic means that home-country approaches to ethics are considered to be superior to those elsewhere in the world and may be applied whenever possible.

When a firm moves toward multinational operations, management's orientation will evolve, as the result of the experiences in host countries, from an ethnocentric viewpoint of an exporter toward a polycentric orientation as its managerial logic-in-use. This orientation recognizes that a firm must adapt to the unique aspects of each national market in which it operates. The logic-in-use is broadened by a willingness to adapt the home-country's ethical system in the various host countries in which the firm operates. This willingness to adapt its home-country ethical system is strengthened as a firm focus astutely on each host country, develops a multilocal approach to its multinational operations, brings host-country national

into management positions, and grants greater autonomy from the home-country parent. All of these things heighten a firm's willingness to adapt and/or to customize its ethical system to fit the culture of a host country.

When a firm evolves to being a global firm, management's orientation becomes geocentric, with an acceptance of and openness to concepts, ideas, processes, and people from throughout the world, including approaches to ethics. The implication of a geocentric orientation is that a firm will be more amenable to addressing values that are inherent in the culture of a host country as a system of ethics is developed.

In developing a framework for global business ethics, a global firm, with a geocentric orientation of its management, is posited to be more open to using a system of global ethics than is an exporter, whose orientation tends to be ethnocentric. In terms of orientation, a global firm generally exhibits a greater readiness to develop ethical systems that appreciate and include the diversity of culture differences found in the world. An exporter, by contrast, is a domestic firm and is posited generally to prefer home-country ethical systems.

Step Two—Differences and Similarities Between Countries

The second step toward a framework for global business ethics is to appreciate and understand the differences and similarities between countries. In global business, there obviously are significant differences between peoples, countries, and cultures. This diversity adds richness to the experience of living on the earth, but may be problematic in establishing an ethical culture in a firm.

Comparing any two countries in regard to ethics in business would find striking differences as well as similarities. For example, consider a comparison of Japan and the United States.

Japan's business culture is characterized (Shimada, 1991) as having excessive corporate competition and a focus on rationality in decision making, based on economic factors at the expense of human factors. Itoh (1991) reported that Japanese managers are criticized for being indifferent to the health of their employees. Hammer, Bradley, and Lewis (1989) found cases of influence-peddling scandals involving leading business executives and Japanese politicians. In fact, breaches in business ethics was suggested by Whenmouth (1992) to be part of the system of doing business in Japan, with unethical behavior having origins deep in the country's cultural tradition.

In comparison, business in the United States has experienced some of the same ethical lapses as in Japan. For example, Labich (1992) presented evidence showing that for some US managers, ethics had an economic basis. These managers became lax in regard for ethics during difficult economic times, but returned to a stronger appreciation of ethics when business conditions improved. The increasing number of whistleblowing cases in the United States argues that something may be remiss in corporate ethics programs (Driscoll, 1992; Dworkin and Near, 1997; Mayer and Joyce, 2002). Research by Sandroff (1990) and others found such ethical abuses as lying to employees and clients, expense account padding, favoritism, nepotism, sexual harassment, discrimination, and taking credit for the work of others are part of US business culture. All of which has led to an increasing number of business firms offering inhouse training in ethics (Hager, 1991), developing games and simulations in ethics (Ireland, 1991), establishing permanent ethics committees (Labrecque, 1990), publishing codes of ethics (Court, 1988), and contracting with ethics' consulting firms for advice and programs, in what Cordtz (1994) has called an *ethicsplosion.* One consulting firm, Transparency International, is reported (Anonymous, 1993b) to have programs to improve ethics and standards of conduct, and to have worked with companies to prevent bribe paying in the conduct of global business.

Step Three—Identify Things of Broad Agreement

While there are differences and similarities in the appreciation for ethics among countries of the world, and while there are differences and similarities in lapses of ethics among businesses from various countries, there are things about ethics to which peoples across the world may agree. This is the third step in the framework. To identify those things, or values, in which there may be common agreement around the world.

Valasquez (1992, p. 30) identified the *global common good* as an area of worldwide agreement. He argued that individuals in international business have a responsibility to contribute to the global common good, including "maintaining a congenial global climate, . . . maintaining safe transportation routes for the international flow of goods, . . . maintaining clean oceans, . . . and the avoidance of global nuclear war. The global common good is that set of conditions that are necessary for the citizens of all or of most nations to achieve their individual fulfillment. . . . "

Beyond the aspects of a global common good to which people in international business might agree, there are certain attributes of life in any society to which a majority might agree (Kehoe, 1994). These include such values and principles (Goodpaster, Note 383-007) as, obeying the law; not harming others; respecting the rights and property of others; never lying, cheating, or stealing; keeping promises and contracts; being fair to others; helping those in need; and encouraging and reinforcing these values in others, all of which Goodpaster called *moral common sense.* These moral values are reaffirmed and enlarged by Scott (2002) in identifying honest communications, respect for property, respect for life, respect for religion, and justice as important organizational moral values.

Another example of attributes to which people throughout the world agree is found in a code of ethics of Rotary International. The attributes to which some 1.2 million Rotarians in 162 countries (Rotary, 2002) agree are: truth telling, fairness to others, goodwill toward others, and acting in ways beneficial to others. These concepts are embodied in a code called the 4-Way Test of Rotary International. The code, consisting of 24 words, is as follows: 1. Is it the truth? 2. Is it fair to all concerned? 3. Will it build goodwill and better friendships? 4. Will it be beneficial to all concerned?

Step Four—Find Voice to Express Agreement

Having identified the things of broad agreement, the fourth step of the framework is to identify a voice or way of expressing those things. Understanding voice is important because it is arguably likely that there are different voices used by people in different countries to express the same value or ethical concept. In fact, within the same country, an ethical concept may be voiced differently (Gilligan, 1982) by men than by women. The challenge is to find a voice or moral language appropriate for each culture wherein a global firm may operate. The challenge further is to recognize when a change in voice is required in order to express an ethical concept in a different culture.

In order to find a voice appropriate for situations in global business ethics, an underpinning of ethical theory is an initial step. In brief, ethical theory might be presented from a teleological or a deontological frame.

Teleological theory is concerned with the *consequences* of an action or business decision. The teleological principle of utilitarianism requires that an individual act in a way to produce the greatest good for the greatest number. In acting in this manner, an individual considers not only self in a decision or action, but the impact of the act on others. An individual applying utilitarianism in decision-making "would determine the effects of each alternative and would select the alternative that optimizes the satisfactions of the greatest number of people." (Kehoe, 1993, p. 16).

Deontological theory is concerned with the *rules* used to arrive at an action or a decision rather than the consequences of the action; that is, deontological theory is rule based, whereas teleological theory is consequences based. The deontological principle of the categorical imperative (Kant, 1785) is: "Act only according to that maxim by which you can at the same time will that it should be a universal law." In other words, the categorical imperative proscribes that individuals only do those things that they can recommend to others. That is, there are certain things that must be done in order to maintain basic humanity in a society, just as there certain things that must be practiced by individuals to maintain order in an organization.

These things make up the shared moral values of an organization and are a part of its ethical culture. For example, a manager who does not participate in bribery because he or she could not admit or recommend it to others may be said to be adhering to the categorical imperative. Likewise, as other individuals in a firm adhere to the categorical imperative, it becomes a shared moral value and a part of the ethical culture of a firm.

Kidder (1994) conceptualized an example of shared moral values. He surveyed "ethical thinkers" from around the world and identified eight shared moral values that have broad application across cultures. These included love, truthfulness, fairness, freedom, unity, tolerance, responsibility, and respect for life.

A second example of shared moral values is by DeGeorge (1994). He suggested that there are moral norms that cross cultures that may be used to develop ethical standards for global business. Examples of such shared moral norms are truthfulness, respect for property, fairness, and trust.

Research by Scott (2002) elevated a third example of shared moral values. Arguing that the most important organizational value for analysis is an organization's moral values, she identified five moral values for organizations—justice, honest communication, respect for property, respect for life, and respect for religion.

Perhaps the most useful example of shared moral values is by Donaldson (1992). He analyzed six moral languages for their appropriateness in global business ethics. The languages were: virtue and vice; self-perfection through self control; maximization of human welfare; avoidance of human harm; rights and duties; and social contract. He argues (Donaldson, 1992, p. 280) that "the former three (virtue and vice; self perfection through self control; maximization of human welfare) are inappropriate for establishing a system of ethics in global business," while the "latter three (avoidance of human harm; rights and duties; social contract) are deontological ethical languages with the capacity to establish minimum rather than perfectionist standards of behavior" and are, therefore, better suited for addressing ethical issues in global business. These moral languages give voice to ethics in global business.

Step Five—Use Voice to Develop Ethical Statements

Generalizing from the conclusions concerning the appropriateness of moral languages for global business ethics, the fifth step of the framework emerges. That step is to use voice to develop ethical statements or codes of ethics.

It is posited that the voice used in a framework for global business ethics should be deontological rather than teleological, and minimum rather than perfectionist. This means that the statements developed in a framework for global business ethics

should be rule based and be minimum in standard. Said another way, simpler and shorter statements are more appropriate in developing a framework for global business ethics. Parsimony must be the guiding principle in using voice to develop ethical statements.

Step Six—Separate Core and Peripheral Values

Being guided by voice to use rule based, minimum in standard, simple, and short statements, a global business organization, as a sixth step, should determine the core values to be included in its ethical framework and in its global code of ethics. Then identify the peripheral values that may be altered or even deleted from its global code of ethics according to the culture of a host country. This means, for example, if a global firm's home country is the United States, and if it operates also in China, India, Mexico, and Russia, its global code of ethics should contain core-value statements of the home country as well as statements common across all the countries, but may contain different peripheral-value statements in each of the host countries.

It is an imperative that individuals in a global firm understand its core values and its peripheral values. Collins (1995) defined a core value as something a firm would hold even if it became a competitive disadvantage. Donaldson (1996) identified three core values that have basis in Western and non-Western culture and religious traditions—respect for human dignity, respect for basic rights, and good citizenship through support of community institutions. He postulated (Donaldson, 1996, p. 53) that core values "establish a moral compass for business practice. They can help identify practices that are acceptable and those that are intolerable—even if the practices are compatible with a host country's norms and laws. Dumping pollutants near people's homes and accepting inadequate standards for handling hazardous materials are two examples of actions that violate core values. Similarly, if employing children prevents them from receiving a basic education, the practice is intolerable" and violates core values.

To separate core and peripheral values, consider this situation. If the core values of a firm include acknowledging human equality, promoting human welfare, providing high-quality products, having fair prices, contributing to the community, and compliance with national laws, these values should be reflected in a firm's global code of ethics and promulgated to all host-country subsidiaries. If, however, a firm believes that relationships among employees, with customers, and with suppliers are best addressed at the country level, these are peripheral values to be addressed in ethical statements developed by employees in each operating location. In brief, a firm, as noted by Laczniak and Murphy (1993), should strive to have a single worldwide policy on ethics to address its core values, those values never to be compromised, but may allow addenda to its worldwide core-value policy on ethics to address peripheral values that are inherent in the culture of a host country.

Step Seven—Writing a Global Code of Ethics

The seventh step of the framework concerns writing a global code of business ethics that will be a central part of a firm's framework for global business ethics. A global code cannot and should not be written at the home-country headquarters. Rather, contributions to the code must be sought from around the world. Individuals from throughout a firm's global expanse must be involved in developing the code. This means that a committee or task force that is charged with developing the code should have representation from each geographic region in which a firm operates, or even, if possible, from each host country. Likewise, individuals from across functions and levels of hierarchy should be included, so that the result is a multi-functional, multilevel, and multinational task force. The goal must be to be as inclusive as possible in developing a global code of ethics.

Global inclusiveness is important so that a code does not contain only the concepts, ideas, prejudices theories, values, and words of a firm's home country. This is part of using voice to develop a global code. A firm's values that are reflected in a code must be stated in a globally inclusive manner. This is not easily accomplished. It can only be accomplished by being as globally inclusive in voice as possible in writing the code. This implies that those charged with developing a global code of ethics must be empowered to be in close and regular contact wherever located in the world. This may mean that a firm regularly uses teleconferencing while developing the code. It also may mean that meetings of the task force are held regularly in various host countries while the code is being developed. Put simply, a global code of ethics cannot and should not be developed solely in a home-country venue.

Step Eight—Promulgating and Using a Global Code of Ethics

The final step of a framework for global business ethics is to promulgate and use the code of ethics. This means that the code must be translated effectively to the language of each host country. In each host country, some process for ethics representation should be arranged. It may be that a manager is assigned responsibility for ethics in addition to other duties, or preferably an ethics officer is designated formally in each country. That individual should be charged with promulgating the code of ethics, encouraging its use, and managing and refining the

firm's framework for global business ethics. The posited result of having a framework of global business ethics is that there should be higher levels of ethical behavior across a global firm when a framework is in place, as was reported by Ferrell and Skinner (1988) with codes of ethics in domestic firms. Simply put, ethics must be made "salient and be part of an ongoing conversation" within an organization (Freeman, 2001). The goal of developing a framework for global business ethics is to have ethics often considered, rather than seldom or never considered in the conduct of global business (Kehoe, 1998).

Conclusion

A mosaic of diversity continues to shine brilliantly across the landscape of global business. It is a landscape of business firms, large and small, operating in various ways in an increasing number of the countries of the world. It is a landscape of diverse cultures, with differing appreciations for and understandings of ethics. It is a landscape of individual managers encountering choices that reflect all the ambiguities, differences, and subtleties of a global mosaic of diversity. It is a landscape of people unified by shared moral values and of global firms in which ethics must be an imperative.

More than 40 years ago, Berle (1954) made a statement that is relevant for today's global corporations. The statement addressed ethics and the responsibilities of management. "The really great corporation management must consider the kind of community in which they have faith and which they will serve and which they intend to help construct and maintain. In a word, they must consider the ancient problems of the good life and how their operations in the community can be adapted to affording or fostering it."

The framework conceptualized in this research is anchored in a concept of shared moral values and developed by using moral languages to give meaning to ethics across cultures. The framework allows for a firm to remain loyal to its core values in situations involving questions of ethics, but allows different peripheral-value statements in host countries. When developing a framework for global business ethics, contributions must be sought from throughout the world. This means that individuals from throughout a firm's global expanse must be involved in developing the framework. Such a global corporate community developed framework will contribute to a concept of ethics being embraced throughout a firm, and to ethics being a word often spoken by employees throughout a firm, rather than a word seldom spoken or never spoken.

A report of the Center for Business Ethics (Hoffman, 2000) noted "business ethics is no longer a set of national initiatives, if it ever was. It is now a global affair." Anywhere a firm operates in the world, its activities must be ethical and adapted to affording or fostering the good life. This is an ethical imperative. Simply yet profoundly stated (Freeman, 2002), "ethics is about the most important parts of our lives and must be center stage" in any activity whether of a business or a personal nature. The practice of ethics in global business is posited to enhance a global corporation, uplift it and its stakeholders, and ensure that its actions foster the good life.

References

Alford, C. Fred (2001). *Whistleblowers: Broken Lives and Organizational Power.* Ithaca, NY: Cornell University Press.

Anonymous (1993a). "The Purging of Italy, Inc.," *Economist,* March 20, pp. 69–70.

Anonymous (1993b). "Clean, Not Laundered," *Economist,* May 8, p. 78.

Arndt, Michael and Susan Scherreik (2002). "Five Ways to Avoid More Enrons," *Business Week,* February 18, pp. 36–37.

Associate Press Report (1997). "Conditions Deplorable at Nike's Vietnamese Plants," *The Daily Progress,* March 28, p. A2.

Ballinger, Jeffrey (1992). "The New Free-Trade Hall," *Harper's,* August, pp. 45–47.

Baumhart, Raymond C. (1961). "How Ethical Are Businessmen?" *Harvard Business Review,* July/August, pp. 6–12.

Becker, Thomas E. (1998). "Integrity in Organizations," *Academy of Management Review,* Volume 23 (1), pp. 154–161.

Berle, A. A. (1954). *The 20th Century Capitalist Revolution.* New York, NY: Harcourt, Brace and World, pp. 166–176.

Berleant, Arnold (1982). "Multinationals and the Problem of Ethical Consistency," *Journal of Business Ethics,* 3, August, pp. 185–195.

Bernstein, Aaron (1999). "Sweatshops: No More Excuses," *Business Week,* November 8, pp. 104–106.

Blodgett, Jeffrey G., Long-Chaun Lu, G. M. Rose and S. J. Vitell (2001). "Ethical Sensitivity to Stakeholder Interests: A CrossCultural Comparison," *Journal of the Academy of Marketing Science,* Volume 29 (2), pp. 190–202.

Boulding, Kenneth (1967). "The Basis of Value Judgments in Economics," in Sidney Hook, ed., *Human Values and Economic Policy.* New York, NY: New York University Press.

Bowie, Norman E. (1978). "A Taxonomy for Discussing the Conflicting Responsibilities of a Multinational Corporation," in Norman E. Bowie, *Responsibilities of Multinational Corporations to Society.* Arlington, VA: Council of Better Business Bureaus, pp. 21–43.

Bowie, Norman E. (1990). "Business Ethics and Cultural Relativism," in Peter Madsen and Jay M. Shafritz, eds., *Essentials of Business Ethics.* New York, NY: Penguin Books, pp. 366–382.

Bowie, Norman E. (1997). "The Moral Obligations of Multinational Corporations," in Norman E. Bowie, ed., *Ethical Theory and Business.* Upper Saddle River, NJ: Prentice-Hall, pp. 522–534.

Bowie, Norman E. (1999). *Business Ethics: A Kantian Perspective.* New York, NY: Blackwell Publishers.

Boyle, Matthew (2002). "How Nike Got Its Swoosh Back," *Fortune,* Volume 145, June 11, p. 31.

Brock, Gillian (1998). "Are Corporations Morally Defensible?" *Business Ethics Quarterly,* Volume 8, October, pp. 703–721.

Buller, Paul F. and Glen M. McEvoy (1999). "Creating and Sustaining Ethical Capability in the Multinational Corporation," *Journal of World Business,* 34 (4), pp. 326–343.

Business Ethics Quarterly (1994, Volume 4, January). Issue devoted entirely to international business ethics, pp. 1–110.

Carroll, Archie B. (1979). "A Three-Dimensional Conceptual Model of Corporate Social Performance," *Academy of Management Review,* Volume 4, pp. 497–505.

Carroll, Archie B. (2000). "Ethical Challenges for Business in the New Millennium," *Business Ethics Quarterly,* Volume 10, Number 1, pp. 33–42.

Cateora, Philip R. and John L. Graham (2002). *International Marketing.* New York, NY: McGraw-Hill Companies, Inc.

Caux Roundtable, Principles for Business. (1995). *Society for Business Ethics Newsletter,* May, pp. 14–15.

Cherry, John (2002). "Perceived Risk and Moral Philosophy." *Marketing Management Journal,* Volume 12, Issue 1, pp. 49–58.

Chonko, Lawrence B. and Shelby D. Hunt (2000). "Ethics and Marketing Management: A retrospective and Prospective Commentary," *Journal of Business Research,* 50, pp. 235–244.

Collier, Jane (1998). "Theorising the Ethical Organization," *Business Ethics Quarterly,* Volume 8, October, pp. 621–654.

Collins, James M. (1995). "Change Is Good—But First, Know What Should Never Change," *Fortune,* May 29, p. 141.

Colvin, Geoffrey (2002). "Wonder Women of Whistleblowing," *Fortune,* August 12, p. 56.

Comstock, Gary L. (2000). *Vexing Nature? On the Ethical Case Against Agricultural Biotechnology.* Boston, MA: Kluwer Academic Publishers.

Connolly, P. J. (2000). "Privacy as Global Policy," *InfoWorld,* September 11, pp. 49–50.

Cordtz, Dan (1994). "Ethicsplosion," *Financial World,* August 16, pp. 58–60.

Costa, John Dalla (1998). The Ethical Imperative: *Why Moral Leadership Is Good Business.* Reading, MA: Addison-Wesley.

Court, James (1988). "A Question of Corporate Ethics," *Personnel Journal,* September, pp. 37–39.

Cragg, Wesley (2002). "Business Ethics and Stakeholder Theory," *Business Ethics Quarterly,* Volume 12, Number 2, April, pp. 113–142.

Crenshaw, Albert B. (2002). "Nortel Executive Quits Amid Accusations," *The Washington Post,* February 12, pp. E1 and E4.

Crosby, Stills and Nash. (1970).

Czinkota, Michael R., Ilkka A. Ronkainen and Michael H. Moffett (2002). *International Business.* Fort Worth, TX: Harcourt College Publishers.

Daniels John D. and L. H. Radebaugh (1993). *International Dimensions of Contemporary Business.* Boston, MA: PWS-Kent Publishing Company, pp. 79–80.

Daniels John L. and N. Caroline Daniels (1994). *Global Vision: Building New Models for the Corporation of the Future.* New York, NY: McGraw-Hill, Inc., p. 12.

Davids, Meryl (1999). "Global Standards, Local Problems," *Journal of Business Strategy,* January/February, pp. 38–43.

DeGeorge, Richard T. (1990). "The International Business System, Multinationals, and Morality," in Richard T. DeGeorge, *Business Ethics.* New York, NY: Macmillan Publishing Company.

DeGeorge, Richard T. (1993). *Competing With Integrity in International Business.* New York, NY: Oxford University Press.

DeGeorge, Richard T. (1994). "International Business Ethics," *Business Ethics Quarterly,* Volume 4, January, pp. 1–9.

Delener, Nejdet, ed. (1995). *Ethical Issues in International Marketing.* New York, NY: International Business Press.

Deresky, Helen (1994). *International Management.* New York, NY: Harper Collins College Publishers, pp. 516–519.

Donaldson, Thomas (1985). "Multinational Decision Making: Reconciling International Norms," *Journal of Business Ethics,* December, pp. 357–366.

Donaldson, Thomas (1989). *The Ethics of International Business.* New York, NY: Oxford University Press.

Donaldson, Thomas (1992). "The Language of International Corporate Ethics," *Business Ethics Quarterly,* Volume 2, July, pp. 271–281.

Donaldson, Thomas (1996). "Values in Tension: Ethics Away From Home," *Harvard Business Review,* September–October, p. 53.

Donaldson, Thomas and T. W. Dunfee (1994). "Toward a Unified Conception of Business Ethics: Integrative Social Contracts Theory," *Academy of Management Review,* April, p. 261.

Driscoll, Lisa (1992). "A Better Way to Handle Whistle Blowers: Let Them Speak," *Business Week,* July 27, p. 36.

Drucker, Peter (1981). "What is Business Ethics?" *The Public Interest,* Spring, pp. 18–37.

Dunfee, Thomas W. (1998). "The Marketplace of Morality: Small Steps Toward a Theory of Moral Choice," *Business Ethics Quarterly,* Volume 8, January, pp. 127–145.

Dworkin, Terry M. and J.P. Near (1997). "A Better Statutory Approach To Whistle Blowing," *Business Ethics Quarterly,* Volume 7, January, pp. 1–16.

Economist Reporter (2002a). "In Praise of Whistleblowers," *The Economist,* January 12, pp. 13–14.

Economist Reporter (2002b). "As Companies Cut Costs They Cut Corners Too. Time to Blow the Whistle?" *The Economist,* January 12, pp. 55–56.

Economist Reporter (2002c). Special Report: Bribery and Business," *The Economist,* March 2, pp. 63–65.

Elins, Michael (2002). "Year of the Whistleblower," *Business Week,* December 16, pp. 106–110.

Engelbourg, Saul (1980). *Power and Morality: American Business Ethics, 1840–1914.* Westport, CT: Greenwood Press.

Ferrell, O. C. (1998). "Business Ethics in a Global Economy," *Journal of Marketing Management,* Volume 9 (1), pp. 65–71.

Ferrell, O. C. and L. G. Gresham (1985). "A Contingency Framework for Understanding Ethical Decision Making," *Journal of Marketing,* 49 (Summer), pp. 87–96.

Ferrell, O. C. and S. J. Skinner (1988). "Ethical Behavior and Bureaucratic Structure in Marketing Research Organizations," *Journal of Marketing Research,* 25 (February), pp. 103–109.

Ferrell, O. C., John Fraedrich and Linda Ferrell (2002). *Business Ethics.* Boston, MA: Houghton Mifflin.

File: Framework for Global Business Ethics, RR&R, 2003.

Fraedrich, John, Debbie M. Thorne and O. C. Ferrell (1994). "Assessing the Application of Cognitive Moral Development Theory to Business Ethics," *Journal of Business Ethics,* 13, pp. 829–838.

Freeman, R. Edward (2000). "Business Ethics at the Millennium," *Business Ethics Quarterly,* Volume 10, January, pp. 169–180.

Freeman, R. Edward (2001). Presentation to the FBI/UVA Annual Meeting, University of Virginia, December 12, 2001.

Freeman, R. Edward (2002). Presentation to Beta Gamma Sigma Ethics Symposium, University of Virginia, February 1, 2002.

French, Warren A. and John Granrose (1995). *Practical Business Ethics.* Englewood Cliffs, NJ: Prentice-Hall, Inc.

Fuller, Joseph and Michael C. Jensen (2002). "Just Say No to Wall Street," *Working Paper 02-01,* Tuck School of Business, Dartmouth College and Harvard Business School.

Geva, Aviva (2001). "Myth and Ethics in Business," *Business Ethics Quarterly,* Volume 11, October, pp. 575–597.

Gilligan, Carol (1982). *In a Different Voice: Psychological Theory and Women's Development.* Cambridge, MA: Harvard University Press.

Goodpaster, Kenneth E. (Note 383-007). "Some Avenues for Ethical Analysis in General Management," *Harvard Business School Note 383-007,* p. 6.

Green, Ronald M. (1993). "Business Ethics in a Global Context," in Ronald M. Green, *The Ethical Manager.* New York, NY: Macmillan Publishing Company.

Griffin, Ricky W. and Michael W. Pustay (2003). *International Business.* Upper Saddle River, NJ: Prentice Hall.

Gustafson, Andrew (2000). "Making Sense of Postmodern Business Ethics," *Business Ethics Quarterly,* Volume 10, July, pp. 645–658.

Hager, Bruce (1991). "What's Behind Business' Sudden Fervor for Ethics?," *Business Week,* September 23, p. 65.

Hammer, Joshua, Bradley Martin and David Lewis (1989). "The Dark Side of Japan, Inc.," *Newsweek,* January 9, p. 41.

Hanafin, John J. (2002). "Morality and Markets in China," *Business Ethics Quarterly,* Volume 12 (January), 1–18.

Hasnas, John (1998). "The Normative Theories of Business Ethics: A Guide for the Perplexed," *Business Ethics Quarterly,* Volume 8, January, pp. 19–42.

Headden, Susan (1997). "A Modest Attack on Sweatshops," *U. S. News and World Report,* April 28, p. 39.

Hinds, M. (1982). "Products Unsafe at Home Are Still Unloaded Abroad," *The New York Times,* August 22, p. 56.

Hill, Charles W. L. (2001). *International Business.* New York, NY: McGraw-Hill.

Hill, Charles W. L. (2003). *Global Business Today.* New York, NY: McGraw-Hill.

Hoffman, W. Michael (2000). *Business Ethics: Reflections for the Center.* Waltham, MA: Center for Business Ethics, p. 6.

Hoffman, W. Michael, A.E. Lange, and D. A. Fedo, eds. (1986). *Ethics and the Multinational Enterprise.* Lanham, MD: University Press of America.

Hosmer, LaRue T. and Feng Chen (2001). "Ethics and Economics: Growing Opportunities for Research," *Business Ethics Quarterly,* Volume 11, October, pp. 599–622.

Ireland, Karin (1991). "The Ethics Game," *Personnel Journal,* March, pp. 72–75.

Itoh, Yoshiaki (1991). "Worked to Death in Japan," *World Press Review,* March, p. 50.

Jensen, Michael C. (2002). "Value Maximization, Stakeholder Theory and the Corporate Objective Function," *Business Ethics Quarterly,* Volume 12, Number 2, April, pp. 235–256.

Johnson, Elmer W. (1997). "Corporate Soulcraft in the Age of Brutal Markets," *Business Ethics Quarterly,* Volume 7, October, pp. 109–124.

Kant, Immanuel (1785). *Foundations of the Metaphysic of Morals,* L. W. Beck, translator. New York, NY: Bobbs-Merrill, 1959, p. 39.

Kaufman, Allen (2002). "Managers' Double Fiduciary Duty: To Stakeholders and To Freedom," *Business Ethics Quarterly,* Volume 12, Number 2, April, pp. 189–214.

Keegan, Warren J. (2002). *Global Marketing Management.* Upper Saddle River, NJ: Prentice Hall.

Kehoe, William J. (1985). "Ethics, Price Fixing, and the Management of Price Strategy," in Gene R. Laczniak and Patrick E. Murphy, eds., *Marketing Ethics: Guidelines for Managers.* Lexington, MA: D. C. Heath and Company, pp. 71–83.

Kehoe, William J. (1993). "Ethics in Business: Theory and Application," *Journal of Professional Services Marketing,* Volume 9, Number 1, pp. 13–25.

Kehoe, William J. (1994). "Ethics and Employee Theft," in John E. Richardson, ed., *Annual Editions: Business Ethics.* Guilford, CT: The Dushkin Publishing Group.

Kehoe, William J. (1995). "NAFTA: Concept, Problems, Promise," in B. T. Engelland and D. T. Smart, eds., *Marketing: Foundations For A Changing World.* Evansville, IN: Society for Marketing Advances, pp. 363–367.

Kehoe, William J. (1998). "The Environment of Ethics in Global Business," *Journal of Business and Behavioral Sciences,* Volume 4, Fall, pp. 47–56.

Kehoe, William J. and Linda K. Whitten (1999). "Structuring HostCountry Operations: Framing a Research Study," *Proceedings of the American Society of Business and Behavioral Sciences,* Volume 5, pp. 1–9.

Keohane, K. (1989). "Toxic Trade Off: The Price Ireland Pays for Industrial Development," *The Ecologist,* 19, pp. 144–146.

Kidder, R.M. (1994). *Shared Values for a Troubled World: Conversations with Men and Women of Conscience.* San Francisco, CA: Jossey-Bass, pp. 18–19.

Kimelman, John (1994). "The Lonely Boy Scout," *Financial World,* August 16, pp. 50–51.

Koehn, Daryl (1992). "Toward an Ethic of Exchange," *Business Ethics Quarterly,* Volume 2, July, pp. 341–355.

Kohlberg, Lawrence (1971). "Stages of Moral Development as a Basis for Moral Education," in C. M. Beck, B. S. Crittenden and E. V. Sullivan, eds., *Moral Education.* Toronto, Canada: University of Toronto Press.

Krugman, Paul (2002). "A System Corrupted," *The Wall Street Journal,* January 18, p. C1.

Kung, Hans (1997). "A Global Ethic in An Age of Globalization," *Business Ethics Quarterly,* Volume 7, July, pp. 17–32. Labich, Kenneth (1992). "The New Crisis in Business Ethics," *Fortune,* April 20, pp. 167–176.

Labrecque, Thomas G. (1990). "Good Ethics Is Good Business," *USA Today: The Magazine of The American Scene,* May, pp. 20–21.

Laczniak, Gene R. (1983). "Business Ethics: A Manager's Primer," *Business,* January–March, pp. 23–29.

Laczniak, Gene R. and Patrick E. Murphy (1985). *Marketing Ethics: Guidelines for Managers.* Lexington, MA: D. C. Heath and Company.

Laczniak, Gene R. and Patrick E. Murphy (1993). *Ethical Marketing Decisions: The Higher Road.* Boston, MA: Allyn and Bacon.

Landauer, J. (1979). "Agency Will Define Corrupt Acts Abroad by U. S. Businesses," *The Wall Street Journal,* September 21, p. 23.

Lantos, Geoffrey P. (1999). "Motivating Moral Corporate Behavior," *Journal of Consumer Marketing,* Volume 16 (3), pp. 222–233.

Lascu, Dana-Nicoleta (2003). *International Marketing.* Cincinnati, OH: Atomic Dog Publishing.

Leopold, Jason (2002). "En-Ruse? Workers at Enron Sat They Posed as Busy Traders to Impress Visiting Analysts," *The Wall Street Journal,* February 7, pp. C1 and C13.

Levitt, Theodore. (1983). "The Globalization of Markets," *Harvard Business Review,* May–June, pp. 92–93.

Mackenzie, Craig and Alan Lewis (1999). "Morals and Markets: The Case for Ethical Investing," *Business Ethics Quarterly,* Volume 9, July, pp. 439–452.

MacKenzie, Debora (1992). "Europe Debates the Ownership of Life," *New Scientist,* January 4, pp. 9–10.

Mayer, Caroline E. and Amy Joyce (2002). "Blowing the Whistle," *The Washington Post,* February 10, pp. H1 and H4–H5.

McCoy, Bowen H. (1983). "The Parable of the Sadhu," *Harvard Business Review,* September/October, pp. 103–108.

McLean, Bethany (2002). "Monster Mess: The Enron Fallout has Just Begun," *Fortune,* February 4, pp. 93–96.

McMaster, Mark (2001). "Too Close for Comfort," *Sales & Marketing Management,* July, pp. 42–48.

Morgenson, Gretchen (2002). "Enron Letter Suggests $1.3 Billion More Down the Drain," *The New York Times,* January 17, pp. C1 & C10.

Murphy, Patrick E. (1988). "Implementing Business Ethics," *Journal of Business Ethics,* Volume 7, pp. 907–915.

Nash, Laura L. (1981). "Ethics Without the Sermon," *Harvard Business Review,* November/December, pp. 79–90.

Nichols, Martha, P. A. Jacobi, J. T. Dunlop and D. L. Lindauer (1993). "Third World Families at Work: Child Labor or Child Care?," *Harvard Business Review,* January–February, pp. 12–23.

Nicholson, Nigel (1994). "Ethics in Organizations: A Framework for Theory and Research," *Journal of Business Ethics,* 13, pp. 581–596.

Nussbaum, Bruce (2002). "Can You Trust Anybody Anymore?" *Business Week,* January 28, pp. 31–32.

O'Mally, Shaun F. (1995). "Ethical Cultures—Corporate and Personal," *Ethics Journal,* Winter, p. 9.

Orts, Eric W. and Alan Strudler (2002). "The Ethical and Environmental Limits of Stakeholder Theory," *Business Ethics Quarterly,* Volume 12, Number 2, April, pp. 215–233.

Paine, Lynn S. (1994). "Managing for Organizational Integrity," *Harvard Business Review,* March–April, pp. 106–117.

Perlmutter, Howard W. (1969). "The Tortuous Evolution of the Multinational Corporation," *Columbia Journal of World Business,* January–February, pp. 11–14.

Post, James M. (1985). "Assessing the Nestle Boycott," *California Management Review,* Winter, pp. 113–131.

Raths, Louis E., Merrill Harmin and Sidney Simon (1966). *Values and Teaching.* Columbus, OH: Merrill Publishing.

Robin, Donald P. (2000). *Questions and Answers About Business Ethics: Running an Ethical and Successful Business.* Cincinnati, OH: Dame, Thompson Learning.

Roddick, Anita (1994). "Corporate Responsibility," *Vital Speeches of the Day,* January 15, pp. 196–199.

Rogers, Hudson P., Alponso O. Ogbuehi, and C. M. Kochunny (1995). "Ethics and Transnational Corporations in Developing Countries: A Social Contract Perspective" in Nejdet Delener, ed., *Ethical Issues in International Marketing.* New York, NY: International Business Press, pp. 11–38.

Roman, Monica (2002). "Deflating those Pro Forma Figures," *Business Week,* January 28, p. 50.

Rossouw, G. J. (1994). "Business Ethics in Developing Countries," *Business Ethics Quarterly,* Volume 4, January, pp. 43–51. Rotary (2002). "Rotary at a Glance," *The Rotarian,* January, p. 44. See also the Rotary International website at www.rotary.org/aboutrotary/4way.html.

Sandroff, Ronni (1990). "How Ethical Is American Business? The Working Woman Report," *Working Woman,* September, pp. 113–129.

Saporito, Bill (1998). "Taking a Look Inside Nike's Factories," *Time,* Volume 151, Issue 12, pp. 52–53.

Schmidt, Susan (2002). "Lawmaker Challenges Skilling's Denials," *The Washington Post,* February 12, pp. E1 and E5.

Schwartz, John (2002). "An Enron Unit Chief Warned and Was Rebuffed," *The New York Times,* February 20, pp. C1 and C4.

Scott, Elizabeth D. (2002). "Organizational Moral Values," *Business Ethics Quarterly,* Volume 12, Number 1, January, pp. 33–55.

Sethi, S. Prskash and Oliver F. Williams (2001). *Economic Imperatives and Ethical Values in Global Business: The South African Experience and International Codes Today.* South Bend, IN: University of Notre Dame Press.

Shimada, Hauro (1991). "The Desperate Need for New Values in Japanese Corporate Behavior," *Journal of Japanese Studies,* Winter, pp. 107–125.

Sidorov, Alexey, Irina Alexeyeva and Elena Shklyarik (2000). "The Ethical Environment of Russian Business," *Business Ethics Quarterly,* Volume 10, October, pp. 911–924.

Singer, Andrew W. (2000). "When it Comes to Child Labor, Toys R Us Isn't Playing Around," *Ethikos,* May/June, pp. 4–14.

Singer, Peter (2002). "Navigating the Ethics of Globalization," *The Chronicle of Higher Education,* October 11, pp. B7–B10.

Skelly, Joe (1995). "The Rise of International Ethics," *Business Ethics,* March/April, pp. 2–5.

Sloan, Allen and Michael Isikoff (2002). "The Enron Effect," *Newsweek,* January 28, pp. 34–35.

Smith, Adam (1966). *The Theory of Moral Sentiments.* New York, NY: Kelley Publishers.

Smith, N. Craig (1995). "Marketing Strategies for the Ethics Era," *Sloan Management Review,* Summer, pp. 85–97.

Sonnenberg, Frank K. and Beverly Goldberg (1992). "Business Integrity: An Oxymoron?," *Industry Week,* April 6, pp. 53–56.

Staff Report (1997). "Nike Suspends a Vietnam Boss," *The New York Times,* p. C3.

Thomson, Roy and Nigel Dudley (1989). "Transnationals and Oil in Amazonia," *The Ecologist,* November, pp. 219–224.

Trevino, Linda K., K. D. Butterfield and D. L. McCabe (1998). "The Ethical Context of Organizations: Influences on Employee Attitudes and Behaviors," *Business Ethics Quarterly,* Volume 8, July, pp. 447–476.

Turner, Louis (1984). "There's No love Lost Between Multinational Companies and the Third World," in W. M. Hoffman and J. M. Moore, eds., *Business Ethics.* New York, NY: McGraw-Hill Book Company, pp. 394–400.

U. S. Foreign Corrupt Practices Act (1977). www.usdoj.gov/criminal/fraud/fcpa/dojdocb.htm

van Tulder, Rob and Ans Kolk (2001). "Multinationality and Corporate Ethics," *Journal of International Business Studies,* Volume 32 (2), pp. 267–283.

Velasquez, Manual (1992). "International Business, Morality, and the Common Good," *Business Ethics Quarterly,* Volume 2, January, p. 30.

Velasquez, Manual (2000). "Globalization and the Failure of Ethics," *Business Ethics Quarterly,* Volume 10, January, pp. 343–352. WSJ Editorial (2002). "Enron's Sins," *The Wall Street Journal,* January 18, p. A10.

Weaver, Gary R., Linda K. Trevino and Philip L. Cochran (1999). "Corporate Ethics Programs as Control Systems," *Academy of Management Journal,* Volume 42 (1), pp. 41–57.

Weaver Gary R. and Bradley R. Agle (2002). "Religiosity and Ethical Behavior In Organizations," *Academy of Management Review,* Volume 27, Number 1, pp. 77–97.

Werhane, Patricia H. (2000). "Exporting Mental Models: Global
    Capitalism in the 21st Century," *Business Ethics Quarterly,*
    Volume 10, January, pp. 353–362.

Whenmouth, Edwin (1992). "A Matter of Ethics," *Industry Week,*
    March 16, pp. 57–62.

White, Anna (1997). "Joe Camel's World Tour," *The New York Times,*
    April 23, p. A31.

Willatt, Norris (1970). "How Nestle Adapts Products to Its Markets,"
    Business Abroad, June, pp. 31–33.

Yip, George S. (2003). *Total Global Strategy II.* Upper Saddle River,
    NJ: Prentice Hall/Pearson Education, Inc.

Zellner, Wendy and Michael Arndt (2002). "The Perfect Sales Pitch:
    No Debt, No Worries," *Business Week,* January 28, p. 35.

Zellner, Wendy, Stephanie F. Anderson and Laura Cohn (2002). "The
    Whistle Blower: A Hero and a Smoking-Gun Letter," *Business
    Week,* January 28, pp. 34–35.

Zellner, Wendy, Michael France and Joseph Weber (2002). "The
    Man Behind the Deal Machine," *Business Week,* February 4,
    pp. 40–41.

Critical Thinking

1. What are important considerations in developing a global code of ethics?

2. Should a firm change its home-country code of ethics when operating in another country? Why or why not?

3. Of the eight-stage framework for developing a global code of ethics presented in the article, what stage do you believe is most critical for a firm operating in the global business arena? Why is it a critical stage?

4. How should a firm promulgate its code of ethics in countries in which it operates?

Internet References

Association of Corporate Council
    http://www.acc.com/legalresources/quickcounsel/daiagcoc.cfm
Ethics Resource Center
    http://www.ethics.org/files/u5/LRNGlobalIntegrity.pdf

Article   Prepared by: Eric Teoro, *Lincoln Christian University*

Opting to Blow the Whistle
or Choosing to Walk Away

ALINA TUGEND

Learning Outcomes

After reading this article, you will be able to:

- Describe challenges involved in reporting unethical behavior on the part of managers.

- Discern motives behind whistleblowing.

- Determine when to refrain from making managerial behavior public.

Whistle-blowers have been big news lately—from Chelsea Manning, formerly known as Pfc. Bradley Manning, to Edward J. Snowden. Yet, for most people, the question of whether to expose unethical or ille- gal activities at work doesn't make headlines or involve state secrets.

But that doesn't make the problem less of a quandary. The question of when to remain quiet and when to speak out—and how to do it—can be extraordinarily difficult no matter what the situation.

And while many think of ethics violations as confined to obviously illegal acts, like financial fraud or safety violations, the line often can be much blurrier and, therefore, more difficult to navigate.

According to the Ethics Resource Center, a nonprofit research organization, the No. 1 misconduct observed—by a third of 4,800 respondents—was misuse of company time. That was closely followed by abusive behavior and lying to employees.

The findings were published in the organization's 2011 National Business Ethics Survey, which interviewed, on the phone or online, employees in the commercial sector who were employed at least 20 hours a week. It has been conducted biannually since 1994.

But offensive behavior that creates a hostile work environment, although often not thought of as unethical behavior, is the leading reason people leave their jobs, said Patricia J. Harned, president of the center. "Abusive and intimidating behavior by supervisors and managers creates a toxic work environment."

So does lying to employees. Lester, who asked that I use only his first name to avoid possible legal issues, worked at a global consulting company for about 3 years, earning high performance ratings. At one point, he said, he accidentally learned that his manager had deliberately lied to deny him a promotion opportunity. Lester spoke to the hiring manager to no avail, and because the company had a strong ethics program—including a specific "no retaliation policy" and a hot line to report ethics complaints—he reported the situation.

An investigation found no wrongdoing, and although Lester appealed the findings, no action was taken against the manager. That is when he says the retaliation began.

"All my direct reports were taken away from me and I was given the most difficult projects with the least resources," he said. "A whole series of things happened, which were unlikely to be a coincidence."

After about 8 months of this, he decided to leave.

Lester's experience may be the reason the misconduct most often seen is not the one most often reported. According to the Ethics Resources Center report, which is sponsored by major corporations like Wal-Mart and Northrop Grumman, less than half of those who observed a boss lying to employees reported it.

On the other hand, while only 12 percent said they had witnessed someone stealing from the company, almost 70 percent of those who saw such activity reported it.

One of the difficulties in cases like Lester's is that no law has been broken. True whistleblowing, according to Stephen M. Kohn, a lawyer and executive director of the National Whistleblowers Center, is when people report seeing or experiencing something at their company that is against the law, rather than cases in which employees feel mistreated, but nothing illegal has occurred.

It appears, however, that an increasing number of employees are willing to come forward in both types of cases. More people are using their companies' ethics procedures to report misconduct, and more people are filing whistle-blower claims.

Mr. Kohn, whose organization refers potential whistle-blowers to lawyers, said there had been a 30 percent increase in the num- ber of people requesting referrals over the last 18 months, which comes to about 1,500 requests a year.

He also said the quality of complaints—with more documentation and from higher-level employees—had increased.

Some of this is because of legislation rewarding whistle-blowers for coming forth and protecting them against retaliation. The most prominent of those is the Dodd-Frank Act, which passed in 2010. Under that act, the Securities and Exchange Commission oversees the Office of the Whistleblower, which in 2012 alone received 3,001 tips.

It may seem counterintuitive that reporting bad behavior would go up during the recession and afterward, when people fear for their jobs. Ms. Harned said, however, that one explanation was that employees were less able to change jobs, so they might be more willing to try to change a negative work culture.

"Historically, when the economy is good, companies take more risks and focus more on the bottom line," Ms. Harned said. "They're not talking about ethics as much."

But, just as reporting is on the rise, so is retaliation. More than one in five employees interviewed said they experienced some sort of reprisal when they reported misconduct, ranging from being excluded from decision-making activities and getting the cold shoulder from other employees to being passed over for promotion.

That is almost double the number who said they were retaliated against in the 2007 study.

Even more alarming, in 2009, 4 percent of those who said they experienced reprisals for reporting wrongdoing cited physical threats to themselves or their property. In 2011, that rose to 31 percent.

"Whistle-blowing does threaten cultures and individuals, even when companies say they want it and think they want it," said Kirk O. Hanson, executive director of the Markkula Center for Applied Ethics at Santa Clara University.

And, he said, it's very easy to rationalize that an action— say, denying a promotion—is not actually payback for reporting misconduct, but because the worker isn't a team player.

So, while it's important to expose unethical behavior, it's also necessary to be very clear why you're doing it—and how to do it right.

"A good thing to ask yourself is, 'Why am I doing this? Am I trying to help the company or just get someone in trouble?' " said Stuart Sidle, director of the Industrial-Organizational Psychology program at the University of New Haven.

You need to ensure that you're not talking yourself out of taking an ethical stand, nor talking yourself into reporting something for the wrong reason, Professor Hanson said.

"Have someone you can bounce dilemmas off who has similar values," he said. "To make sure you're not rationalizing not doing anything, and to make sure there's a genuine problem— someone to help you be strong but also to test your realities."

In general, employees should follow the proper channels, like addressing the issue with the person directly supervising the supposed culprit, said John M. Thornton, a professor of accounting ethics at Azusa Pacific University.

Along the same lines, think very hard before going public.

"I question someone trying to report externally before reporting internally," Mr. Sidle said. It's too easy, now, he said, to put up a video of bad behavior on YouTube or lash out on Facebook without ever speaking with the people who might be willing to resolve the problems.

On the other hand, don't shy away from reporting bad behavior because you don't want to be seen as that worst elementary school insult—a tattletale.

"You don't want a culture of tattling, but you do want a culture of telling if something is harming the company and the community," Professor Sidle said.

And companies need to be specific in how they talk about ethics, he added.

"It's useless just to talk about unethical behavior," he said. "Everyone is against fraud. Everyone is against disrespectful behavior, but how is it defined? Leadership has to give exam- ples. If someone asks you to backdate something because the client asked, it's unethical, even if it's commonly done."

And, finally, whistle-blowers should know that most cases are not settled in their favor. "This may be attributable to injustices in the system, or lack of merit or proof of the alleged wrongdoing," Professor Thornton said.

For good or for bad, most of us will never face the decisions that Mr. Manning and Mr. Snowden have. But that doesn't mean our choices—to confront or to ignore—aren't important.

"Some will always cheat on their expense reports," Professor Hanson said. "Some will never cheat. Most of us are in the middle. It's a constant struggle to do the right thing."

Critical Thinking

1. Is reporting unethical behavior ever an unethical act? Why or why not?

2. What are the challenges inherent in whistleblowing?

3. What advice would you give to someone who is considering whistleblowing?

Internet References

U.S. Department of Labor
http://www.whistleblowers.gov/

U.S. Equal Employment Opportunity Commission
http://www.eeoc.gov/laws/types/facts-retal.cfm

U.S. Securities and Exchange Commission
http://www.sec.gov/whistleblower

Article   Prepared by: Eric Teoro, *Lincoln Christian University*

The Unexpected Cost of Staying Silent

Not blowing the whistle may seem like the easy way out, but those who choose silence pay a price.

AMY FREDIN

Learning Outcomes

After reading this article, you will be able to:

- Recognize that individuals who remain silent about wrongdoing in organizations often regret doing so.
- Recognize various deterrents to whistleblowing, enabling-possible reporting improvements.

". . . and another massive fraud was just uncovered today thanks to a whistleblower who came forward with critical information. . ." We've all heard these reports on the news and read about them in the newspapers, but this type of activity wouldn't happen in *my* organization, right? And even if it did, certainly *my* employees would quickly take corrective action, right? Let's take a look at the current landscape for organizational wrongdoing, including fraud, as well as the prevalence of whistleblowing in response to these activities. The findings alone may be surprising.

To bring these topics a little closer to home, additional analysis outlines the situations of wrongdoing some of our fellow IMA members encountered. Many individuals in the survey did blow the whistle in these wrongdoing cases, but others chose not to report the situations. This article looks further at their reasons for staying silent and their subsequent feelings of regret associated with that decision.

What Do the Surveys Say?

PricewaterhouseCoopers (PwC) has conducted several global studies of economic crime over the past decade. Most recently, its 2011 study reports data from nearly 4,000 companies worldwide, including 156 from the United States. (See www.pwc.com/gx/en/economiccrime-survey/index.jhtml for PwC's 2011, 2009, and 2007 Global Economic Crime Surveys.)

Data from the 2011 study indicates that 34 percent of all companies (45 percent of US companies) reported having uncovered a significant economic crime during the previous 12-month period. The term "significant" means the crime had a definite impact on the business, either from direct, tangible damage or from collateral or psychological damage. These crimes occurred in companies of all sizes and industries. The noted wrongdoings included such instances as cybercrime, bribery and corruption, accounting fraud, and, most frequently, asset misappropriation.

Just 2 years earlier, more than 3,000 companies worldwide (71 US companies) responded to PwC's 2009 survey where 30 percent of companies (35 percent of US companies) reported experiencing a significant economic crime over the previous 12-month period. Considering both of these recent surveys, the prevalence of these crimes is disturbing, to say the least. The loss amounts are staggering as well. In 2011 (and 2009), 54 percent (44 percent) of US companies estimated their fraud losses to be between $100,000 and $5 million, with another 10 percent (8 percent) reporting that their losses amounted to more than $5 million.

PwC also identified detection sources for these crimes. In 2009, 34 percent of the incidences worldwide were initially found because of internal or external "tips," but the largest source of detection during that time frame came from companies' own internal controls, which accounted for 46 percent. In 2011, the global survey reported similar rankings but an even larger disparity between these two detection methods, with only 23 percent of frauds being detected by "tips," while 50 percent were detected from a variety of internal control procedures. Kalaithasan Kuppusamy and David Yong Gun Fie reported similar rankings in their October 2004 article,

"Developing Whistleblowing Policies: An Aid to Internal Auditors," in *Accountants Today.* They reported global survey results where auditors ranked first and whistleblowers ranked second in terms of detection sources for economic crime.

Though detail for US detection sources in 2011 wasn't reported, the sources of detection in the US in 2009 looked very different from the global results. "The single most common way that fraud was detected among US survey respondents was through tip-offs," the report notes, where whistleblowers alerted officials to 48 percent of the crimes; internal controls initially detected 28 percent of the crimes during this time period.

With the prevalence of crime and the importance of whistleblowing well documented, it might lead you to believe that more and more individuals are coming forward to report organizational wrongdoing. But what percentage of individuals who either know about or suspect wrongdoing come forward? Going back to 1992, a US federal government survey of its own employees reported that as many as 50 percent of individuals who were aware of a crime chose to remain silent.

A slightly later study, "Whistle-Blower Disclosures and Management Retaliation" by Joyce Rothschild and Terance Miethe, published in the February 1999 issue of *Work and Occupations,* reported a similar level of nonreporting, but does that level still apply today? As we head into a new era where whistleblowers have the potential to be rewarded financially for their information because of the recently instituted DoddFrank Wall Street Reform and Consumer Protection Act, it seems appropriate to take an even more current look at the landscape around those who observe organizational wrongdoing.

The IMA Study

In an effort to understand this issue from an insider's perspective, I surveyed attendees at IMA's Annual Conference & Exposition in 2007. Attendees could complete an anonymous survey, which included questions predominantly related to whistleblowing and internal controls, in exchange for a chance to win one of 10 $50 cash prizes. Of the 75 individuals who completed the survey, 45 reported having observed wrongdoing within their organizations, and 27 of these 45 individuals stated that they reported this information to the appropriate authorized party, suggesting a 60 percent report rate.

The 60 percent rate suggests we may be making strides in encouraging whistleblowers to come forward. Yet five of the 27 individuals who blew the whistle on one situation admitted to staying silent on at least one other. The remaining 18 of the 45 individuals who had observed one or more incidences of wrongdoing didn't report any of them. If this last group of 18 nonreporters is analyzed on its own, it suggests that the nonreporter rate is 40 percent. But if the five individuals who both reported and stayed silent on different issues are allowed to be included in both groups, then the nonreporter rate goes up to 51 percent (23 out of 45). At this level, we're back to where we startedthe 50 percent range

Table 1   Instances of Reported Wrongdoing

Type of Activity Observed	No. of Reports	Examples Noted
Theft of Company Property/Cash	2	Theft of company computer
		Mishandling of petty cash
Unauthorized/Inappropriate Use of Company Assets	5	Unauthorized use of company vehicle
		Misappropriation of funds
		Inappropriate use of grant money
		Purchase misuse
Financial Statement Manipulation	5	Irrelevant advertising expenditures that weren't approved
		Financial Statement Manipulation 5 Misstated product line P&L
		Aggressive estimates affecting income
		Income statement misrepresentation
		Financial statement misstatements
		Overstatement of inventory value

(conitnued)

Table 1 Instances of Reported Wrongdoing *(continued)*

Type of Activity Observed	No. of Reports	Examples Noted
Claiming Personal Expenses for Reimbursement	4	Airfare for spouse purchased with company credit card Inappropriate personal spending on company credit card Improper expense submission
Sexual Harassment	2	Sexual harassment of a coworker Sexual harassment
Inappropriate Human Resources/Payroll Practices	4	Fraud in the selection process Hiring spouse of executive Back pay being withheld inappropriately Inappropriate untaxed bonuses
Other	5	Kickbacks Overbilling client Employee using counterfeit money in vending machine Inappropriate use of cash-basis accounting Violation of corporate risk management policy
TOTAL	27	

of reporting and nonreporting that previous studies have documented.

In order to better understand the situations behind these reports (and nonreports), the survey asked respondents to describe incidence(s) of wrongdoing that they observed. Table 1 outlines the situations on which individuals blew the whistle. These reported wrongdoing activities varied greatly from mishandling petty cash to misrepresenting the company's income statement to sexual harassment.

Table 2 describes the other situations—the ones on which individuals remained silent. These unreported situations of wrongdoing also varied greatly—from an employee stealing company supplies to manipulating revenues and expenses to claiming personal expenses for reimbursement. When comparing the situations in Tables 1 and 2, the uncanny crossovers are hard to dismiss. The situations described in both tables are very similar, suggesting that it isn't just the event's nature or the significance that drives an individual to report-or not report-wrongdoing.

Table 3 provides a closer look at the survey respondents to see if there are any key demographic differences between those who reported wrongdoing and those who didn't. This information is provided for the entire group of survey respondents along with comparison detail for the two different reporter groups (reporters, the 27 who reported at least one situation of wrongdoing; nonreporters, the 23 who stayed silent on at least one instance of wrongdoing). There doesn't appear to be much difference in the ages and length of time at current companies of those who blew the whistle as opposed to those who stayed silent. The average age across the board was approximately 47, and average time

with their current company was also quite steady at approximately 8 or 9 years.

But there are some gender differences between the groups. Though 55 percent of the entire sample was male, only 48 percent of those blowing the whistle were male. Further, of the individuals who remained silent, 70 percent were male. A meta-analysis by Jessica Mesmer-Magnus and Chockalingam Viswesvaran, "Whistleblowing in Organizations: An Examination of Correlates of Whistleblowing Intentions, Actions, and Retliation," in the Spring 2005 issue of the *Journal of Business Ethics,* looked at four specific studies on actual whistleblowers and noted a similar gender difference across those studies: Women blew the whistle more often than men did.

In addition to a gender difference in my study's respondents, the remainder of the data shows that these individuals come from businesses of all types and sizes and that the whistleblowing reports are spread fairly evenly among all such companies. Further, both the reporter and nonreporter groups appear to be composed of similar individuals in regard to their certifications held and degrees completed: The vast majority are either a CMA® (Certified Management Accountant) or CPA (Certified Public Accountant) or both, and the majority in both groups also have a master's degree. In other words, even these highly educated individuals with valued credentials and experience find it difficult to deal with wrongdoing in the workplace.

Although this detail portrays the background information of all respondents as well as the wrongdoing situations that they observed, the survey asked more probing questions of the silent observers. Since the rate of whistleblowing has remained constant at around 50 percent for at least the past 18 years, there

Table 2 Instances of Unreported Wrongdoing . . . and Regret Associated with Staying Silent

Type of Activity Observed	No. of Similar Reports	Examples Noted	Level ofRegret Experienced*
Theft of Company Property/Cash	2	Employee stealing supplies from the company Unauthorized purchases; incorrect recording of cash	no regret some regret
Inappropriate Use of Company Assets	1	Accessing pornography on work computer	little regret
Financial Statement Manipulation	5	Inappropriate month-end adjustments Accounting estimate adjustments for bad debt	great regret no regret
		Manipulating revenue and expenses	some regret
		Earnings manipulation	some regret
		Income smoothing using accrual manipulation	little regret
		Personal travel of children	great regret
Claiming Personal Expenses for Reimbursement	4	Personal travel of children	great regret
		Misclassifying expense reports	little regret
		Personal assets purchased by company	no regret
		Personal expenses purchased on corporate card	little regret
Sexual Harassment	1	Sexist comments	little regret
Inappropriate HR/Payroll Practices	3	Inappropriate time-sheet reporting	little regret
		Profit-sharing calculations unverifi able	little regret
		Reporting payments to employees as travel vs. wages to avoid payroll taxes	little regret
Other	7	Collusion within upper management; sharing inside information	great regret
		Executive cover-up	some regret
		Fraudulent information reported on tax returns	great regret
		Controller cover-up on missing equipment	little regret great regret
		Noncompetitive supplier selected	no regret
		Sabotage of a new process change	great regret
TOTAL	**23**		

* Subjects were asked if they were currently experiencing (or had in the past experienced) any regret associated with their decision to stay silent. They were asked to respond in one of the following ways: no regret, little regret, some regret, and great regret.

must be something more that we can learn from these nonreporterssomething that can help us "break through" to future observers that may give them the courage to come forward with their information.

One such survey question asked these individuals to explain why they chose to remain silent. Table 4 reports the reasons they gave. Not surprisingly, the most common reason for not blowing the whistle was fear of retaliation in one form or another, including job loss and difficult working conditions.

Others noted reasons such as the wrongdoing wasn't serious enough to worry about; they didn't feel they had enough proof to bring the allegation forward; and/or they felt somebody else would report the situation. Two individuals further noted that they voluntarily left the company because of what was going on.

Table 3 Survey Respondents

	All		Reporters		Nonreporters	
Age (in years)						
Mean	47.5		46.7		49.1	
Range	27 to 71		29 to 67		30 to 71	
Tenure with Organization (in years)						
Mean	8.6		9		8.3	
Range	0.25 to 31		2 to 20		0.75 to 30	
	N	**Percentage**	**N**	**Percentage**	**N**	**Percentage**
Gender						
Male	41	55 percent	13	48 percent	16	
Female	33	44 percent	14	52 percent	7	
Missing Data	1	1 percent	0		0	
Total	75		27		23	
Industry Membership						
Manufacturing	27	36 percent	10	37 percent	7	30 percent
Professional Services	17	23 percent	7	26 percent	6	26 percent
Education	7	9 percent	2	7 percent	5	22 percent
Government	5	7 percent	1	4 percent	1	4 percent
Pharmaceuticals/Healthcare	4	5 percent	1	4 percent	0	0 percent
Other/Missing	15	20 percent	6	22 percent	4	17 percent
Total	75		27		23	
# of Employees in Company	20	27 percent	11	41 percent	6	26 percent
Less than 100	19	25 percent	5	19 percent	6	26 percent
101 to 500	10	13 percent	5	19 percent	5	22 percent
501 to 2,000	11	15 percent	1	4 percent		13 percent
2,001 to 10,000	13	17 percent	4	15 percent	3	13 percent
More than 10,000	2	3 percent	1	4 percent	3	0 percent
Missing	75		27		0	
Total					23	
Certifications Held						
CMA (w/o CPA)	22	29 percent	8	30 percent	7	30 percent
CPA (w/o CMA)	16	21 percent	6	22 percent	3	13 percent
CMA & CPA	20	27 percent	8	30 percent	5	22 percent
Others (no CMA or CPA)	3	4 percent	1	4 percent	1	4 percent
None/Missing	14	19 percent	4	15 percent	7	30 percent
Total	75		27		23	
Highest Degree Completed						4 percent
Associate's	1	1 percent	1	4 percent	1	30 percent
Bachelor's	29	39 percent	10	37 percent	7	61 percent
Master's	41	55 percent	16	59 percent	14	4 percent
Doctorate	3	4 percent	0	0 percent	1	0 percent
Missing	1	1 percent	0	0 percent	0	
Total	75		27		23	

Table 4 Reasons for Not Reporting the Wrongdoing

Reason Given	Number of Similar Reports
Fear of job loss and/or other retaliation	10
Not that big of a deal	4
Didn't have enough proof	3
Thought somebody else would report it	2
Chose to leave the company instead	2
Other	5
Total*	26

* Three individuals each gave two reasons for staying silent, thus the total adds up to 23 + 3 = 26.

. . . the most common reason for not blowing the whistle was fear of retaliation in one form or another . . .

Regret from Not Blowing the Whistle

But what have these individuals experienced since their decision to remain silent? Did they avoid the retaliation they were hoping to avoid, or were there other negative consequences associated with staying silent, too? One question asked these silent observers whether they were currently experiencing (or had in the past) any regret associated with their decision to remain silent. This data speaks for itself. Presented alongside the unreported situations in the last column of Table 2, the vast majority of silent observers, 19 of the 23 individuals who chose not to report the wrongdoings, acknowledge having experienced at least some regret (rated as either little, some, or great) associated with their decision to remain silent.

It further appears that these individuals have experienced regret-to varying degrees-for many different types of wrongdoing situations. Not only did some experience regret for the "bigger" issues, such as "fixing" the numbers or theft of property, but individuals also experienced regret for letting "smaller" issues go unreported, including such things as bypassing proper procedures in order to justify a purchase or letting some personal expenses count for reimbursement.

Tone at the Top

It's clear that there's no easy way to deal with wrongdoing in the workplace. Once an individual becomes aware of illegal and/or unethical activity, there are ramifications for reporting and not reporting it. Unfortunately, organizational wrongdoing occurs in companies of all sizes and in all industries. Further, given that many businesses today find themselves in fragile financial positions with lower-than-desired headcounts, there are fewer resources to allocate toward enhanced internal controls and ethics training.

Once an individual becomes aware of illegal and/or unethical activity, there are ramifications for reporting and not reporting it.

But there's still something companies can do, at relatively no cost to them, to combat and prevent fraud and wrongdoing. Businesses can espouse an ethical culture, one that truly is motivated from the top tiers of the organizational chart, to show their employees that they mean business. The importance of a company's "tone at the top" certainly it isn't a new phenomenon (see "Tone at the Top: Insights from Section 404" by Dana Hermanson, Daniel Ivancevich, and Susan Ivancevich in the November 2008 *Strategic Finance*). And this is getting even more pronounced attention as a fraud prevention factor in today's fastpaced, risk-laden marketplace. PwC captured this message loud and clear when it concluded its 2011 global economic crime survey with the following statement: "Establishing the right 'tone at the top' is key in the fight against economic crime."

No Easy Way Out

The data in this article suggests that the level of whistleblowing has stayed relatively constant over the past two decades at around 50 percent and gives reasons as to why the remaining 50 percent chose to remain silent on these issues. Yet through this analysis it becomes clear that these silent observers don't come out unscathed because they have to live with their decision, knowing that some individuals are benefitting at the expense of others. They have to live with their regret-knowing that their silence may be perpetuating fraud, harassment, law violations, and the like, within that company. The stress associated with this regret may be a cost that they didn't anticipate, but it's a cost nonetheless. Perhaps the potential for financial rewards will now give some of these otherwise silent observers enough incentive to come forward with their information. And perhaps these and other reward opportunities will eventually give all whistleblowers the compensation they desire and deserve to help offset the personal costs that come with whistleblowing.

One thing is certain, though. We can all learn something from the survey respondents. Blowing the whistle on organizational wrongdoing isn't an easy thing to do, but staying silent on these issues may not be an easy way out, either.

Critical Thinking

1. Comment on the methodology used in the IMA Study reported in the article. Are the results of the study generalizable given its methodology? Why or why not?

2. Examine Table 4 in the article. Of the reasons given for not reporting wrongdoing (i.e., not blowing the whistle), which of the reasons do you find most compelling? Why? Which the least compelling? Why?

3. Examine Table 2 in the article. What might be the reasons for a finding of great regret versus a finding of no regret? Make a list of possible reasons for feeling or not feeling of regret for use in class discussion.

4. Examine Table 1—Instance of Reported Wrongdoing. Develop a table or a chart in which you analyze the seriousness of the reported wrongdoing. Then, relate your analysis of Table 1 to the results reported in Table 2. What conclusion might you draw from Tables 1 and 2?

Internet References

New York Times
http://www.nytimes.com/1987/02/22/us/survey-of-whistle-blowers-findsretaliation-but-few-regrets.html

Reuters
http://www.reuters.com/article/2012/02/17/us-citigroup-whistlebloweridUSTRE81G06Y20120217

The Guardian
http://www.theguardian.com/money/2014/sep/23/whistleblower-bankpersonal-cost-sec

---

AMY FREDIN, PhD, is an assistant professor of accounting at St. Cloud State University in St. Cloud, Minn. She also is a member of IMA's Central Minnesota Chapter. You can reach her at (320) 308-3287 or ajfredin@stcloudstate.edu.

Article   Prepared by: Eric Teoro, *Lincoln Christian University*

Unethical Behaviors in the Workplace

Abuse of Social Media in the Workplace on the Rise

Steven Mintz

Learning Outcomes

After reading this article, you will be able to:

- Describe five types of unethical behavior in the workplace.
- Describe ethical issues related to violating company Internet policies.

I recently read a piece about the five most unethical behaviors in the workplace. Arthur Schwartz points out that each day roughly 120 million people walk into a workplace somewhere in the U.S. Within the past year, almost half of these workers personally witnessed some form of ethical misconduct, according to a recent survey conducted by the Washington, D.C.-based Ethics Resource Center (ERC).

Schwartz points out that the issue is not workers being privy to the CFO committing fraud. More likely, it's someone who lied to a supervisor or handed in a false expense report. Listed below, according to the ERC study, are the five most frequently observed unethical behaviors in the U.S. workplace.

1. **Misusing company time**

   Whether it is covering for someone who shows up late or altering a time sheet, misusing company time tops the list. This category includes knowing that one of your co-workers is conducting personal business on company time. By "personal business" the survey recognizes the difference between making cold calls to advance your freelance business and calling your spouse to find out how your sick child is doing.

2. **Abusive behavior**

   Too many workplaces are filled with managers and supervisors who use their position and power to mistreat or disrespect others. Unfortunately, unless the situation you're in involves race, gender or ethnic origin, there is often no legal protection against abusive behavior in the workplace.

3. **Employee theft**

   According to a recent study by Jack L. Hayes International, one out of every 40 employees in 2012 was caught stealing from their employer. Even more startling is that these employees steal on average 5.5 times more than shoplifters ($715 vs $129). Employee fraud is also on the uptick, whether its check tampering, not recording sales in order to skim, or manipulating expense reimbursements. The FBI recently reported that employee theft is the fastest growing crime in the U.S. today.

4. **Lying to employees**

   The fastest way to lose the trust of your employees is to lie to them, yet employers do it all the time. One out of every five employees report that their manager or supervisor has lied to them within the past year.

5. **Violating company Internet policies**

   Cyberslackers. Cyberloafers. These are terms used to identify people who surf the Web when they should be working. It's a huge, multi-billion-dollar problem for companies. A survey conducted recently by Salary.com found that every day at least 64 percent of employees visit websites that have nothing to do with their work.

The ERC study points out that most American workers and employers do the right thing. The survey reveals that most follow the company's ethical standards of behavior, and are willing to report wrongdoing when it occurs, except if it relates to the company's Internet use policy.

These results are retrospective and do not reflect the increasing trend of employees' use of social media at work for personal purposes. According to a *Forbes study,* 64 percent of employees visit non-work related websites daily, and wasted the most time on these social sharing sites (in descending order):

Tumblr–57 percent
Facebook–52 percent
Twitter–17 percent
Instagram–11 percent
SnapChat–4 percent

The question is how much control an employer should have over its employees' use of social media. This is an emerging issue and one where the rules and ethical guidelines have not caught up with technology. One of the most difficult things for employers to monitor is what an employee is looking at on his/her computer screen. Short of walking around frequently and checking it out, as a possible deterrent to improper use, an employer has to trust that employees will use good judgment when it comes to the use of social media in the workplace.

Part of the problem with defining social media abuse is how common Internet use is in our daily personal and professional lives. In an age when employers expect workers to respond to client emails immediately and social networking sites reload with new information every minute, it's often hard to define the limits between normal and abusive. Businesses need to be proactive in the workplace with establishing these limits, creating a clear and comprehensive acceptable use policy and communicating it to employees through presentation and workshops. Good communication can generate a workplace-wide consensus on the behavior that falls outside acceptable boundaries.

Most of all the Internet use policy should be tied to the general issue of ethics in the workplace. The use and abuse of social media in the workplace is an excellent way to give life to the provisions in a code of ethics.

Two of the five most unethical practices relate to the abuse of social media at work: violating company Internet policy and misusing company time. Those who excessively surf the Internet at work for personal reasons are stealing from their companies. They are being paid for work when they are not doing so. The ethics policy must be clear on this matter. In the end it is no different from coming in late; leaving early; or taking long lunch hours and being paid for that time.

Critical Thinking

1. In addition to the unethical behaviors outlined in the article, develop a list of unethical behaviors. Why are these behaviors unethical?

2. What types of unethical behaviors are you most prone to commit? Do you justify any of them? How can you safeguard against committing them?

3. What should you do when you witness a coworker violating one of the five unethical behaviors? Why?

Internet References

Academia
http://www.academia.edu/5164148/Positive_and_negative_deviant_work place_behaviors_causes_impacts_and_solutions_Introduction_to_deviant_behavior

Ethics Alarm
http://ethicsalarms.com/2013/11/05/workplace-ethics-62-things-that-are-legal-but-22-of-them-are-unethical/

Houston Chronicle: Small Business
http://smallbusiness.chron.com/examples-unethical-behavior-workplace-10092.html

TU Jobs
http://www.tujobs.com/news/323116-the-10-most-common-examples-of-unethical-behavior

Article   Prepared by: Eric Teoro, *Lincoln Christian University*

Too Much Information?

The BMF's HR guru, Kate Russell examines the ethics of using social media profiles in the recruitment process.

KATE RUSSEL

Learning Outcomes

After reading this article, you will be able to:

- Describe ethical issues related to using social media research in hiring decisions.

- Describe the risks of using social media research in hiring decisions.

While most employers continue to use traditional methods to recruit new employees, there is a growing trend to utilise social media sites as part of the recruitment process. On-line job portals are already overtaking printed job ads in popularity with job seekers, and with many young people far more likely to view their Facebook and Twitter feeds than to read a newspaper on a regular basis, social media can only become even more important to recruiters over the next few years.

This raises two important questions. Is it ethical for business owners to access the personal social media profiles of prospective employees during the recruitment process? If so, how can employers ensure that discrimination is avoided?

Let's start by considering why both recruiters and job seekers are using social media.

Spread the Word

The key attraction for recruiters is that social media can spread the word about an available position to a wide network of people, usually at little or no cost. Meanwhile, those looking for a new position can leverage their contacts and their time to best effect.

The business networking site, LinkedIn, is one of the most popular social platforms for both those offering and those seeking employment. It enables job seekers to network with their own contacts and with a far wider group of people linked to those contacts. It also allows them to follow their targeted employers and quickly learn of any jobs they post.

The benefit for employers is the wealth of information available about the qualifications and experience of job seekers, and the wide network that can be accessed to find potential candidates.

Facebook was created to facilitate personal communications but it is widely used by organisations to create a presence to reflect their brand and develop a community of "fans". Once a business has established a network, they may also view this as useful medium to post jobs and find potential candidates.

As a medium to advertise positions, this is all well and good. The risk occurs when the process moves from sourcing to screening applicants.

Accurate Decisions

All recruiting managers want to find out as much as they can about prospective applicants and the more relevant data you have, the better able you are to make an accurate decision. The potential problem arises when recruiters use irrelevant information gleaned from social media sites to screen or eliminate candidates from consideration. Too much general information may cause you to make judgements about an individual that is irrelevant to whether or not they are a good candidate for your position.

Despite—or perhaps due to—complex privacy settings, people add information to their social media pages without too much thought about who can see it. Facebook pages, for example, may include a great deal of information that reveals protected characteristics (age, gender, religion, sexual orientation, etc).

> **"The key attraction for recruiters is that social media can spread the word about an available position to a wide network of people, usually at little or no cost"**

These protected characteristics will rarely be relevant to an ability to do the job, but if for example, you assume a mum with three kids can't travel and do a field sales representative's role because of her domestic circumstances and you block the appointment because of that, you will have acted unlawfully.

Similarly, information about what individuals like to do in their spare time, their interests and any common links you may have through other friends and acquaintances may tell you whether you are likely to get on with them—or not–but it doesn't say anything about their ability to do the job you are recruiting for.

Feedback

A job applicant is entitled to ask why they were turned down for a job or not given an interview. You must be able to give an objective answer, or you will leave yourself open to a claim.

It's a sad fact that there are bounty hunters who will repeatedly exploit weak recruitment processes to claim against companies that don't hire them.

If you are going to use social media as part of the assessment process, it is important to keep to the facts and focus on what is relevant to the job.

This means ensuring that your job description and person specification are properly thought through and justifiable. Then

if you do collect data online, confine the basis of your decision to the objective requirements of the job description and person specification.

Critical Thinking

1. Develop a set of ethical guidelines for using social media research in hiring decisions? Defend your set of guidelines.
2. If individuals post information on the open web, do they have a right to privacy regarding that information? Why or why not?
3. Is there material you posted on the web that you regret? That you should regret? What can you do about it?

Internet References

Ethics Sage
http://www.ethicssage.com/2015/04/is-it-ethical-for-employers-to-use-social-media-in-hiring-and-employment-decisions.html

HRZone
http://www.hrzone.com/talent/acquisition/social-media-screening-is-it-ethical

Society for Human Resource Management
http://www.shrm.org/publications/hrmagazine/editorialcontent/2014/0914/pages/0914-social-media-hiring.aspx

Society for Human Resource Management
http://www.shrm.org/publications/hrmagazine/editorialcontent/2014/1114/pages/1114-social-media-screening.aspx

KATE RUSSELL heads the BMF Employment Plus service that delivers practical HR solutions to BMF members of all sizes.
Follow Kate on Twitter@ KateRussellHR or Facebook www.facebook.com/russell-hrconsultingltd
The BMF Employment Plus Service includes a detailed review and regular updates of your contracts of employment and employee handbook, expert briefings, and telephone advice. Russell HR Consulting can also offer on-site help if needed.

Dozens of Companies Are Using Facebook to Exclude Older Workers from Job Ads by Julia Angwin, Noam Scheiber, and Ariana Tobin

131

Article

Prepared by: Eric Teoro, *Lincoln Christian University*

Dozens of Companies Are Using Facebook to Exclude Older Workers from Job Ads

JULIA ANGWIN, NOAM SCHEIBER, AND ARIANA TOBIN

Learning Outcomes

After reading this article, you will be able to:

- Understand how companies have discriminated against older workers when utilizing Facebook recruitment ads.

- Understand facets regarding liability for age-based discrimination.

A few weeks ago, Verizon placed an ad on Facebook to recruit applicants for a unit focused on financial planning and analysis. The ad showed a smiling, millennial-aged woman seated at a computer and promised that new hires could look forward to a rewarding career in which they would be "more than just a number."

Some relevant numbers were not immediately evident. The promotion was set to run on the Facebook feeds of users 25–36 years old who lived in the nation's capital, or had recently visited there, and had demonstrated an interest in finance. For a vast majority of the hundreds of millions of people who check Facebook every day, the ad did not exist.

Verizon is among dozens of the nation's leading employers—including Amazon, Goldman Sachs, Target, and Facebook itself—that placed recruitment ads limited to particular age groups, an investigation by ProPublica and *The New York Times* has found.

The ability of advertisers to deliver their message to the precise audience most likely to respond is the cornerstone of Facebook's business model. But using the system to expose job opportunities only to certain age groups has raised concerns about fairness to older workers.

Several experts questioned whether the practice is in keeping with the federal Age Discrimination in Employment Act of 1967, which prohibits bias against people 40 or older in hiring or employment. Many jurisdictions make it a crime to "aid" or "abet" age discrimination, a provision that could apply to companies like Facebook that distribute job ads.

"It's blatantly unlawful," said Debra Katz, a Washington employment lawyer who represents victims of discrimination.

Facebook defended the practice. "Used responsibly, age-based targeting for employment purposes is an accepted industry practice and for good reason: it helps employers recruit and people of all ages find work," said Rob Goldman, a Facebook vice president.

The revelations come at a time when the unregulated power of the tech companies is under increased scrutiny, and Congress is weighing whether to limit the immunity that it granted to tech companies in 1996 for third-party content on their platforms.

Facebook has argued in court filings that the law, the Communications Decency Act, makes it immune from liability for discriminatory ads.

Although Facebook is a relatively new entrant into the recruiting arena, it is rapidly gaining popularity with employers. Earlier this year, the social network launched a section of its site devoted to job ads. Facebook allows advertisers to select their audience, and then Facebook finds the chosen users with the extensive data it collects about its members.

The use of age targets emerged in a review of data originally compiled by ProPublica readers for a project about political ad placement on Facebook. Many of the ads include a disclosure by Facebook about why the user is seeing the ad, which can be anything from their age to their affinity for folk music.

The precision of Facebook's ad delivery has helped it dominate an industry once in the hands of print and broadcast outlets. The system, called microtargeting, allows advertisers to reach essentially whomever they prefer, including the people their analysis suggests are the most plausible hires or consumers, lowering the costs and vastly increasing efficiency.

Targeted Facebook ads were an important tool in Russia's efforts to influence the 2016 election. The social media giant has acknowledged that 126 million people saw Russia-linked content, some of which was aimed at particular demographic groups and regions. Facebook has also come under criticism for the disclosure that it accepted ads aimed at "Jew-haters" as well as housing ads that discriminated by race, gender, disability, and other factors.

Other tech companies also offer employers opportunities to discriminate by age. ProPublica bought job ads on Google and LinkedIn that excluded audiences older than 40—and the ads were instantly approved. Google said it does not prevent advertisers from displaying ads based on the user's age. After being contacted by ProPublica, LinkedIn changed its system to prevent such targeting in employment ads.

The practice has begun to attract legal challenges. On Wednesday, a class action complaint alleging age discrimination was filed in federal court in San Francisco on behalf of the Communications Workers of America and its members— as well as all Facebook users 40 or older who may have been denied the chance to learn about job openings. The plaintiffs' lawyers said the complaint was based on ads for dozens of companies that they had discovered on Facebook.

The database of Facebook ads collected by ProPublica shows how often and precisely employers recruit by age. In a search for "part-time package handlers," United Parcel Service ran an ad aimed at people 18–24. State Farm pitched its hiring promotion to those 19–35.

Some companies, including Target, State Farm, and UPS, defended their targeting as a part of a broader recruitment strategy that reached candidates of all ages. The group of companies making this case included Facebook itself, which ran career ads on its own platform, many aimed at people 25–60. "We completely reject the allegation that these advertisements are discriminatory," said Goldman of Facebook.

After being contacted by ProPublica and *The Times*, other employers, including Amazon, Northwestern Mutual, and the New York City Department of Education, said they had changed or were changing their recruiting strategies.

"We recently audited our recruiting ads on Facebook and discovered some had targeting that was inconsistent with our approach of searching for any candidate over the age of 18," said Nina Lindsey, a spokeswoman for Amazon, which targeted some ads for workers at its distribution centers between the ages of 18 and 50. "We have corrected those ads."

Verizon did not respond to requests for comment.

Several companies argued that targeted recruiting on Facebook was comparable to advertising opportunities in publications like *AARP The Magazine* or *Teen Vogue*, which are aimed at particular age groups. But this obscures an important distinction. Anyone can buy *Teen Vogue* and see an ad. Online, however, people outside the targeted age groups can be excluded in ways they will never learn about.

"What happens with Facebook is you don't know what you don't know," said David Lopez, a former general counsel for the Equal Employment Opportunity Commission who is one of the lawyers at the firm Outten & Golden bringing the age-discrimination case on behalf of the communication workers union.

"They Know I'm Dead"

Age discrimination on digital platforms is something that many workers suspect is happening to them, but that is often difficult to prove.

Mark Edelstein, a fitfully employed social media marketing strategist who is 58 and legally blind doesn't pretend to know what he doesn't know, but he has his suspicions.

Edelstein, who lives in St. Louis, says he never had serious trouble finding a job until he turned 50. "Once you reach your 50s, you may as well be dead," he said. "I've gone into interviews, with my head of gray hair and my receding hairline, and they know I'm dead."

Edelstein spends most of his days scouring sites like LinkedIn and Indeed and pitching hiring managers with personalized appeals. When he scrolled through his Facebook ads on a Wednesday in December, he saw a variety of ads reflecting his interest in social media marketing: ads for the marketing software HubSpot ("15 free infographic templates!") and TripIt, which he used to book a trip to visit his mother in Florida.

What he didn't see was a single ad for a job in his profession, including one identified by ProPublica that was being shown to younger users: a posting for a social media director job at HubSpot. The company asked that the ad be shown to people aged 27–40 who live or were recently living in the United States.

"Hypothetically, had I seen a job for a social media director at HubSpot, even if it involved relocation, I ABSOLUTELY would have applied for it," Edelstein said by e-mail when told about the ad.

A HubSpot spokeswoman, Ellie Botelho, said that the job was posted on many sites, including LinkedIn, The Ladders, and Built in Boston, and was open to anyone meeting the qualifications regardless of age or any other demographic characteristic.

She added that "the use of the targeted age range selection on the Facebook ad was frankly a mistake on our part given our lack of experience using that platform for job postings and not a feature we will use again."

For his part, Edelstein says he understands why marketers wouldn't want to target ads at him: "It doesn't surprise me a bit. Why would they want a 58-year-old white guy who's disabled?"

Looking for "Younger Blood"

Although LinkedIn is the leading online recruitment platform, according to an annual survey by SourceCon, an industry website. Facebook is rapidly increasing in popularity for employers.

One reason is that Facebook's sheer size—two billion monthly active users, versus LinkedIn's 530 million total members—gives recruiters access to types of workers they can't find elsewhere.

Consider nurses, whom hospitals are desperate to hire. "They're less likely to use LinkedIn," said Josh Rock, a recruiter at a large hospital system in Minnesota who has expertise in digital media. "Nurses are predominantly female, there's a larger volume of Facebook users. That's what they use."

There are also millions of hourly workers who have never visited LinkedIn and may not even have a résumé, but who check Facebook obsessively.

Deb Andrychuk, chief executive of the Arland Group, which helps employers place recruitment ads, said clients sometimes asked her firm to target ads by age, saying they needed "to start bringing younger blood" into their organizations. "It's not necessarily that we wouldn't take someone older," these clients say, according to Andrychuk, "but if you could bring in a younger set of applicants, it would definitely work out better."

Andrychuk said that "we coach clients to be open and not discriminate" and that after being contacted by *The Times*, her team updated all their ads to ensure they didn't exclude any age groups.

But some companies contend that there are permissible reasons to filter audiences by age, as with an ad for entry-level analyst positions at Goldman Sachs that was distributed to people 18–64. A Goldman Sachs spokesman, Andrew Williams, said showing it to people above that age range would have wasted money: roughly 25 percent of those who typically click on the firm's untargeted ads are 65 or older, but people that age almost never apply for the analyst job.

"We welcome and actively recruit applicants of all ages," Williams said. "For some of our social-media ads, we look to get the content to the people most likely to be interested, but do not exclude anyone from our recruiting activity."

Pauline Kim, a professor of employment law at Washington University in St. Louis, said the Age Discrimination in Employment Act, unlike the federal antidiscrimination statute that covers race and gender, allows an employer to take into account "reasonable factors" that may be highly correlated with the protected characteristic, such as cost, as long as they don't rely on the characteristic explicitly.

The Question of Liability

In various ways, Facebook and LinkedIn have acknowledged at least a modest obligation to police their ad platforms against abuse.

Earlier this year, Facebook said it would require advertisers to "self-certify" that their housing, employment, and credit ads were compliant with antidiscrimination laws, but that it would not block marketers from purchasing age-restricted ads.

Still, Facebook didn't promise to monitor those certifications for accuracy. And Facebook said the self-certification system, announced in February, was still being rolled out to all advertisers.

LinkedIn, in response to inquiries by ProPublica, added a self-certification step that prevents employers from using age ranges once they confirm that they are placing an employment ad.

With these efforts evolving, legal experts say it is unclear how much liability the tech platforms could have. Some civil rights laws, like the Fair Housing Act, explicitly require publishers to assume liability for discriminatory ads.

But the Age Discrimination in Employment Act assigns liability only to employers or employment agencies, like recruiters and advertising firms.

The lawsuit filed against Facebook on behalf of the communications workers argues that the company essentially plays the role of an employment agency—collecting and providing data that helps employers locate candidates, effectively coordinating with the employer to develop the advertising strategies, informing employers about the performance of the ads, and so forth.

Regardless of whether courts accept that argument, the tech companies could also face liability under certain state or local antidiscrimination statutes. For example, California's Fair Employment and Housing Act makes it unlawful to "aid, abet, incite, compel, or coerce the doing" of discriminatory acts proscribed by the statute.

"They may have an obligation there not to aid and abet an ad that enables discrimination," said Cliff Palefsky, an employment lawyer based in San Francisco.

The question may hinge on Section 230 of the federal Communications Decency Act, which protects internet companies from liability for third-party content.

Tech companies have successfully invoked this law to avoid liability for offensive or criminal content—including sex trafficking, revenge porn, and calls for violence against Jews. Facebook is currently arguing in federal court that Section

230 immunizes it against liability for ad placement that blocks members of certain racial and ethnic groups from seeing the ads.

"Advertisers, not Facebook, are responsible for both the content of their ads and what targeting criteria to use, if any," Facebook argued in its motion to dismiss allegations that its ads violated a host of civil rights laws. The case does not allege age discrimination.

Eric Goldman, professor and codirector of the High Tech Law Institute at the Santa Clara University School of Law, who has written extensively about Section 230, says it is hard to predict how courts would treat Facebook's age-targeting of employment ads.

Goldman said the law covered the content of ads, and that courts have made clear that Facebook would not be liable for an advertisement in which an employer wrote, say, "no one over 55 need apply." But it is not clear how the courts would treat Facebook's offering of age-targeted customization.

According to a federal appellate court decision in a fair-housing case, a platform can be considered to have helped "develop unlawful content" that users play a role in generating, which would negate the immunity.

"Depending on how the targeting is happening, you can make potentially different sorts of arguments about whether or not Google or Facebook or LinkedIn is contributing to the development" of the ad, said Deirdre K. Mulligan, a faculty director of the Berkeley Center for Law and Technology.

Critical Thinking

1. Describe the assumptions underlying age-based discrimination. What do you think about those assumptions? Are they valid? Invalid? Why?

2. Examine a series of recruitment ads on Facebook and other platforms that appear to discriminate based on age. Describe how the discrimination is taking place, for example, terminology, implicit messages, placement of ads, and so on.

Internet References

Chicago Tribune
http://www.chicagotribune.com/business/ct-biz-age-discrimination-lawsuit-dale-kleber-0930-story.html

Sherman Law
https://www.johnshermanlaw.com/signs-of-age-discrimination-in-the-workplace/

The New York Times
https://www.nytimes.com/2017/12/20/business/facebook-job-ads.html

Article   Prepared by: Eric Teoro, *Lincoln Christian University*

The Murky Ethics of Data Gathering in a Post-Cambridge Analytica World

SARAH STEIMER

Learning Outcomes

After reading this article, you will be able to:

- Understand ethical challenges associated with data gathering.
- Understand some of the issues that Facebook experiences with data gathering ethics.
- Understand some of the tenets of the General Data Protection Regulation.

Marketers Can Lead the Way in a Post-Cambridge Analytica World, Where Data Collection Rules Are Murky and Consumers Are Creeped Out

Facebook changes its policies frequently, like a child switching up the rules to a game of his own making: a sly update when it's personally beneficial, a knee-jerk pivot when in trouble. Everyone else—the platform's users and advertisers—is left scampering and contorting to comply.

The Cambridge Analytica scandal shed a light on the social platform's inner workings perhaps more than any algorithm or design update prior. *The Guardian* and *The New York Times* found the data firm paid to acquire Facebook users' personal information through an outside researcher, Aleksandr Kogan, who created a data-harvesting personality quiz app that told users (in fine print) that it was collecting the information for academic purposes—a claim Facebook did not verify and was not true. Although only 305,000 people participated in the quiz

and consented to having their data harvested, their friends also had their profiles scraped, bringing the estimated number of those affected to 87 million.

Facebook rescinded the ability to obtain data from friends of consenting users without their permission in 2015, but it's unclear if companies that engaged in this sort of data collection deleted the information they pulled before the access was denied. The old policy was part of Facebook's open platform style, which saw CEO Mark Zuckerberg inviting developers to build their apps on the website.

Cambridge Analytica's ability to circumvent the rules left consumers feeling uneasy (even though most marketers were well aware of this practice already). What followed was a cascade of realizations about Facebook's fast and loose policies. For instance, apps like the personality quiz aren't the only way that companies harvest user profiles: In April, Facebook's Chief Technology Officer Mike Schroepfer told Slate that he believes most users on Facebook could have had their public profile data harvested by third parties through contact information. The comment was related to a Facebook feature that allowed users to search for other users via phone number or e-mail address, a practice that Facebook says was abused by hackers who scoured Facebook using lists of contact information to locate and grab users' public profile information. The feature was subsequently disabled, but Schroepfer said, "we believe most people on Facebook could have had their public profile scraped in this way."

The ability to collect more granular data continues to grow, sometimes faster than guidelines can be written. In a blow to Facebook's freewheeling practices, Zuckerberg was called to Congress. Europe handed down its own set of data collection rules, too. As Facebook policies continue to morph, marketers are mulling over whether the social platform is still the golden child of online ad targeting, or if guidance and filtering could help Facebook reach its potential.

Facebook-Advertiser-User Codependence

Facebook needs advertising to sustain its business, advertisers need Facebook users to sell their products, and Facebook users need the platform to remember their aunt's birthday. It's Facebook's codependent world, and we're all just living in it.

Users' reliance on the platform hasn't been monetized (for now), but advertisers and Facebook itself can put a dollar sign on their relationship: In its first quarterly earnings report since the Cambridge Analytica news broke, Facebook reported $11.8 billion in advertising revenue, a 50 percent increase since the same period last year.

On the marketing side, Facebook remains a great deal for advertisers. The cost per thousand impressions on Facebook is $5.12 (compared with LinkedIn at $16.99, Instagram at $4.20, Pinterest at $3.20, and Snapchat at $2.95), according to data science and martech firm 4C's "The State of Media Q1 2018" report. Facebook also yields the highest click-through rates at 1 percent (compared with Pinterest at 0.48 percent, Snapchat at 0.37 percent, LinkedIn at 0.25 percent, and Instagram at 0.17 percent), making its cost-per-click of 48 cents the most efficient when compared with other social media platforms. The accuracy of its ad reporting, however, has recently been questioned. Facebook has admitted to measurement issues, including miscalculations of average watch time of videos, organic reach of posts, video ad completion rate, average time spent on instant articles, and referral traffic from Facebook to websites and mobile apps.

Even if users' attachment to Facebook can't be financially quantified, perhaps the fact that they didn't peel themselves off the platform after the Cambridge Analytica story is illustration enough. Facebook lost about 2.8 million U.S. users under age 25 last year, but it still boasts more than 1 billion daily active users. And despite the momentary media commotion, the #deleteFacebook movement didn't catch fire. A Reuters/Ipsos survey of 2,194 American adults following the Cambridge Analytica news found about half of Facebook users said they did not recently change the amount that they used the site, and another quarter reported they were using it more. Only the remaining quarter said that they were using it less, had stopped using it, or deleted their account entirely.

The codependence among all parties may be one reason why the ethics of data collection have become murky. Though Cambridge Analytica's data gathering might have been a shock to users, many in the marketing industry were well aware of the practice.

Alexandra Samuel, an independent technology writer and the former vice president of social media for Vision Critical, wrote an article in The Verge about the siren song of shady data-gathering tactics, such as those used by Cambridge Analytica. She wrote that Facebook's "generous access" to friend data was known to many marketers and software developers, as was the tactic of disguising data-mining as fun apps, pages, or quizzes.

"I don't think we can generalize about whether, when, and why specific companies or marketers venture into unethical or ethically nebulous territory when it comes to data collection and targeting," Samuel wrote in an e-mail.

She says a marketer's willingness to dive into these waters can depend on their business model; whether they're working in a company or industry with clear guidelines around how data are collected and managed; their level of tech knowledge (that is, do they know what kind of data are available or have the skills to collect and use it?); and their own personal ethics.

In her Verge article, Samuel wrote that it may be difficult to reform the industry of data collectors and marketing shops, which have grown to maximize the amount of data collected and the precision of ad targeting. "Social networks and other advertising platforms may set up various processes that notionally screen out data aggregators or manipulative advertisers, but as long as these companies run on advertising revenue, they have little incentive to promote transparency among data brokers and advertisers," she wrote.

Facebook Reels It in

One of the only controls on shady user privacy practices may be the fear of bad publicity, Samuel says.

"At this point, the real check [would be] the availability of competitive platforms that behave better," she says. "There certainly is a market opportunity for a social media platform to build a user base on the strength of respect for privacy, though so far none of those efforts have really taken off. I do believe it's just a matter of time before that happens. The fear of that alternative may motivate Facebook and others to make some real changes."

Whatever the motivation, Facebook has moved to take some interest in user privacy. There were rumblings, prompted by Facebook COO Sheryl Sandberg, of making a paid version of Facebook where users would not see ads. More immediately, Facebook tweaked its advertising program.

Marketers on Facebook could traditionally leverage three types of data streams for ad targeting: data gathered by Facebook, which could include information on users' habits and usage of the platform, web browsing history, and cellular location; data that advertisers collected themselves and uploaded, such as names and e-mail addresses of the customers who visit their stores; and data provided by third parties. This final source, from companies known as data brokers, includes insights gleaned by firms such as Acxiom, Oracle, Epsilon, and Experian. These companies build profiles by gathering data over a period of years from government and public records, consumer contests, warranties and surveys, and private commercial sources (namely, loyalty programs and subscription lists).

At the end of March, Facebook made an unusual and succinct announcement: it plans to shut down "partner categories," a product that "enables third-party data providers to offer their targeting directly on Facebook." "While this is common industry practice, we believe this step, winding down over the next six months, will help improve people's privacy on Facebook," the statement read.

The decision centers around the idea that Facebook has less control over where and how third-party data aggregators collect their data, which is risky. This wouldn't have stopped the Cambridge Analytica debacle, but the development could have major repercussions for the broader digital advertising ecosystem. Should others in the industry follow Facebook's lead and distance themselves from data brokers, it could also mean an increase in transparency into their work with personal data.

Kristen Walker, a marketing professor at California State University, Northridge, cautions that this move may be less privacy-oriented and more lip service from Facebook.

"If they were really concerned about ending this service to improve people's privacy, they'd explain how it violated people's privacy," Walker says. "And how does it violate people's privacy? Is it the storage, the use, the rental? Maybe the real concern for Facebook, beyond meeting [General Data Protection Regulation] guidelines, is maintaining people's trust with illusions of transparency and concern for their privacy. And, really, isn't Facebook a data broker, anyhow? The entire distribution system and access to consumer data are undergoing a change. Whether it is an improvement for privacy or not is still a question."

Walker says ending partner categories doesn't necessarily mean that Facebook won't use these partners or access their data to boost targeting; it may just mean that marketers won't have visible access to that information.

"It actually could mean less transparency at a certain level for marketers who may be interested in the source of Facebook data they use to target consumers," Walker says. "Marketers want access to consumers and data broker info can help, but this service makes Facebook less of a dealer and more an intermediary. Nothing's stopping them from buying the data and repackaging it as theirs for marketers to utilize."

In another move to improve customer privacy (feigned or otherwise), Facebook is also changing its "custom audiences" policy by adding a tool that will require advertisers to verify that they gained consent to use e-mail addresses uploaded to the platform. Custom audiences allow advertisers to target users on the site by uploading e-mails, phone numbers, and other information and cross-referencing it against Facebook user profiles. The permissions tool Facebook is developing will require an advertiser, along with the agencies or other organizations that obtain the information, to confirm that the third-party data in a custom audience has been responsibly sourced.

There's a strong chance that these moves were at least hastened in response to Cambridge Analytica and General Data Protection Regulation (GDPR), the latter of which restricts how personal data are collected and handled and focuses on ensuring that users comprehend and consent to the data collected about them. The European Union (EU) rule requires companies to spell out why data are being collected and whether it will be used to create profiles of people's actions and habits. Consumers in the EU have to opt in, not search for ways to opt out; and they have a right to access the data companies store about them, to correct inaccurate information, and to limit the use of decisions made by algorithms.

Whatever the reason for change, it's not entirely clear whether these policy shifts increase transparency. It may be up to marketers to come armed with flashlights in the social media swampland.

The Argument for Draining (or at Least Straining) the Swamp

It's not easy convincing marketers that not all data are worth gobbling up and storing, but Cambridge Analytica and GDPR may be enough to urge marketers to consider the quality of what they collect and their ethical responsibilities.

"Millennials grew up in digital, meaning they had to learn all the things the hard way about what you should and shouldn't put out in the public space," says Jessica Best, director of data-driven marketing at Barkley. "We're in that space on the advertising side right now, where we actually have to think about what we should and shouldn't do morally, ethically in data. We're going to start to take some responsibility. There's a lot of excess data being stored in unsecure ways right now in vendor databases and company databases. We're going to have to be a little bit more responsible, and I think that's going to be a good thing."

Although the trend has been toward increased personalization in marketing, there comes a point where the environment begins to feel creepy to the customer. There's a difference between seeing ads from a company you previously purchased from and receiving targeted communication that speaks very directly to your lifestyle from a brand you never interacted with.

There's precedent for this, Best says. "People have not liked being marketed to since about two years after marketing became a thing. The difference is that the scalable level to which we're able to use and activate data has become alarming. [. . .] What's scary is the level to which somebody can cultivate a profile of me and understand my 'why,' or the algorithm can construct this fairly accurate representation of what will motivate me. That's where we're not accustomed to it yet: We've scaled past the comfort level of those on the receiving end. It's become creepier faster than it's become acceptable."

In theory, any marketer could spend time on Facebook learning about users and their interests, but technology has allowed this to happen on a much larger scale, and faster. In this way, the data become almost weaponized—especially if used in a manner that could cause harm.

At Cal State, Northridge, Walker's research has explored the difference of shared data and surrendered data, advocating for controls on the amount and type of information that social media users provide. The amount of data coming down the pipeline is too much and not always accurate. Placing some sort of filter or slowing the trickle of information could result in more robust and appropriate targeting.

"What if we asked consumers what information they'd like us to know?" Walker says, "because I can guarantee you that if I know what you want me to know, that's going to help me address and serve your wants and needs."

Not only could marketers see their dollars go further, but consumers would likely appreciate seeing ads that are relevant to their lives. When Facebook made it possible for users to access the list of advertisers that uploaded their information, it was clear that not all marketers may benefit from such gratuitous access (this author included, after finding the vast majority of political groups or candidates with my information weren't remotely relevant to me in location or ideology). When marketing works well, it works for the advertiser and the consumer.

Regulating the Flow of Data—In Plain Sight

No one is expecting consumers to take the lead on how their data are collected, stored, and used, as the nature of technology is to help them multitask more and move faster. In short, they're too busy and too overwhelmed to stop and read paragraphs of technical language before downloading an app that provides a few minutes of mental escape. The onus falls on marketers to guide data policies.

The industry is defensive of its ability to self-regulate, and most marketers in the U.S. hope to continue on this route, even

as overseas legislation is enacted. Sentiment among Americans differs from their European counterparts: privacy is viewed as a privilege in the United States and as a right in the EU. As such, marketers in the states have been freely roaming the information highways.

Yet this isn't the first time that advertisers have grappled with issues of audience deception. To potentially avoid legislation in the United States, digital marketers may want to focus on increased transparency and ethical behavior as it relates to personal data. In fact, advertisers can serve as guides for the relatively young technology industry.

"It's going to require demanding quality data," Walker says. "Then it's going to require someone to stand up and say, 'We can help you with this.' Marketers understand that we're supposed to avoid deception, and we see a lot of newer industries learning that the hard way."

Despite the new policy guidelines set by Facebook, experts caution against expecting the social media giant or others in the tech industry to lead the way on data regulation. Marketers will need to play the role of middleman, filtering the rivers of customer data that pour through social media and choosing what is quality and how to use it ethically. Being transparent to consumers will be a balancing act: data collection must have consumers' approval, but to avoid the "ick" factor of seemingly creepy ad targeting, the curtain can't be pulled away completely to reveal all of marketing's tricks.

Best cites a greeting card company as a theoretical example for striking an appropriate balance. Based on a consumer's buying behavior (e.g., purchasing a "Congratulations on your new baby boy!" card), the company would know if a household has a young child. Rather than speaking directly to that knowledge ("Here's a perfect onesie for 3-month-old Timmy!"), advertisers can simply show appropriate products. The ads are relevant, but not invasive.

"I believe this entire conversation has really been about the marketer self-regulating," Best says.

As marketers use data to create segments and personas, it's their job to regulate just how much information is collected and be transparent about the ways it's used.

Thinking like a Market Researcher

Market researchers are quick to point out that Cambridge Analytica is not a market research firm, but the data-driven industry's principles may be worth a review by digital marketers.

A core tenet of market research ethics is transparency. Firms like Forrester, Nielsen, and Kantar follow guidelines that require researchers to be up front with subjects: providing interviewees with clear descriptions of their work, keeping recorded conversations classified, and generally withholding all personally identifiable information. These are ethics that allow for segmentation, not personalization.

Julia Clark, senior vice president of public affairs in the United States for Ipsos, emphasizes the need in market research for informed consent, in which research participants provide information with knowledge of how that data will be used and by whom.

"The first thing I think of when I think of ethics in research is the ethical responsibility we have toward participants and respondents," Clark says. "That means protecting their information and data and utilizing the best data control protocols. It also means not stressing them out. You don't want to administer a survey that's going to leave them with a real sense of unease or ask them questions that are going to make them so uncomfortable they want to stop."

GDPR seems to take a cue from these guidelines and gets at the heart of a modern challenge for market researchers: how to ensure that people do not suffer adverse consequences as marketing relies increasingly on secondary data, defined as information collected for another purpose and subsequently used in research, versus primary data collection (surveys).

"One stream is useful but messy," Clark says of secondary data. "The other (primary data) is very clean but probably not as comprehensive and loose. Navigating between those two is at the crux of all of this." Reg Baker, executive director of Marketing Research Institute International, says the industry is working to expand the ethics that cover primary data to also address secondary data. He says it is essential that no one is harmed related to the use of data, whether obtained in person, on the phone, through Facebook posts, or via Amazon transactions.

The International Chamber of Commerce and European Society for Opinion and Marketing Research revised its International Code in 2016 to account for this concern, adding a new article addressing secondary data. The code defines harm as "tangible and material harm (such as physical injury or financial loss), intangible or moral harm (such as damage to reputation or goodwill), or excessive intrusion into private life, including unsolicited personally targeted marketing messages."

This last point, perhaps appealing to advertisers, is what market researchers want no part of. It's one of the industry's historic principles, and it has no plans to change that in the digital era.

"We don't deliver data to clients that allows them to identify individual data records and associate them with a person," Baker says. "As part of the research, we may develop a profile on a whole bunch of people whom we have information on, but that remains protected and confidential, and it's not what we would deliver to a client. We're here to help companies make decisions, a bet based on the information about the marketplace. But we're not in the business of actually giving them the weapons to go at individuals so that they can change their behavior or sell them something."

That's the business Cambridge Analytica was involved in. The company mined users' data and created profiles, then used those profiles to reallocate advertising and other communications. It was a full feedback loop. This is compared with market research where the data are used to create segments. Individuals whose data were used in the research might receive the segmented marketing communication, but never in a personally targeted manner.

"We (market researchers) are capturing the information, but we are not deploying that directly back to the person we captured it from," Clark says. "It's being aggregated, it's being anonymized."

General Data Protection Regulation What Is It?

The regulation is a new set of rules from the EU that are designed to improve individuals' control over their personal data. The rules replace the 23-year-old Data Protection Directive 95/46/EC and aim to harmonize data privacy laws across Europe.

GDPR affects organizations located within the EU, but it also applies to organizations located outside of the region if they monitor the behavior of EU data subjects. It applies to all companies processing and holding the personal data of subjects residing in the EU, regardless of the company's location.

Under the regulation, personal data are defined as any information related to a natural person or "data subject" that can be used to directly or indirectly identify the person. It can be a name, a photo, an e-mail address, bank details, posts on social networking websites, medical information, a computer IP address, or a host of other identifiers.

Parental consent will be required to process the personal data of children under the age of 16 for online services.

How Are Marketers Affected?

Organizations need to pay attention to the rules: penalties could lead to fines as high as $24.6 million or 4 percent of global annual revenue, whichever is larger.

GDPR limits the amount of data that marketers can collect on European consumers, who have more options about what data companies can see about them. Customers must be able to give consent, and implied consent is unacceptable. The consent must be informed, specific, unambiguous, and revocable. That means consent may not be within long-winded terms and conditions that use complex legal language. The customer is also given the right to remove their consent at any time.

The type of data collected must be adequate, relevant, and limited to what is necessary for the intended purpose of collection. Information may not be used in a way that would be incompatible with the intended purpose for which it was collected. Data may not be shared or transferred to another organization without consent from the person to do so.

Customers also reserve the right to be forgotten, meaning they may request that their personal data be removed from any database or cookie pool. Marketers will need to have processes that can erase collected data should a user submit a request for withdrawal. Users also reserve the right to correct or update any data.

Additionally, the data that an organization obtains from a consenting user must be protected. Any data breaches must be reported within 72 hours to all consumers and respective bodies.

Critical Thinking

1. Describe the ethical challenges associated with data gathering. How would you resolve competing claims that arise in those challenges, for example, need for marketing information to better serve customers and personal privacy?

2. Choose an organization. Describe its data gathering needs and interests. Develop a data gathering ethics policy for that organization.

3. Review regulations and/or policies regarding data gathering. What are their strengths and weaknesses?

Internet References

Forbes
https://www.forbes.com/sites/kalevleetaru/2017/10/16/is-it-too-late-for-big-data-ethics/#25003a493a6d

PLOS One
https://journals.plos.org/plosone/article?id=10.1371/journal.pone.0187155

Vox
https://www.vox.com/policy-and-politics/2018/3/23/17151916/facebook-cambridge-analytica-trump-diagram

Article   Prepared by: Eric Teoro, *Lincoln Christian University*

As Data Gets Bigger, So Do the Risks

HAL CONICK

Learning Outcomes

After reading this article, you will be able to:

- Understand ethical issues regarding the collection and usage of big data.

- Understand ethical issues regarding the collection and usage of big data with respect to minors.

- Understand ethical issues regarding the use of big data aggregators.

As the rules and ethics of Big Data grow alongside other technology, industry professionals see the potential but data ethicists see the potential for harm.

Big Data is snowballing, whether the ethics, protection, and security are in place or not. The number of internet users will rise from two billion in 2016 to five billion in 2020, according to Amy Mushahwar, counsel and chief information security officer with ZwillGen PLLC. More people means more devices, which leads to far more data points created, she said at the 2016 Association of National Advertisers Advertising Law & Public Policy Conference.

"To make all this work, consumers need digital literacy now more than ever," she said to a panel of three other industry professionals, including staff from Google, AT&T, and Oracle Corporation. While the rise of data means opportunity, it also means far more threats, she said.

Pedro Pavón, senior corporate counsel with Oracle Corporation, said mobile has been and will continue to be a huge development for businesses, specifically for its ability to target users wherever they are.

Government Intrigue

The level of access businesses have to personal data has perked up the ears of government officials and made privacy professionals wary of its potential for a serious breach and privacy invasion.

Jeff Brueggeman, vice president of public policy with AT&T, mentioned during the session that the Federal Communications Commission (FCC) and the Federal Trade Commission (FTC) are looking to put greater protections on data, with an FCC report that "treats all data the same."

The new FCC rules, which were proposed in late March, would apply to broadband Internet service providers and not allow companies to share consumer data with third-party aggregators or for marketing or promotions.

"We have to live with the Internet that we have," Pavón said, adding that he believes the guidance for data security and protection needs to come from within the industry—for example, from a group like the Digital Advertising Alliance—lest they lose control. "Some of these rules might create some very serious challenges to continue to provide meaningful ads and content."

Mushahwar said there needs to be a paradigm shift about privacy, as there are plenty of positive and innovative things that can be done with data, which deserve discussion as much as the "creepy nature" of cross-device data collection.

While the FTC and FCC, as well as many privacy professionals, have stressed the need for more transparency, privacy, and security for consumers, members of the panel said this is something already taken very seriously by the industry at large. Ted Souder, head of industry and retail at Google, said data protection is "100% top of mind" for his company, but also very challenging.

"It's really become cyber warfare," Souder said. "It's a really big, serious issue, so much that I've heard people [with the CIA] say cyber warfare is right up there with naval and land warfare."

The Future and Its Ethical Implications

Big Data and the Internet of Things will soon bring a new challenge to the ethical collection of data: wearable technology. Engagement with data and technology is changing more quickly than the rules and ethics, and Pavón wonders how consumers will be able to consent to being tracked in the future, as these devices will be screenless. They'll be with users wherever they go and constantly communicating with other devices.

"That's the world we're heading to in other aspects of our lives. You just won't know what's interacting with you," he said.

The opportunities will be there, but what's ethical? What's not? How can an industry with so much data at its disposal move forward and avoid a widespread breach that has potential to affect millions of people?

Marketing Insights spoke with experts in the Big Data ethics field to find out what's happening now, what's next, and what may soon be changing. Click below to view these interviews in full:

Bill Schmarzo, chief technology officer at EMC Global Services, on the ethics of using Big Data in marketing and communications.

Jason Hong, creator of Privacy Grade and an associate professor at the Carnegie Mellon School of Computer Science, on the ethics of collecting data from children.

Kirsten Martin, assistant professor of strategic management and public policy at The George Washington University, on the ramifications of data security as it flows from companies to third-party aggregators.

Setting Big Data Boundaries: Collecting Too Much Can Hurt, Transparency Can Help

The rapid growth of Big Data has meant more targeted and location-based marketing. Gartner reported in September 2015 that more than 75 percent of companies plan to invest in Big Data by 2017. However, Millward Brown Digital reported in July 2015 that companies' confidence in the use of Big Data is down from 39 percent in 2014 to 14 percent in 2015.

Bill Schmarzo

Bill Schmarzo, chief technology officer at EMC and author of *Big Data: Understanding How Data Powers Big Business*, is better known as the "Dean of Big Data," and for good reason. Schmarzo has been working in the Big Data space for years and created the MC Big Data Vision Workshop methodology, which links an organization's business initiatives, thereby helping organizations become more confident in their use and collection of Big Data.

What's the solution to this Big Data problem, and how can it be ethically implemented and used? *Marketing Insights* spoke with Schmarzo on how Big Data can be used both ethically and successfully by organizations and marketers.

Q: When It Comes to Big Data for Marketing and Communications, Do You See Any Unethical Things Happening?

A: The first thing that jumps to mind is typical in this space: The technology is ahead of the ethics. We tend to be really reactive in that space. We do things and realize after the fact they were stupid and figure out how to apologize profusely for that. I don't think that's unusual for technology. Whether you're talking Big Data, mobile, or the first experiences with e-mail and website marketing, we tend to think about the customer or consumer interest second and the technology first. It always ends up biting us in the butt.

Q: Have You Seen Any Industry Improvement of That Practice?

A: Even e-mail started off as really powerful, and we soon abused it and turned it into spam. Websites are the same way, too. Some make really nice use of the real estate on the screen and present marketing messages in a tasteful way, but then you have some that are just cluttered, and they try to trick you into clicking on buttons you don't want to. I run into websites all the time with interesting articles, but there's a button you push to advance and it ends up being a button for an ad. When I see those kind of websites, I try to never go back there again. . . . More and more, we're abusing the customer because we have the technology to do that, and we think about the customers after the fact. Big Data is guilty of that, as well.

Q: Is the Current Data-for-content Trade a Good Deal for Customers? Does This Afford Them Better Marketing, Advertising or News Content?

A: They do at first, then I think it gets watered down. We recommend to clients that they really understand what their customer needs are and try to be relevant to those needs. There's probably no better example of that than Netflix. Netflix watches your viewing patterns and makes recommendations, and they seem to do a nice job of not only recommending movies they know you're going to like, but they also seem to throw in serendipity. Throw in a movie, sometimes at random, then see how you react to it. Do you actually click on it and watch it? Netflix understands the power of using Big Data to deliver a very relevant and compelling customer experience.

Q: Do You Think It's Harder to Retrofit Big Data Ethics and Best Practices If You Come Out of the Analog, Pre-Internet Age?

A: I've never thought about it before, but I think it might be. One of the areas we see being the first to adopt Big Data across many of our clients is marketing. Organizations that have a direct marketing background are some of the first to jump on Big Data. They understand the importance of being relevant.

Culturally, some of these organizations are really good about it, and some of them are horrible about what they will show customers. One of things I love to talk about is the Target incident. Everyone knows about the Target incident and the underage girl being served ads and coupons for baby products and [pregnancy]. To me, that's the classic example of not thinking ahead about your customer.

Organizations have data governance in place; they're using it to manage their data and make sure it's accurate and in compliance. . . . What we're trying to do is take it one step further and think about decision governance. Think about the decisions you want to drive with your customers and what info you have about those customers that gives you the right to act on it. If you find out things about your customers that do not fall within that realm that you want to act on, then you should not act on it.

Say you're in the health insurance space and find out some of your customers are looking at websites talking about cancer. What do you do? Or you're an employer like EMC and you have employees who are married, but going to dating sites. What do you do? As an organization, you need to think about the decisions you want to make and make certain you've got rules in place with this decision governance approach that makes sure the whole organization is being respectful of how they make those decisions and how they use data.

I was doing a project with a large university. As you can imagine, large universities can track all these data about their students. I know when they got to the library, how long they're there, what classes they go to, if they skip a class, their performance in class. I even have a pretty good idea, by looking at social media, what they're doing in their free time. Let's say you've done this and you've got a really good insight on students and what they're doing. What if, by virtue of doing that, you can identify students who might need tutoring, who might need some sort of intervention in order to help them be successful? . . . The first question is, if you can identify, by virtue of analyzing students' in-classroom performance and out-of-classroom behaviors, someone who is going to struggle, should you intervene?

The vast majority of people in the meeting said, "It's our responsibility to intervene." . . . But let's say by that same data you think that student is abusing either drugs or alcohol. What would you do then? I could hear the room talk: "Well, where's the line?" and one person said, "There isn't a line, it's the murky middle."

We don't know what to do. We haven't thought through it. There are ethical ramifications, there are legal ramifications, and there are liabilities. One person suggested we shouldn't even do that analysis because if we know it and don't act on it, we set ourselves up for a liability.

Going through that process of understanding what decisions you want to make and how you will leverage data . . . ahead of time is critical, otherwise you risk doing some analysis that opens you up to all kinds of bad things.

Q: That Has to Help Them Become More Ethical. It Seems a Lot of Companies Are Collecting Data They Really Have No Use for.

A: The decision governance is all about being ethical. Being ethical will help you identify ahead of time some data sources you just shouldn't go get because they will open up big problems.

Another rule we have is the mom rule. That is, if you are ever in question about a decision to make, what would your mom do? The mom rule helps keep things honest. If I know someone is doing XYZ and I'm going to use that to exploit them, what would your mom think? Well, your mom would probably think you're a bad person, so you don't do that.

Q: Have You Noticed Companies Getting Better, Becoming More Ethical with Regard to Big Data?

A: Organizations are much more aware of it. We build data lakes for clients—that's the environment upon which we do a lot of our data science work. There are a lot of thoughtful discussions about what goes into that data lake, what data we need to mask, who has access to what data, and how they are going to use that. Organizations are becoming a little more respectful of that data. Maybe the Target example was kind of a wake-up call for people. Something that was . . . done with the best of intentions, but it worked out to be such a PR disaster for Target. Everyone said, "I don't want that to happen to me." Maybe we can thank Target for being the whipping boy and showing the marketplace you need to be thoughtful on this.

Q: What about on the Consumer Side; Is There Something like the Target Breach from the Consumer Side? The Target Story Scares Businesses, but How Can Consumers Get More in Tune with Big Data?

A: The industry has made opting out such a horrible process that people are just willing to take all the spam that comes in. The industry hasn't really given the consumer any sort of option. I don't know if the consumers will ever amass as a group and strike back. I doubt it. It's going to be rules and regulations, unfortunately, that have to keep some things in alignment. It's going to be more Target situations or when personally identifying information gets leaked and someone has to pay a huge fine that will change their behaviors.

Q: It Seems like the FTC and FCC Are Looking at Tighter Regulations Now. Does the Industry Need to Take the Lead Here?

A: The industry should definitely take the lead in this. If they let someone else dictate, they're not going to like what happens. That's why organizations need to have decision governance strategy and owner and related policies. If they don't take actions and monitor themselves, government is going to do it, and the government does things for political reasons, so no one is going to like what the government does. They're going to make decisions that make consumers unhappy and companies unhappy, so if companies are smart, they should police themselves.

Q: Do Companies That Decide to Become More Transparent Have an Advantage over Those That Don't?

A: I think so. Not only would it help them become more ethical to be open with customers and let them opt out, but it would allow the ability to flag things you're interested in. [As a customer], I'm interested in [Golden State] Warriors basketball, [Chicago] Cubs baseball, and University of Iowa football. If they knew those were my areas of passion and interest . . . they could then service me more accurately.

Q: Seems That Has Cross-platform Potential for Both Sides.

A: We're starting to see these kinds of conversations. Imagine you're a financial services organization and you have a bunch of investors. You'd like to create a retirement readiness score [that asks], "How ready are you to retire?" Like a FICA score but for retirement. Most banks or investment firms may know all about what you have with them, but they don't have any idea what other assets you have—checking accounts, IRA, and other investing. If they're trying to create a whole retirement-readiness strategy for you, the more they know about you, the better they could serve you. The only way to pull that off is if you are open and transparent.

In a conversation with a client about that, one of the things we came across was that when you think about retirement readiness, how long you are going to live is really important. Suddenly that financial services organization becomes very interested in your personal health, your diet, and your wellness. Maybe they can pull data to monitor your stress, your BMI from the fitness band on your wrist. But it's got to be an open and transparent environment, otherwise your customers will never go for it. They'll think you're going to use it against them.

Q: What Do You See Happening over Next Few Years? What Are the Big Changes That May Be Coming?

A: With respect to ethics, I think you're going to see that a few organizations are going to realize that there's more to gain from transparency and openness than not. I wouldn't be surprised to see a financial services organization or two embrace that holistic retirement readiness approach and become much more open and transparent—to really put the customers' interest first.

Like Taking Data from a Baby: The Ethics of Big Data from Children

When parents let their children download an app, privacy probably isn't high on the list of concerns. After all, why would an app like "My Talking Tom" or "Bakery Store" need any personal information?

However, PrivacyGrade.org reviewed the privacy and data collection of more than 1 million free apps in the Google Play store and ranked them. The worst rated apps, the D-list, featured many apps that seem to be specifically for children, including the aforementioned "Bakery Store" and "My Talking Tom," as well as "Fashion Story," "Happy Farm," and "Rail Rush."

Jason Hong, an associate professor at Carnegie Mellon University's Human-Computer Interaction Institute and leader of PrivacyGrade, worked on research this year titled "Identifying and Analyzing the Privacy of Apps for Kids." He and three Chinese researchers explored privacy for children in creating a learning model for predicting whether a mobile app was designed for children. The paper says this is an important step toward better enforcement of the Children's Online Privacy Protection Act (COPPA).

"We evaluated our model on 1,728 apps from Google Play and achieved 95 percent accuracy," the research's abstract says. "We also applied our model on a set of nearly 1 million free apps from Google Play, and identified almost 68,000 apps for kids."

Marketing Insights spoke with Hong about how apps for kids can be made more securely and ethically, especially with regard to data collection.

Q: What Is the State of Privacy and Protection for Kids Right Now? Is the Industry in a Good Ethical Spot or Is There Work to Be Done for Improved Protection?

A: We reported on these two FTC reports published a few years ago. . . . What they found is that there's just not a lot of information for parents as far as what these apps are doing and the data they collect. A lot of them probably are violating the law right now, such as COPPA. You're not supposed to collect certain types of data for children under 13 unless you have explicit consent form the parents.

Q: What Is There in Place to Stop Bad Actors from Doing That? Is There Anything Other than the Possibility of Getting Caught?

A: [COPPA]'s basically the main thing; the FTC is the main enforcer. That's also where we're trying to help out with PrivacyGrade. We're trying to make it so this information becomes more apparent and, parents can have more information—and it can nudge the developers to do better, too. That's one of the features we're working on now, to make it so app developers can upload their app to our website. We can scan it and we can also offer advice as to how to fix the app and exist within COPPA.

Q: Looking at the Bigger Picture, What Is the Biggest Ethical Problem with Collecting This Type of Online Data from Kids and Teens? What's the Worst Case Scenario?

A: There have already been some data breaches outside of apps. For example, VTech makes these physical [smart] toys for kids. There was a data breach recently where a lot of the kids' information was stolen. In response, what VTech put into their new terms and conditions was basically saying, "You can't sue us if there's a data breach." That's pretty egregious.

That's just the short-term version of things. Most of the people that are trying to collect data probably aren't malicious. They're probably doing it for advertising or personalization. A lot of the app developers don't realize COPPA exists.

In the longer term, the system is just going to be a lot more pervasive around the use of social media, cyber bullying, and accidental leaks of information. A lot of these systems like Google [are] trying to make user models of who the person is and what their interests are. There's a lot of potential there for abuse of data or accidental use of the data as well.

Q: A Lot of Adults in General Aren't Aware This Is Happening, so What Chance Does That Leave Children?

A: That's roughly right. That's one of the main motivations for why we created PrivacyGrade, to get a lot of our research out there and make it easier for people to understand, but also [make] journalists [aware] and to influence app developers.

A lot of these [D-grade] apps disappear, but we've also seen some of the apps' grades improve over time. I don't know if we can take credit for that, but I think that's a positive sign that people are starting to become a lot more aware of these issues.

A lot of app developers don't even realize that their apps are collecting data. It sounds crazy, but it turns out that there are these things called third-party libraries that are collecting the data. Imagine if an app is made out of blocks; some of these blocks are made by other developers. For example, ad networks, or Facebook or Twitter, and so on, instead of you having to retro and code to connect to Facebook, you just grab this Facebook library. If you need to make revenue, instead of just trying to figure out your own ad system, you just grab the ad library and plug it in. It turns out it's usually those third-party ad libraries that want the data, not the app.

Q: Is There Any Awareness of Which Apps Are Using Which Libraries?

A: Right now that's invisible. That's why we have it as one of the pieces of information on PrivacyGrade.

Q: Is That Ethical to Have It Hidden like That? Does That Need to Change as a General Feature of Data Collection, from Children or Otherwise?

A: There definitely are some egregious libraries we've seen. Some of them are trying to use audio data, some of them are trying to use your contact list. Most of them are trying to get your location data so they can do personalized ads. A lot of people are still surprised. They don't even know their apps are doing that.

When we explain it, about half the people we talk to say, "Because it's a free app, I can understand that." The other half are surprised. [They say], "Why do they even do it in the first place?" If there were a lot of more transparency and awareness

of this, then I think it'd be mostly OK. If people understand they're getting a free app because they're getting advertisements, I suspect most people would be OK with that, but there's also a limit of how far you can go before it starts getting really creepy, too. Do you really need my location every 10 seconds or every minute, versus just once? A lot of these smartphones can get your location within hundreds of meters rather than your exact location.

Q: What Was the Biggest Surprise You Found in Your Research?

A: Most apps are mostly OK. A lot of apps actually don't collect that much data, but it seems the most popular apps do.

Q: Is There a Correlation Between Popularity and Data Collection?

A: I'm not sure. I suspect it's partly because what a lot of the popular apps try to aim for is that [they put] a lot of money into developing this app and then [they go for] a "freemium" model or an advertising model. There's a very long tail of apps; some are made by hobbyists or universities where they don't really need to collect that kind of data to make it work.

Q: COPPA Deters People Somewhat, and You Said Some Are Improving, but Is It Enough to Shift How These Apps Collect the Data? Are There Other Steps Needed for Better Ethics on Data Collection from Children?

A: We, as an entire community of people, need to look at the whole ecosystem for privacy. The analogy I've been using is that privacy is a lot like spam e-mail 20 years go. You used to get lots of spam [and you] had to filter it out of your inbox; all the burden of managing spam was on you as an end user. But over time, there are better e-mail filters, your ISP and e-mail service providers help get rid of spam. . . . Nowadays, you may see only one or two spam e-mails per day.

That's the analogy for how we need to grow this entire ecosystem. We need to make it much easier for developers to do the right thing. A lot of developers don't know what to do about privacy, and they sometimes don't realize their apps are collecting lots of data. We also need to make it easier for ad networks to make revenue, but how do you do it in a more privacy-sensitive way? That's going to require a lot of advances in technology.

We also need to make it easier for third parties, like the FTC or for Consumer Reports or the EFF [Electronic Frontier Foundation] . . . to do their jobs, too.

At the very end, we also have end users. How do you make it easier for end users to do things? Have them as the very last part of the whole chain. That way, the burden is not on them.

Q: Let's Say Data Collection from These Apps Stays the Same for Years on End. What Would Happen over the Next 5–10?

A: Companies may see lower adoption rates for these apps and their products because people are just too worried and don't know what's going on. We've seen the small effect of that on the web and e-commerce. Some people are refusing or trying to scrub all their data to protect their data there. It's really hard to know. You can't really tell what's going on.

Right now, the problem is only ads, but tomorrow, there will be a lot more problems. [Think about] mobile health data; phones can access cars and garage doors through the Internet of Things. Your phone is going to know so much about you, and that's going to be the hardest part. That's also the part I'm sure the advertisers would like to know: how do you do this in a safe manner? That's the key.

We, as an entire community, need to figure out how we get the benefit of these apps while minimizing concerns and making people feel like they're empowered. Because most of these apps are not meaning to creep people out or scare people—neither are the ad networks—they're just trying to make a buck off of things. It's fair for them to make a buck off their hard work. But how do you do this in a very reasonable way that everyone feels like they have control over and they understand? That's a really big challenge.

Big Data Aggregators: Are They Unethical, Insecure, or Just Creepy?

The "creepy" label has not dissipated from the Big Data world, even as data has shown a certain level of value for the consumer. There's still an overarching worry from many about why and how they are being tracked.

Kirsten Martin, assistant professor of strategic management and public policy at The George Washington University, wrote in the MIS Quarterly Executive, in a piece titled "Ethical Issues in the Big Data Industry," that there are plenty of questionable uses of Big Data, such as price discrimination, location-based tracking, and using data for admissions decimation at universities, among other issues.

One security concern in Big Data is the data aggregators or data brokers, which get information from customer-facing businesses or websites and move it on in the Big Data supply chain.

"Survey firms, academic research teams, government agencies, or private firms may also contract with a data broker directly to use data to supplement survey research, make employment decisions, and investigate possible criminal activity," she wrote in the MIS Quarterly article.

Marketing Insights spoke with Martin about the ethical implications of these Big Data aggregators, as well as security and identity protection.

Q: What Are Some of the Important Points Companies Should Remember When It Comes to Big Data Ethics, Security, and Identity Protection?

A: There're a few folks that need to have a concern. There is the concern around the original collector of the data—the gatekeeper—that's any website or app you use, the person you trust to hand over your data. [Gatekeepers] have an obligation and responsibility to make sure that it's transparent as to what data they're collecting and, furthermore, where it's going. We find that people don't have an issue with those front gatekeepers. In consumer-facing organizations that are collecting a decent amount of data, [consumers] just assume it's being used for proper purposes.

The thing [consumers] don't know is going on, and don't particularly like when they find out it's going on, is when [their data is] handed off to the unseen data aggregators, the data brokers. They're behind the scenes and don't have any customer-facing relationship whatsoever. There's no agreement between the consumers and those organizations. It's almost a pass-through from the gatekeepers, if that makes sense.

Q: What's Ethically Problematic with These Data Aggregators?

A: It's not that they have the data, it's the security. They do have the obligation [to secure data] if they decide to hold individual-level row data or data attributable to an individual. . . . If it's based on my phone, then it's the equivalent of having my social security number. It's not really that different if you can identify me with [row data] if you identify me by name.

If they decide to hold individual-level data, there is an added burden of responsibility that they have to carry with that. I'd argue they should carry a cost of only having certain types of individuals being able to access individual row data—like a data professional or someone that has some form of certification—like they have for census data. . . .

Everyone can get individualized data now. You could just be, as they say, two hoodies in a garage creating an app and you get access to that data. There's no stopping an individual from getting data-aggregator data. They can get very individualized info . . . We don't have any cost associated with that.

Part of the problem is there's not added protection around this individualized data. The reason the market is not taking care of it . . . [is because] people that use back-end marketing, data aggregators, and data brokers will say people are giving [them] their data. If I don't like what the data aggregator is doing, there's no market mechanism for me to pull my data and say, "I don't trust you," which is how the market fixes these problems. But we don't have the customer-facing ability to pull our business from [data aggregators] because we don't have a relationship with them.

I'm not saying you need to have a rule; there are ways to let the market figure this out. But right now, I, as a consumer, have no ability to pull my data back from that data aggregator if I don't like the way they're treating that data. That's why the markets are not quite working. What we want as a consumer is not showing up. You'll hear people say, "What's the point? They're going to get my data anyway. There's nothing I can do." . . . That's a systematic issue as to why we're unable to put consumer pressure as individuals in the market place.

There's another way. If I don't like what ESPN is doing with my data—if I don't think they're using trusted partners and don't like the limits the data aggregators have put on the data—I could just not go to ESPN.com. We put pressure on Nike to have good outsourcing policies with who makes their shoes, so there are ways. Even though I don't have a relationship with who Nike uses to make their shoes, I can put pressure on Nike. . . . There are templates within businesses to actually fix this, we're just not used to thinking about [websites] as an information supply chain. Right now, we're not putting pressure on ESPN to say, "Who is tracking the data, and who do you think is a trusted partner to have my data?" But we can, and I actually think we will.

Q: What Will It Take for People to Want to Know Who Has Their Data and Where It's Going?

A: There are two possibilities: one is you could have a first mover—someone who thinks, I'm going to make a difference and I'm going to create a new data-use policy sheet that explains visually who gets access to your data and at what level. It'd have to be a big enough company that they'd have market power over one of the data aggregators to say, "I'm no longer using you because you don't have the right controls over data." They could say, "I'm only using data aggregators that have this level of data professionalism." They could say, "This is the criteria by which I'm picking my partners for data and who I'm going to sell my data to." If one company does that, we'd look at them and say, "ESPN is doing that, why aren't you, Deadspin?" . . .

While people inside marketing or privacy scholars know exactly what's going on and we can visualize where the data are, 90–95 percent of the population do not get that. I liken it to the 1980s when people denied steel companies were polluting the rivers. It took a long time for us to say, "I think there's a problem here," and start getting mad. I don't think it will take that long because we are able to communicate what is going on better now with the Internet, get into files, and find out how data are being used. I think events where info from a data aggregator are used to create harm [are if] you find out you aren't getting into your university of choice because of friends or where someone uses the data to harm someone else. If that can link back to a specific data aggregator, that's going to cause a problem.

› Join us at the AMA Annual Conference October 5-7

Q: Is There Potential for a Large-scale Breach from the Way Big Data Moves from Gatekeepers to Aggregators?

A: If something like that happened and a senator like Al Franken, who is into data privacy, puts forward a substantive bill that says something like, "You cannot give data to third parties," that

would hurt a lot of people, right? Everything would come to a screeching halt. But then maybe they'd say, "OK, we should just have better transparency instead." There's always the threat of substantive regulation to get [data aggregators] into alignment.

Even if there is a breach, my concern is that I don't know . . . what people could do about it. Most people don't know who uses that data aggregator. . . . I have an add-on on my browser that shows the data aggregators that are accessing me at any one time, but most people don't have that. They don't actually see who is tracking them and turn them off and say, "No, you can't track me here."

Even if you found out that [a data aggregator] is breached. . . [people] aren't going to know which sites not to go to. This is where it comes back to this issue of a systemic glitch where the market is not able to do its job because we don't have a relationship with them. We're not holding the gatekeepers accountable . . . and forcing them to actually say who they're using and who they're not.

Q: Is There a Way to Get Companies to Disclose Which Aggregators They're Using?

A: Consumers aren't getting much info. The notices are bad. There are a million studies saying notices don't work, people don't read them, they project whatever they want onto them, and they're almost a blank slate. People don't understand even when they're trying to be clear. But there is one place where companies have figured out how to give substantive information in a very clear and concise way, and that's in their 10Ks, their annual reports. SEC filings are easy to read and very substantive and very specific because investors actually demand it. It's required. In order to get people to invest in your company, you need to show them that you know what you're talking about and be very clear about it.

Companies claim they can't be clear [when it comes to Big Data]. It's too complicated. And I always think, I've read Goldman Sachs' 10Ks, and that's complicated, but it's not that complicated.

Another place that will be interesting is a whole movement around data risk and data security on corporate boards. . . . It's a new form of risk that needs to be addressed for investors; they need to understand what the risk is, not only behind pollution and your product quality and accounting, which has always been there, but data risk and security, too.

Q: Do Investors Have Leverage to Get Transparency on a Greater Level Than Your Average Consumer?

A: Yes, and they're worried about hackers, so they want [more information security professionals] on boards of directors. . . . But what would be interesting is if in addition to information security . . . they also want to know whom you're passing your data to and whom you're getting your data from. Are they trusted partners? And if they started asking those same questions as a point of vulnerability for investors because consumers could leave if they're upset by it, then that would be another way for people to demand to know more through the investor class.

Q: To Pull Back a Bit, What Benefit Do Data Aggregators Get from This Transaction? Is It Money from Data? Better Targeted Ads?

A: That is a good question. I don't think the agreements are public. There are two ways [they might be structured]. One is you get flat-out paid for being able to track users; you're selling access to your users. . . . The other thing would be an agreement that says, "If you use my ad network, you must feed into it."

Q: You Spoke to Risk and Reward in Your Paper—Is the Risk of Big Data Worth It?

A: I don't think so, and I don't think if it was up to the market, the market would think so either.

It's definitely not worth it to [consumers]. We could get hypertargeted ads [without being tracked]. When you're watching TV, I don't get an individual ad based on what I shopped for that day. There is a technique to do that, but they know that would upset me. We can have very effective ads without violating people's privacy.

I don't think it's worth it for the consumers, and I'm not convinced it would be worth it for the apps or the websites. The trust violation for the consumer is just not worth it given the [potential] harm of the back-end data aggregators and data brokers. The people getting the free lunch are the data aggregators and the data brokers. They have no pressure on them to not use the data in the wrong way, so there's a moral hazard there. They take all this risk, and there's no market pressure on them not to do it.

Q: It Seems There's a Message from the Data-aggregator End That Consumers Aren't Fully Entitled to Privacy Anymore. Do You Think That's Correct?

A: There's a term called the . . . information exchange. It means we let the website have access to our information in return for a lower access price [for content] or it's free. We disclose information, but we always disclose it within a term of use.

There have been studies that ask what the limit of the costumer exchange is, and it turns out [people are] OK with companies using data for things like research or process improvements or better targeted products. When [data aggregators] go in, [consumers aren't] bargaining that you'd get access to their photos. Just because we use an app or use a website and let [aggregators] have access to our data because we trust them, it doesn't mean they can do anything they want with the data. There's an asterisk next to it with "these qualifying uses in mind."

But this is where it's similar to the companies that used to claim there was no way to make steel without dumping crap in the river or there's no way to make Nike shoes without using slave labor in other countries. [Aggregators say], "You don't understand, this is just how it has to occur." These types of arguments have been made in the past, and then when consumers or investors put pressure on them, [companies] say, "We can find another way to do it." And then they figure it out.

There are solutions. Only trusting data scientists that have a certain professional degree [is one solution]. That would be expensive. That would stop the two guys that create an app from getting access to all that data, but that's OK. They would just partner with someone who is a trusted data professional, and I'm ok with that. There may be additional costs to getting access to that data. It's not going to be perfect, but it would at least slow down the free flow of the data and the idea you can do whatever you want with it.

Critical Thinking

1. Summarize the ethical issues regarding the collection and usage of big data. What do you find especially problematic? Why?

2. How can businesses balance their need for data and privacy concerns?

3. How can individuals safeguard against violating others' privacy with data they personally possess?

Internet References

ResearchGate
https://www.researchgate.net/publication/273772472_Ethical_Issues_in_Big_Data_Industry

Royal Statistical Society
https://www.rss.org.uk/Images/PDF/influencing-change/2016/rss-report-opps-and-ethics-of-big-data-feb-2016.pdf

Unicef
https://www.unicef-irc.org/publications/907-children-and-the-data-cyclerights-and-ethics-in-a-big-data-world.html

---

HAL CONICK is a staff writer for the *AMA*'s magazines and e-newsletters. He can be reached at hconick@ama.org or on Twitter at @HalConick.

Article   Prepared by: Eric Teoro, *Lincoln Christian University*

The Facebook–Cambridge Analytica Scandal Was a Half-century in the Making

Marketers Have Long Used Our Most Intimate Desires to Sell Us Things

DAN GUADAGNOLO

Learning Outcomes

After reading this article, you will be able to:

- Understand the role that psychographics has played in the history of marketing.
- Understand facets of the relationship between psychographics and big data.

Alarmed Americans are up in arms about the Facebook–Cambridge Analytica scandal. Many have called for boycotts of Facebook, and on Tuesday, senators grilled chief executive Mark Zuckerberg on his plans to protect users' privacy during heated hearings on Capitol Hill (today, House members got their turn).

But the work that Cambridge Analytica did with Facebook data is the logical culmination of more than a half-century of marketing techniques. Psychographic profiling like the work done by Cambridge Analytica—basically, the use of personality information to predict and influence behavior—has given marketers the ability to use the most intimate of insights and details into our lives to sell us goods, services, and even presidents. While social media data have offered them even more information to hone profiles and micro-target what they sell us, marketers have long been capitalizing on our most intimate desires to tantalize us into opening our wallets.

Psychographics emerged from the intersection of two trends in psychology and marketing in the late 1940s and early 1950s:

the field of motivational research and the growing use of standardized personality inventories in marketing and management. This method goes beyond clustering us based on where we shop or on the demographics contours of our user profiles. Psychographics cluster us into groups based on psychological factors, like whether we are more meek or aggressive, more externally or internally motivated, all to better construct advertisements to sell us things.

Most famously associated with psychologist Ernest Dichter, motivational research probed how a person's unconscious desires motivated consumer decision-making. Dichter's famous "depth interviews" brought research participants into a state of reflection as they spoke about their daily use of everyday consumer goods. From this, he mined their responses for unconscious associations between product details, packaging or shopping experiences, and the consumer's inner desires.

Through these conversations, Dichter helped advertisers envision the "image" of their product in the consumer's mind. For example, Dichter found Ivory soap had a somber ritualistic cleansing character that would, as the advertising campaign which followed promised consumers, "wash your troubles away."

During the 1960s, marketers began combining these motivational research techniques with the standardized-types approach from personality inventories, like the well-known Myers–Briggs or the Minnesota Multiphasic Personality Inventory. These inventories were originally developed to help both corporate management and the U.S. military make better personnel decisions. When fused with the desires uncovered in motivational research, however, the tests could be used to create "psychographic" profiles that sorted and classified people into different personality categories. This psychographic profiling could determine whether one set of consumers were likely to be aggressive and achievement-oriented, while others might be team builders who focused on building relationships.

The psychographic profiling solved a budding problem in the marketing world. A litany of marketing and advertising thinkers argued that broad demographic differences, such as ethnicity, sex, age, or gender, were obsolete as sole indicators of shared values, interests, and desires. Psychographic profiling offered a tantalizing alternative, promising corporate advertising executives the power to uncover the most unlikely of consumer markets out of the most arbitrary of social patterns.

Psychographics would also resolve two tensions that had plagued marketing and advertising for much of the 20th century: demographics told marketers who their buyers were, either through anecdotal or survey data, but not why customers bought what they did. Knowing the why allowed for more targeted brands and advertising appeals that spoke to habits and behaviors as much as to demographics.

Psychographics, then, were born out of the search by eager advertising executives and market researchers for more comprehensive ways of probing consumers' decision-making faculties. The field promised to bring life to what were often imagined to be lifeless statistics documenting ordinary people's preferences and habits. Statistical techniques might suggest that correlations as banal as a person's preference to go camping, desire to avoid confrontation, or favorite type of mustard revealed stronger shared behaviors for clustering consumers into like-minded groups than demographic lines. As one marketer put it, psychographics on a massive scale held enormous value: More than simply organizing data, the real power would be in finding "order in the data."

By the 1980s, psychographics were lauded as the future of consumer-market research, working their way into every step of product engineering and development.

Perhaps, the most well-recognized psychographic research emerged out of the Stanford Research Institute—the company that later developed the first iterations of Apple's onboard AI, Siri. SRI opened in 1946, consulting on organizational management and developing long-range forecasting and risk management strategies for corporations and the state. Through their Values and Lifestyles Surveys, SRI developed testing techniques that deployed a 30-item questionnaire used to verify categories and consumer types based on shared values and interests.

SRI associate Arnold Mitchell offered an example of the power of psychographics in his 1983 book "*The Nine American Lifestyles.*" Through the 1970s, investment bank

Merrill Lynch's advertising featured thundering herds of bulls (ostensibly representing a bull market) captured in the tag "Bullish on America." But in the 1980s, SRI's psychographic profiling suggested to Merrill Lynch that it needed to attract "achievers"—outwardly directed, materialistic high rollers who valued external status symbols and exclusivity—one of the nine American lifestyles documented by Mitchell.

As a result, the company rebranded itself as "Merrill Lynch: A Breed Apart." The firm replaced the thundering herd of bulls with imagery that reflected financial predicaments that a well-off achiever might encounter. These images ranged from a lone bull seeking shelter in a cave to avoid a financial storm to a single bull carefully navigating a shop full of fine china. The psychographic profiling suggested the image of a singular bull navigating both quaint and seemingly insurmountable tasks would speak to the thrill ride lifestyles of investors in the world of 1980s high finance.

In the interim 30 years, psychographics have changed, both in their approach and the nature and amount of data available. Mitchell's nine lifestyle categories derived from surveys administered to 1,600 people asking respondents to agree or disagree with statements like "I like to think I'm a bit of a swinger" or "I feel I get a raw deal out of life." By the 1990s, however the rise and mass adoption of the Internet and the emergence of database marketing, which compiled consumers interactions with particular firms to develop profiles documenting addresses, lifetime purchasing history, and communications with the company like submitting complaints, transformed psychographics.

The arrival of social media platforms like Twitter and Facebook and various other apps in the 2000s provided even greater reams of data for psychographic profilers. These platforms captured our friends, our collective likes and dislikes, our status updates, our locations, our countless photos, products and services we like, stories we read, and websites we visit.

Marketers mine these data to produce micro-targeted ads. By the late 2000s, this data collection allowed for the personalization of each of our Internet environments, including the advertisements we encounter when we scroll, click, or like one another's uploaded photos and status updates.

Platforms like Facebook, available to anyone over the age of 13 since 2006, offer us the promise of community and interconnection. But to their clients—advertisers, political parties, merchandisers, and the like—they offer something else: not only who we are through our data but also how we think and feel. When sorted and counted, "order in the data" is not simply a demographic phenomenon of selling consumer markets on the basis of identity. It is psychological, as well.

Although Cambridge Analytica is a massive example of data misuse, it has by no means revealed anything beyond the norm of advertising and marketing practices over the past half-century. The culture of online manipulation stems directly from a history of corporate America aggressively investing in categorizing us all—not simply our demographic profiles, but our ways of thinking, as well.

Critical Thinking

1. What are ethical issues associated with psychographic research? With psychographic usage by marketers?

2. What differentiations can you make, if any, between the historical use of psychographics and the use of big data today? Describe any similarities and differences between the ethical challenges faced by both methodologies.

Internet References

CB Insights

https://www.cbinsights.com/research/what-is-psychographics/

CXL

https://conversionxl.com/blog/psychographics/

International Journal of Communication

http://ijoc.org/index.php/ijoc/article/view/6706/2197

DAN GUADAGNOLO is a PhD candidate in the department of history at the University of Wisconsin–Madison.

Article   Prepared by: Eric Teoro, *Lincoln Christian University*

Advertisers Sip Rosé and Ponder Ethics in South of France

Sapna Maheshwari

Learning Outcomes

After reading this article, you will be able to:

- Understand ethical issues related to marketing and technology platform usage.
- Understand that ethical lines with respect to company partnerships can be blurry.

CANNES, France—A who's who of marketing and media convened on yachts and in the gardens of luxurious chateaus here last week as musicians like Jon Bon Jovi and the Killers performed at hotels and sandy beaches temporarily renamed after companies like Google and Spotify. There was a "blockchain yacht" and a "blockchain villa" and more rosé than any group of people could, or perhaps should, want to drink.

The occasion was the annual Cannes Lions advertising festival and the goal, as usual, was to fete the industry's best marketing while conducting meetings that could ultimately influence how vast sums of ad dollars are spent. But paired with the heady exuberance this year was a growing sense of unease among some marketers about what kind of return they are actually getting once they pour money into big technology platforms—and also what sort of societal problems they may be unwittingly financing in the process.

The mere presence of Tristan Harris, the tech ethicist who has been called "the closest thing Silicon Valley has to a conscience," showed some of that concern.

Mr. Harris, who joined the festival at the behest of the agency Hearts & Science, and Scott Hagedorn, the agency's chief executive, appeared on a panel for clients where they discussed smartphone addiction, the feelings of depression and anxiety that social media can produce in teenagers, and the methods that popular apps like Facebook use to harness human attention so they can serve more ads to people.

"We don't want to be scorching the playing field when we're extracting attention," Mr. Harris said in an interview. "It would just suck the air out of democracy and there's no shared truth and then it's like, great, we can advertise to people, but they're lonely, depressed, and they don't believe in facts. No one wants that world."

Mr. Hagedorn, who acknowledged that some might look askance at advertisers taking up the cause of ethical persuasion, said he heard Mr. Harris on a podcast last year when his agency was manually reviewing tens of thousands of YouTube videos to figure out what kind of content its clients' ads were appearing with.

"I ended up basically giving myself PTSD because I saw so many horrible things," Mr. Hagedorn said. "We've been, as an industry, blindly telling clients that being 'video neutral' is fine—you can follow the eyeballs from platform to platform—and I think we've been unaware, or not paying attention potentially, to what we're monetizing and funding."

While Google and Apple have announced initiatives around well-being, Hearts & Science has been motivated to help research how people are engaging with their phones—it says that the average person checks apps 88 times a day—and the effectiveness of ads placed next to misinformation and racist or explicit content.

In a separate move, Keith Weed, the chief marketing officer of Unilever, said that the company would look to avoid working with social media personalities who buy followers. (*The New York Times* this year detailed the financial incentives of such behavior and showed that the black market for fake accounts can use personal information from real people without their knowledge.)

"Digital advertising as an industry has grown really, really rapidly and the unintended consequences of that sort of rapid growth means there are things happening that no one had anticipated," Mr. Weed said in an interview. He said he expected to work directly with platforms like Instagram on such issues, adding that social media sites are grappling with a decline in trust.

Jon Kaplan, the global head of sales at Pinterest, said that he had observed "a growing backlash" against automated, data-driven advertising. In an interview on a pier that the company rented for the week, which welcomed "friends of the Pin," he recalled the disenchantment of major advertisers at an industry gathering last year.

"Every story was like, we thought this was the panacea, and while it has its place, we may have over-rotated into that kind of data-driven marketing," he said. "And there's kind of no soul and no creativity and no real brand love associated with that."

Still, the power of tech was clear throughout the week. It wasn't just companies like Google, which hosted a client dinner on Wednesday where Duran Duran performed. Spotify and Hulu transported guests to a chateau that is typically used for weddings, serving drinks, and offering a discussion with stars like the actress Samira Wiley. At the same time, the major ad agency holding companies said that they sent fewer people than in years past.

The big tech companies also had an unexpected neighbor on the beach—Big Tobacco. Philip Morris International hosted a concert by the band St. Lucia and served drinks by robot bartenders. As the week closed, the company issued "a bold call to action for the creative, media and communications communities" to support its efforts in advertising tobacco products.

Wendy Clark, the chief executive of DDB Worldwide, said that in the 1990s, the beachfront space now ruled by tech had been dominated by ad agencies. She was optimistic, however, about technology forcing advertisers to come up with increasingly creative ways to reach people.

"The best ads don't feel like ads," she said. Terms like "advertising" and "marketing" have come to mean less, she said, recounting a meeting she had during the week with a young YouTube influencer. "She would never describe herself as a marketer, but she's a modern-day marketer," Ms. Clark said.

As marketers and media types considered the industry's power shifts—including those resulting from the #MeToo movement—there was ample chatter about the attendance of Martin Sorrell, the British tycoon who abruptly resigned in April from WPP, the ad giant he built and which he led for three decades.

Mr. Sorrell spoke at two events and discussed his newly formed marketing services company on the heels of a report in *The Wall Street Journal* that alleged his departure was preceded by a company investigation into whether he visited a brothel and used WPP money to pay a prostitute. Mr. Sorrell denied the allegation at an event last week. (When approached by a *Times* reporter in a hotel lobby on Thursday, Mr. Sorrell said he was busy working.)

Many in attendance were also interested to see what kind of profile Vice would have this year. The company was the subject of a *Times* investigation into allegations of sexual misconduct in December and more recently faced serious questions about its business in a *New York Magazine* report.

Still, Shane Smith, Vice's cofounder, appeared to remain popular with the ad industry, judging by the long line to enter the company's annual party.

As more reports have emerged about misconduct of varying levels at advertising or media companies, it has posed a challenge for brands.

Marc Pritchard, the chief brand officer of Procter & Gamble, the world's biggest advertiser, said in an interview that, generally, such situations are "few and far between," but that when they do arise, the company has to examine whether they are "isolated incidents or is there a pervasive pattern that you need to do something about."

Mr. Pritchard added that the company has been working to build up its own databases to make its digital ads more precise and pointed to new partnerships it announced last week with Katie Couric and Queen Latifah.

"The bigger thing we're pushing on," he said, "is we're just trying to take more control over things."

Critical Thinking

1. Describe questionable ethical practices you have witnessed with respect to marketing and technology platform usage. Why do you consider those practices ethically questionable?
2. How can businesses and marketing firms safeguard ethics when utilizing technology platforms?

Internet References

American Advertising Federation
    https://www.aaf.org/_PDF/AAF%20Website%20Content/513_Ethics/IAE_Principles_Practices.pdf
Communications of the ACM
    https://cacm.acm.org/magazines/2017/10/221320-internet-advertising/fulltext
El Profesional de la información
    http://www.elprofesionaldelainformacion.com/contenidos/2017/mar/06.pdf
Raconteur
    https://www.raconteur.net/hr/brands-control-digital-advertising

Article   Prepared by: Eric Teoro, *Lincoln Christian University*

Untrustworthy Memories Make It Hard to Shop Ethically

REBECCA WALKER RECZEK, DANIEL ZANE, AND JULIE IRWIN

Learning Outcomes

After reading this article, you will be able to:

- Understand difficulties associated with personal ethics and personal consumption behavior.
- Understand steps that can be taken to promote ethical consumer behavior.

Imagine a shopper, Sarah, who is concerned about child labor and knows about groups like the Fair Wear Foundation that certify which brands sell ethically produced clothing. Hours after learning that fashion giant H&M reportedly sells clothing made by children in risky workplaces in Burma, she goes shopping. Completely forgetting about what she just heard, she buys an H&M dress.

What happened? Sarah either forgot about that child labor allegation, or she mistakenly recalled that H&M was on Fair Wear's list of ethical brands—which it isn't. Either way, how could she make such an error?

We are interested in how actual purchasing can be different from consumers' own values. Our research shows that even though most consumers want to buy ethically sourced items, it's hard for them to heed these sentiments, especially when adhering to their sentiments requires remembering something.

Selective Memories

It's not easy to shop ethically in the United States. Nearly all the clothing sold here is imported. Although not all imported clothing is made in exploitative workplaces, companies that demonstrably benefit from unfair and even dangerous labor practices abroad continue to flourish.

Prior consumer psychology research has shown that people dislike thinking about unethical issues associated with their purchases. When you buy a new sweater, you probably don't want to contemplate the harsh reality that it might have been made by exploited workers. And you may be tempted to come up with rationalizations to avoid thinking much about these issues.

In fact, consumers may do their best to remain ignorant about whether a product is ethical or not, simply to avoid the anguish they would experience if they were to find out.

Unethical Amnesia

We wanted to learn what consumers would do if they had to face the truth.

Perhaps, they might just forget that truth. After all, memory is not a particularly accurate recording device. For example, recent psychological research suggests that people experience "unethical amnesia"—a tendency to forget when they have behaved unethically in the past.

So would shoppers also prefer to forget when a company exploits workers or engages in other unethical actions? We predicted that they would.

In a series of studies described in an article published in the *Journal of Consumer Research*, we explored why consumers' memories might fail them when it comes to recalling whether products are ethical. It turns out that there is a predictable pattern for what consumers are likely to remember (or forget) about the ethicality of products.

In general, we found that consumers are worse at remembering bad ethical information about a product, such as that it was produced with child labor or in a polluting manner, than they are at remembering good ethical information—such as that it was made with good labor practices and without much pollution. Our findings should trouble the many companies now vying for the ethical consumerism market and the people who buy those products.

Avoiding Feeling Torn

To test our hypothesis, we studied how well 236 undergraduates would remember manufacturing information about six wooden desks. We did not select any of the participants for these studies based on whether they did or did not see themselves as ethical consumers.

We told these students that half of the six brands of desks were made from wood sourced from endangered rainforests and that the rest came from wood sourced from sustainable tree farms.

After they had several opportunities to study and memorize the descriptions, the participants completed unrelated tasks for approximately 20 minutes. Then, we displayed only the desks' brand names and asked the students to recall their descriptions.

The participants were significantly less likely to correctly remember when a desk was made with rainforest wood compared to when it was made with sustainable wood.

They either did not remember the wood source at all or wrongly recalled that the desk was made from sustainable wood.

Did that suggest shoppers just don't want to remember unpleasant information about brands?

To find out, we looked into how accurately the students would remember other attributes of the desks, such as their prices. We found that they didn't make the same kinds of errors.

People generally strive to act morally, which in this case would mean remembering whether products are ethically sourced or not and then presumably acting accordingly. However, people also do not want to feel bad or guilty.

And no one enjoys feeling torn. The easiest way for conscientious shoppers to avoid this inner conflict is to yield to their consumerist whims by forgetting details that might trigger ethical concerns.

Do These Jeans Make Me Look Unethical?

In another study, we had 402 adults participate in an online experiment. As part of a shopping task, this group, which averaged 38 years old and included slightly more women than men, read about a pair of jeans. Half of them saw jeans made by adults. The others saw jeans made by children.

Consistent with our other findings, people who saw the child-labor jeans were significantly less likely to remember this detail compared with people who had seen the jeans made by adults.

Notably, participants who saw the child-labor jeans said they felt more uncomfortable. We determined that this desire to not feel uncomfortable again led participants to forget about the child labor detail.

I Don't Remember and I Feel Fine

In another online experiment, we presented 341 adults (with the same demographic profile) with one of two scenarios.

Half of them read about a consumer who, when trying to recall a description of jeans they were interested in purchasing, forgot whether the jeans were ethically made. The other half read about a consumer who instead remembered whether the jeans were made ethically, but chose to ignore this information.

It turns out that participants judged consumers less harshly for buying jeans they forgot were made by children rather than when they remembered but ignored this information.

So, maybe consumers forget when products are made unethically so they can buy what they want without feeling (as) guilty.

Reminding Consumers

How can marketers help consumers make more ethical choices?

One possibility is to continually remind them, even at point of purchase, of their products' ethical attributes. That is what companies such as Everlane, a clothing company that has built social responsibility into its business model, and the outdoor apparel giant Patagonia already do.

Also, companies can concentrate on the bright side, describing how happy their well-paid workers are and how their contractors are good environmental stewards instead of pointing out the bad things their competitors do. Based on what we learned, that approach would make ethical consumers less likely to subconsciously dodge this issue.

How can consumers make more ethical choices?

For starters, they can forget about relying on their memories when they shop. They can use guides like the one Project Just has created to assess their next purchase, and they can also make notes to themselves about brands to avoid. The key is to realize our memories are not perfect and that shopping without a plan may lead us away from our values.

Critical Thinking

1. Describe times you violated your personal ethics/values when purchasing products or services. Why did you violate your personal ethics/values?

2. Describe ways to foster ethical consumer behavior. What makes those ways ethical? Effective?

3. Research companies engaged in promoting ethical consumer behavior. What are these companies doing differently than their competitors regarding consumer behavior ethics?

Internet References

Ethical Consumer

https://www.ethicalconsumer.org/

Harvard Business Review

https://hbr.org/2015/01/ethical-consumerism-isnt-dead-it-just-needs-better-marketing

ResearchGate

https://hbr.org/2015/01/ethical-consumerism-isnt-dead-it-just-needs-better-marketing

Science Direct

https://www.sciencedirect.com/science/article/pii/S0148296315005998

Article

Prepared by: Eric Teoro, *Lincoln Christian University*

Marketing to Children: Accepting Responsibility

GAEL O'BRIEN

Learning Outcomes

After reading this article, you will be able to:

- Describe the debate between McDonald's and industry watchdogs regarding McDonald's marketing practices to children.

- Understand the potential impact of marketing to children.

- Discuss who is primarily responsible for the marketing messages children receive—parents or companies.

For all the significant achievements companies are making as corporate citizens, the issue of their real impact on society—and what as a result society may actually need back from them—raises the question of whether we are adequately defining what is expected by being socially responsible.

The issue of marketing to children really brings that into focus; with food marketing a timely lens, the issue of **obesity** a hot health care crisis, and McDonald's handling of responsibility, as one of the world's largest fast food chains, a case in point.

As background, McDonald's Happy Meals for children with toys has come under attack. San Francisco is one of the cities that has voted to **ban selling toys with fast food** for children that exceed certain levels of salt, fat, calories and sugar. McDonald's was accused of **deceptive marketing practices to children** over the lure of toys as an inducement to buy Happy Meals. Healthy alternatives are available, apple slices in place of fries and milk instead of soda—if kids are willing to eat them. But, there is still the issue of **high sodium content in burgers**.

At McDonald's May 17, 2011 shareholder meeting, activists focused attention on McDonald's marketing to children. In February 2011, in anticipation of McDonald's shareholder meeting, **Corporate Accountability International** launched a campaign to fire Ronald McDonald, the clown mascot for the last nearly 50 years, and encourage headquarters to stop marketing to children by delivering petitions to individual restaurants. They also asked the chain to address directly the relationship of fast food to obesity. Beginning the campaign in a **Portland, Oregon suburb**, by May they had gathered 20,000 parents' and community residents' signatures on petitions which they delivered to the shareholder meeting.

In Oregon, McDonald's threw down the gauntlet, and affirmed Ronald's job security, saying he is "the heart and soul of Ronald McDonald House Charities, which lends a helping hand to families in their time of need." The response demonstrated how McDonald's infuses the emotional and the marketing: Ronald, the symbol to families dealing with sick and dying children, is also the brand, signifying the food and fun atmosphere to eat it in.

A letter signed by 600 health professionals and organizations, critical of the link between fast food and obesity, was read at the shareholder meeting. It had run as full page ads in newspapers across the country. In addition, **shareholder Proposal 11**, by the Sisters of St. Francis of Philadelphia, requested McDonald's undertake a report on its "policy responses to public concerns about the linkage of fast food to childhood obesity, diet-related diseases and other impacts on children's health." The proposal was soundly defeated.

In **his remarks at the meeting**, CEO Jim Skinner asserted the company's right to advertise freely, to offer its menu and lifestyle selections, and leave to parent's the right to chose what their children eat, saying it is up to personal responsibility. McDonald's **Corporate Social Responsibility (CSR) information indicates** the company serves "a balanced array of quality food products and provides the information to make individual choices."

Marketing to children, whether the subject is food, toys, clothes or anything else raises enormous concerns for Susan Linn, director and cofounder of a national coalition of health care professionals, educators, parents, and others called the **Campaign for a Commercial-Free Childhood**.

"There is no ethical, moral, social, or spiritual justification for targeting children in advertising and marketing, said Linn recently at a **Conscious Capitalism Conference**. Linn, who also teaches psychiatry at Harvard Medical School, cited obesity and a number of other issues impacting children and society that stem from targeting kids, including youth violence, sexualization, underage drinking and smoking, excessive materialism, and the erosion of creativity.

"Kids are inundated with advertising in a way never before, she said in an interview. "I don't believe in any advertising to children."

The food industry has been effective in limiting the Federal Trade Commission's ability to regulate marketing to children, and unless Congress changes the rules, companies selfregulate. I asked Linn what protection the **Children's Food and Beverage Initiative** provides. Linn indicated it didn't provide any because it has no actual authority and the standards are voluntary.

The Coalition advocates that children be able to develop a healthy relationship to food, but McDonald's, Linn says, entices kids not because of the food but because of the toys and the message of happiness that is part of their advertising.

Marketing to children is inherently deceptive because kids take things literally and media characters play a big role in their lives, Linn says. They don't understand persuasive intent until they are 8 years old; and the brain's capacity for judgment isn't developed until their 20s which makes them very vulnerable as marketing targets.

Of course parents are accountable for educating their children about responsible choices and healthy foods. And, they have the choice not to take their kids to McDonald's. Except . . . if you serve **more than 64 million people in 117 countries each day** and many of your restaurants are open 24/7, the chain has created a compelling draw.

Add to that, a **recent report** by Yale University's Rudd Center for Food Policy and Obesity that more fast food marketing dollars for toys are being spent (to get kids in the door) while marketing efforts to promote healthy meals haven't really increased.

I asked Cheryl Kiser, the former managing director of Boston College's Center for Corporate Citizenship for her take on marketing to kids. "CSR has had an enormous influence helping companies reduce their global footprint by addressing human rights and other issues," said Kiser, now the managing director of **Babson College's Lewis Institute**. But "companies are socializing kids and the imprint on those kids is not necessarily creating common good outcomes."

"Having a young over-sexualized population of kids who have no awareness of the implications or consequences of their choices is unhealthy," she adds. "Foods appealing to kids because they are tasty, high fat and zero nutrition is also unhealthy. When we start to imprint early in behaviors and consumer choices things that don't lead to personal and common good, and that need to be corrected in teen years by good CSR programs, is CSR doing its job?"

Critical Thinking

1. What limits, if any, should be imposed on businesses regarding marketing to children? Explain your rationale.

2. To what degree are parents responsible for the marketing messages to which their children are exposed? Why are they thusly responsible?

3. Debate with a colleague or fellow student on the permissibility of marketing to children.

Internet References

Association for Consumer Research
   http://www.acrwebsite.org/search/view-conference-proceedings.aspx?Id511328

Campaign for a Commercial-Free Childhood
   http://www.commercialfreechildhood.org/

Wall Street Journal
   http://online.wsj.com/news/articles/SB10001424052748703509104576329610340358394?mod=dist_smartbrief&mg=reno64-wsj&url=http%3A%2F%2Fonline.wsj.com%2Farticle%2FSB10001424052748703509104576329610340358394.html%3Fmod%3Ddist_smartbrief

GAEL O'BRIEN is a *Business Ethics Magazine* columnist. Gael is a thought leader on building leadership, trust, and reputation and writes **The Week in Ethics**.

Article

Prepared by: Eric Teoro, *Lincoln Christian University*

Marketing's Ethical Line between Social Media Habit and Addiction

HAL CONICK

Learning Outcomes

After reading this article, you will be able to:

- Understand ethical challenges associated with social digital marketing.
- Understand facets of addiction, and how addiction relates to social digital marketing.

Where Is the Ethical Line in Marketing between Hooking a Customer and Getting Them Hooked?

Media is an open door to the public mind, Edward Bernays wrote in his landmark 1947 essay "The Engineering of Consent."

"Any one of us through these media may influence the attitudes and actions of our fellow citizens," he wrote. "The United States has become a small room in which a single whisper is magnified thousands of times."

Seventy years later, the door to the public mind is wide open. The thousands of whispers have been multiplied by billions into a deafening roar of smartphones and social media. Consumers can stay in touch with the people and brands they love, meeting new ones along the way. In turn, marketers are now privy to consumer data they dared not dream could exist even 15 years ago—what consumers' preferences are, how much they weigh, what sexual acts they prefer, and the contents of their contact list. Marketers can reach consumers in their home, at work, in the car, and anywhere they happen to take their devices—which, for many, is everywhere. As technology has made communication easy and life convenient, it has placed a two-by-five-inch glowing screen at the center of both.

U.S. teenagers spend nine hours per day using media devices for enjoyment, Common Sense Media reports, which adds up to more than 136 days of the year—not even including media time spent on homework or school. Globally, the average adult spends two hours per day on social media networks, Social Media Week reports, up from 15 minutes per day in 2012. Even if this latter number remained static, that would mean a lifetime average of five years and four months on social media—a number surely higher in the United States, where 77 percent of people own a smartphone and 69 percent use some form of social media.

In this ecosystem, demand for a new kind of rehabilitation has emerged. Facilities, such as reSTART Life in Washington state and Paradigm Malibu in California, have popped up across the country to treat social media and technology addiction in children and adults.

Addictive qualities aside, social media could not thrive if it wasn't so uniquely—for lack of a better word—social. Humans are social animals who ache for connection with others. Mauricio Delgado, associate professor of psychology at Rutgers University, explained to Marketing News in 2014 that social media activity—likes, retweets, and comments—activates the brain's reward center in the same way as a hug, smile, or compliment. Social media interactions are positive reinforcement, he says, bringing favorable effects and drawing users back again and again.

Ashlee Humphreys, associate professor at Northwestern University's Medill School of Journalism and author of Social Media: Enduring Principles, says users are hooked on this social feedback, longing for the dopamine high it creates. "We are always looking for how the social environment is responding to what we do," Humphreys says. "Social media—let's just say even more concretely the smartphone you carry around with you—allows you to get that social feedback, interact socially, and put out social feedback 24/7."

Humphreys cites an argument from Barry Wellman, sociologist and director of the NetLab Network, who says humans are now "networked individuals." This means people actively seek online social capital, but physical group settings—such as bowling leagues—have become less common. An example of network individualism at work is someone posting for emotional support on Facebook when a loved one is sick; those friends who respond may not be lifelong friends, but they may give an on-demand bandage for an emotional wound.

Social media seems to walk the line between a way to socialize, an annoying habit, and an addiction. Marketers may play an ethical role in ensuring consumers don't cross the line from habit to addiction. To find the ethical line, we must first look at how social media can adversely affect people.

The Dark Side

It would be fallacious to say social media or smartphones are a net negative for society, as many studies have shown the power and positivity of human connection on these platforms. However, as Aristotle said in *The Nicomachean Ethics*: "Virtue lies in our power, and similarly so does vice."

The vice of social media can be shown in recent studies, including:

- German researchers from Humboldt University and Darmstadt's Technical University report one in three people felt more dissatisfied with their lives after browsing Facebook—particularly those who browse without contributing.
- A study published in *Psychological Science* reports subjects had the highest "self-control failure rate" with social media—higher than sports, spending, and sex. Wilhelm Hofmann, lead author of the study and an assistant professor of behavioral science at The University of Chicago Booth School of Business, told *The Guardian* that human desires for social media may be harder to resist "because it feels like it does not 'cost much' to engage in these activities, even though one wants to resist."
- A study in the journal *Psychological Reports: Disability & Trauma* found technology addictions share features with substance and gambling addiction. Social media addictions may result in "academic failure, sleep deprivation, social isolation, health issues, and many other impairments for adolescents and young adults;

they also result in reduced work performance and marital discord and separation for adults." Researchers found that these addictions activate the amygdala-striatal brain system—which creates the drive for impulsive behavior—but do not seem to activate the prefrontal cortex, the part of the brain that controls inhibition. Thus, there are shared traits between the digital world and drugs, but it may be unfair to say a social network like Facebook or Twitter is tantamount to a drug like cocaine or alcohol, as posited by recent news headlines covering this study.

James Roberts, a professor of marketing at Baylor University who has spent much of his career looking at the "dark side" of consumer behavior, says the most concrete example of technology's addictive qualities is the willingness of many to risk their lives by using a device while driving. The U.S. Centers for Disease Control and Prevention reports more than eight people are killed and 1,161 are injured each day from an accident involving a driver distracted by screens. For scale, this is just less than $\frac{1}{3}$ of the number of people killed or injured from accidents involving alcohol.

Aside from physical safety, Roberts says people risk their own relationships by "phubbing"—phone snubbing—which entails paying attention to a device in the middle of an interaction with a romantic partner. In one of Roberts' studies, 70 percent of people say phubbing hurts their ability to interact with their partner. This seems to follow people into the workplace, as Roberts says a study currently underway by his team is finding "phubbing" can also harm employer–employee relationships and job status.

"When you perceive your partner to be spending more time and paying more attention to their phone, that undermines your relationship satisfaction, so you are less happy," Roberts says. "And if you are less happy, you are more likely to report higher levels of depression, stress and anxiety."

The Internet is set up to be addictive, Roberts says. Companies want consumers to be clicking from page to page, to be interrupted and distracted. That's what keeps the proverbial cash register ringing. "The Internet has been created by people much smarter than me with the sole purpose of keeping you moving and keeping you off balance," he says. "You're always being interrupted. You're clicking and you're making more money for the advertisers."

At the center of the social digital movement are brands profiting from the Internet's addictive structure. Products by brands, such as Apple, Facebook, Microsoft, Twitter, and Google, are almost irresistibly entertaining on their own. Then, factor in brand-sponsored commentary, games, videos, posts, contests, images, virtual-reality simulations, notifications, and messages—all optimized by personalized consumer data—and you have something far more transfixing than any TV show or movie. But does this level of consumer absorption make the product addictive or simply a habit? That may depend on how one defines the terms "addiction" and "habit."

Nir Eyal, an entrepreneur and author of *Hooked: How to Build Habit-Forming Products*, says a habit—which can be good or bad—is an action performed with little or no conscious thought. Addiction, on the other hand, is always bad and defined by Eyal as a persistent and compulsive dependency that actively harms the user. Similarly, Roberts sees behavioral addiction as any action a person continues to perform despite negative consequences. Where they differ shows their biggest disagreement: Eyal believes only a small percentage—2–5 percent—of the population is hooked, while Roberts believes the number is anywhere between 50 percent and 66 percent of U.S. citizens. Researchers from the aforementioned study in Disability & Trauma believe anywhere from 0.7 percent to 11 percent of the population is addicted to technology.

A matter for marketers, then, is what role brands are playing in the increased consumption of social media. Are brands simply practicing good marketing or are they taking advantage of their advanced knowledge of what makes the average human brain tick? Could the virtue of good marketing—which as Aristotle noted lies in power—turn into a vice?

The Shift from Mere Exposure to Experiential Marketing

Since the start of the 21st century, there's been an important psychological shift in marketing. The mere-exposure effect—defined by PsychCentral as a preference for people or things simply because they're familiar—dominated advertising and marketing in the 20th century. The theory works like this: the more a brand exposes itself to consumers on TV, in magazines, in newspapers, or on billboards, the more consumers grow familiar with the brand. Exposure and familiarity mean increased sales.

However, many modern companies don't rely on the mere-exposure effect anymore, according to Eyal. Consider how rarely you see billboards or ads for Snapchat or Facebook. Instead, brands use experiences to implant themselves in the consumer's mind; using an app, playing a game, watching a video, or reading content.

"The products themselves change consumer behavior and tastes; it's through forming habits with the product," Eyal says. "The product experience itself is what makes people use them more. That's different. That's news. That's something only this century that we've seen."

The best products don't win, Eyal says, but products that have monopoly of the mind do. Take the phrase "search engine," for example: Does anyone's mind immediately think Yahoo or Bing? Without much conscious thought—perhaps as simple as the unconscious stroke of the letter "G" on the keyboard—Google likely flashes to mind.

How do brands win monopoly of the mind? Eyal breaks down the four basic steps of the hook model: a trigger, an action, a reward, and an investment. Brands identify the consumer's initial trigger and the trigger's accompanying emotions, in the process allowing consumers to easily collect rewards. The hook for rewards becomes more enticing on a variable schedule instead of a fixed schedule; Eyal says this is the same psychology at work as pulling the handle of a slot machine. The best example of this may be the social media newsfeed, which users continuously scroll through and pull down to refresh. What pulls the hook model together is investment, the final step of experiential marketing, which Eyal says can only be done by interactive products.

"What's happening is this tectonic shift where products are being made not only by the company but by the user," Eyal says. "When customers put something in a product—like data or content and they increase followers or reputation—they're literally crafting the product with the company. So if [another user] were to log into my Facebook account or Pinterest account, it would be really boring [for them] because it's been tailored to me based on the data I've given the company. That's something that a box of Cheerios can't do yet. These companies are literally making the program with you based on your data and that's a really big deal. That's a sea change."

This sea change has not come by mistake, as companies now know more about the consumer than ever before. Michael Quinn, author of Ethics for the Information Age and dean of the College of Science and Engineering at Seattle University, says data collection and privacy is the biggest issue in digital ethics today. "Sophisticated algorithms now allow governments and private entities to construct sophisticated profiles of individuals," Quinn says. These individual profiles are, in turn, used to appeal and sell the experience to consumers by social media platforms, third-party aggregators, and brands.

Cal Newport, associate professor of computer science at Georgetown University and author of Deep Work, said in a 2016 TED Talk that companies now use "attention engineers," a principle borrowed from Las Vegas casinos, to make products as addictive as possible. "That is the desired use case of these products—you use it in an addictive fashion because that maximizes the profit that can be extracted from your attention and data."

Tristan Harris, a former Google design ethicist and founder of Time Well Spent—described by its website as "a movement to align technology with our humanity"—says product designers "play your psychological vulnerabilities (consciously and unconsciously) against you in the race to grab your attention." To maximize a product's addictive nature, Harris writes that tech designers link a user's action—refreshing their newsfeed—with a variable reward, such as a match, notification, or prize.

However, not every brand sets out to be a peddler of an addictive product. Harris is careful to argue that most of these "slot machines" emerge by the accident of good design. Even so, he says companies like Apple and Google now have an ethical responsibility to reduce intermittent variable rewards in exchange for a less addictive reward system through better, more humane design.

"For example, they could empower people to set predictable times during the day or week for when they want to check 'slot machine' apps, and correspondingly adjust when new messages are delivered to align with those times," he writes.

The Difference and the Line

For Eyal, the ethical line between habit and addiction is rather dark. He believes marketers must be allowed to make good products that hook consumers, especially with innovative technology.

"I'm not a Luddite. I love these technologies," he says. "They make the world a much better place. But you can't separate the tenets that make the product good with the tenets that make it potentially addictive." People will get addicted to anything sufficiently good. You can't help it, he says.

This doesn't mean marketers, programmers, and brands don't have an ethical responsibility to the consumer, he says; they do. Eyal says he won't consult with gambling websites, porn websites, or alcohol companies because he doesn't believe they responsibly deal with addiction. Brands in the digital realm know who the addicts are because of the data they collect.

"Facebook, Zynga, and all social games know how much time [consumers] are spending online," Eyal says. "If they wanted to . . . reach out and ask them, 'Hey, can we help you dial it back?' they could. And if [consumers] say, 'No,' frankly there's not much we can do. But if they say, 'Yes,' if they say, 'You know what, I really need some help here,' we can help. . . . Many unethical companies don't respect that. But that's something an ethical company has a responsibility to do."

So ethical responsibility does somewhat fall on brands, but making an addictive product or creating new consumer habits is the job of marketing—in a way, Roberts says. In his introduction to marketing classes, Roberts tells students that marketing is all about behavior modification or getting people to do what you want them to do.

"I hate to put the responsibility on marketers," Roberts says. "Marketers are just using our increased understanding of habits and addictions and the way the brain works. We're putting that to good use to create habit-forming behavior, so I don't see really an ethical issue. . . . It is a reflection that the science of marketing has just taken leaps forward with our increased understanding of how our brains work."

Roberts stops and thinks for a moment before reversing course. Perhaps, there is an ethical problem, he says, one where the marketer's knowledge of the customer is so advanced that people can be duped, trained, or conditioned to do what brands tell them to do. After all, the understanding of the human brain has never been better. While it's the marketer's job to ensure a sticky website, platform, blog, or app, is there not also an ethical responsibility to the consumer's health?

"Maybe we're getting to that ethical gray area," he says. "Maybe we really do need to at least be thinking about or considering that a lot of the stuff that we're doing is creating addictions or hardwired patterns of behavior. And maybe that needs to be rethought."

Digital addiction is a multifaceted issue, ridden with caveats, complexities, and questions. In the end, Roberts believes marketers must act ethically, and consumers must take responsibility for their own actions, habits, and addictions. The thought brings him back to another Marketing 101 talking point: Caveat emptor. Let the buyer beware.

SIDEBAR: Are You Addicted?

There are six signs of behavioral addiction—which can include technology, sex, or gambling—according to Roberts. These signs are:

- **Salience:** A behavior becomes deeply ingrained within a routine. Smartphones lie next to the bed, social media is swiped daily.
- **Euphoria:** Users get a feeling of giddiness or anticipation with each notification, comment, or buzz. Roberts' website says people may find themselves often picking up their smartphone when bored or taking calls and texts—or perhaps pretending—to avoid social situations.
- **Tolerance:** People feel an increasing need to have a bigger dose, that is, more time than one may care to spend on Facebook or Twitter.
- **Withdrawal Symptoms:** Stress, anxiety, sadness, or panic are the touchstones of separation from a behavioral addiction; technology is no exception.
- **Conflict:** Does smartphone use cause arguments with friends or lovers? Are you texting and driving?

- **Relapse:** Have you ever unsuccessfully attempted to stop or cut back on use of technology?

Visit Roberts' website for the full quiz and see: Are you addicted to smartphones or social media?

SIDEBAR: Heavy Investments

Facebook, the world's largest social platform has approximately two billion users worldwide and is accessed daily by 76 percent of its American user base, according to Pew Research Center. Marketers, who spent $11.7 billion on Facebook and other social media networks in 2016, are expected to spend $13.5 billion in 2017, $15.4 billion in 2018, and $17.3 billion in 2019, according to Forrester Research.

Marketers are also investing a lot of time at work in social media, according to Social Media Examiner. While 58 percent are spending between 1 and 10 hours on social media, 19 percent are spending in excess of 20 hours a week on social—5 percent of which say they spend more than 40 hours per week marketing to customers on social media.

Critical Thinking

1. Describe examples of social digital marketing that you believe were ethically exemplary, ethically questionable, or clear violations of ethical norms. Why do you classify the given example as you do?

2. Describe the responsibilities of marketers and consumers regarding social digital marketing. How can both parties improve their ethical practices regarding such marketing?

3. Based on the questionnaire in the article, describe yourself with respect to social media addiction. What are the ethical implications of your self-assessment? What specific steps can you take to safeguard against social media addiction?

Internet References

Center for Digital Ethics and Policy
https://www.digitalethics.org/
Yahoo Small Business
https://smallbusiness.yahoo.com/advisor/30-signs-social-media-addiction-133619535.html

Article   Prepared by: Eric Teoro, *Lincoln Christian University*

What Designers Could Learn from Lawyers, Doctors, and Priests

Designers Working with AI Must Navigate a Raft of Moral Dilemmas—and They Need a Code of Ethics to Do It, Writes Argodesign's Mark Rolston

MARK ROLSTON

Learning Outcomes

After reading this article, you will be able to:

- Understand ethical challenges encountered by designers.
- Understand how a given profession can appropriate ethical norms from other professions.

Design today faces a new generation of problems that carry an entirely new ethical burden created by the impact of new technologies such as AI and ubiquitous surveillance. It didn't used to be that way—a product's ethical disposition was easy enough to see at face value. A toaster never had another purpose in life other than to toast bread. The lines were clean and simple.

Now, AI, surveillance, and what I call "dark interactions" are transforming even the most prosaic design task into one rife with potentially dark outcomes.

In response, designers have been making the case that we have a new obligation to act responsibly in the face of new ethical challenges—that we should be "agents of positive change." Sounds like a good idea, right? But how exactly is this supposed to work? It's time to look deeper into the subject—and to mine wisdom from professions with long-established ethical guidelines.

Toward a Design Code of Ethics

I don't think most professionals in the industry have anything resembling a conscious or formal plan for how they will navigate these new waters. What is an "agent of positive change"? What exactly does a designer's responsibility look like? Is it merely a personal filter for the projects we take or reject? Is that even practical? Imagine if every doctor you encountered treated your problem differently, some willing to save your life, others refusing it. It wouldn't work, which is why they have a code of ethics. Designers need something similar. We must define an ethical framework, and adopt it industrywide.

Let me illustrate how difficult it is to navigate our industry without a code of ethics, using two projects I encountered just this last year. The first is that we were approached by a gaming company to create a gambling machine. For us, it was an easy line to draw. We don't want to be part of that. It was an example of what I'd call a first-order ethical choice: the intention of the design was clear, and at face value, we didn't agree with it. So we passed on the project. It's important to note that we could afford to pass up that work; most designers don't always have that luxury. How firm might our ethical stance be if we needed the work?

A second design challenge provided more of a conundrum. A startup approached us with a technology that would allow it to track movement in a given physical space, such as in retail or in the home. That data could be used in many scenarios for clear benefits. But in our eyes, there were also drawbacks. Tracking individuals could be construed as a breach of privacy, or at the very least, a creepy intrusion into our expectations of public space. This is exactly the kind of project where there is no clear ethical line—at least not yet. It's what we can call a second-order ethical challenge: the technology itself isn't bad, and in fact has many positive applications, but it also carries the potential to be used for objectionable purposes.

A design code of ethics would guide us in each unique situation. It would also help us advise and navigate the companies that task and pay us to solve these new challenges.

What Can We Learn from Other Professions?

The design industry is not alone in facing ethical choices in our jobs. Many established professions have robust ethical systems already worked out. I've picked out three examples from iconic roles in Western culture: the priest, the doctor, and the lawyer. They all face moral dilemmas in their work, and they all have clear models for resolving those dilemmas.

The Priest

Priests guide and encourage their congregations, and they can wield enormous influence over the moral choices of their parishioners. But in modern Western culture, the priest's guidance exists only as a recommendation, an ideal to strive toward. (Modern religious organizations often don't live up to their own ethical codes, which is a risk our industry also faces.)

The takeaway: It's foolish to think that we can fully control the design choices industry makes. Similarly, the priest does not control people's choices. When church is over, parishioners go their own way and make their own decisions, which may or may not comport with what they heard from the pulpit. As designers, we may be able to shape the contours of the world, but as with modern religion, our ethical framework works best as a set of ideals rather than any rule of force.

The Doctor

All MDs take the Hippocratic oath at the start of their profession. By doing so, they agree to treat everyone who requires medical assistance, regardless of which side of the war they're on, where they come from, or how much money they have. Doctors commit to treating a thief with a gunshot wound just as they would treat a child with a broken arm. The Hippocratic oath also commits doctors to "do no harm" to a patient. In other words, doctors have to recognize that there are times where intervening in a situation might be more harmful than doing nothing at all.

Finally, it's important to understand that doctors' ethical model has evolved over time. Doctors used to wear patchouli in their masks and use leeches for bloodletting. They used to believe in the four humors. But their craft is constantly evolving to adopt new ideas and technologies. They learned how to give bone marrow transplants and triage in times of war and famine. As the science has evolved, so too has the code of ethics.

The takeaway: Just as patients go to doctors, clients come to designers with complex problems, and we're tasked with solving those problems. Our first priority is not to make the problem worse, and if we don't see a way forward, we have to speak up and recommend a different approach. We also have to mindful that a solution that makes sense today might not meet our ethical standards in the future, and we have to be willing to adapt.

The Lawyer

Lawyers pose the clearest parallel to how designers operate today. In the law, regardless of people's innocence or guilt, they are afforded an attorney to help them navigate their rights. It's an agnostic service model, and it's crucial to ensure fairness. Society would be doomed without lawyers to defend people.

The takeaway: Clients task designers to solve problems, and it's not up to us to attach innocence or guilt to the product or outcome of the work. We represent our clients. Some of us may pick and choose clients based on a moral outlook, but this brings me back to the original conundrum: *You* may be fortunate enough to turn down work, but the client will just find another designer.

It's not a question of being for or against designing for good. That work is going to be done. Design for evil people, products, and things—or more likely, things that will become evil—will happen. It may be our highest calling to interact with things that are questionable in order to drive a better outcome, rather than simply accepting or rejecting work based on our personal feelings.

So What's Next?

The industry needs a clear declaration of the business purposes of design and to promote a dialogue about what role designers should take. It begins with documentation. Medicine has a system of articles, studies, and schooling—an entire institution for building its craft. Lawyers have the law. Designers today are limited to conventions and intuition—often routinized by the corporations that hire them. Imagine if Google's Material Design became the law, or Apple's Human Interface Guidelines. I'm not recommending that. But that's one end of the spectrum. Waffling with our feelings is at the other end of the spectrum; neither is acceptable.

As technology seeps into everyday life, designers have to figure out where they fit in. Design for technology cannot be placed solely into good or bad buckets. It's true that there are unsolved moral and ethical questions around new technologies—especially those as profoundly impactful as AI. We need to grapple with all of the implications of the ceaseless march forward, both good and bad, and we need a method to do it so we can come together to make a better world for everyone.

Critical Thinking

1. Describe product designs that could become problematic regarding ethics. What is it about the designs that create the ethical challenge?

2. Choose a product. Develop a design code of ethics for that product.

Internet References

Ethics for Designers

https://www.ethicsfordesigners.com/

Fast Company

https://www.fastcompany.com/90143739/7-designers-draw-their-code-of-ethics

Slate

https://slate.com/technology/2018/08/ethics-in-design-what-exactly-does-that-mean.html

Article   Prepared by: Eric Teoro, *Lincoln Christian University*

Rethinking the Ethics of Photoshop

Retouching Is Its Own Form of Fake News. Can an Oath Change a Problem That Stretches from Fashion to Product Design?

KATHARINE SCHWAB

Learning Outcomes

After reading this article, you will be able to:

- Understand ethical issues regarding retouching images.

- Understand how some designers are responding to the ethical challenges of image retouching.

Ten years ago, a set of five oaths called the Designers Accord aimed to establish a code of ethics around sustainability in the design industry. More than 1,000 design firms and organizations voluntarily adopted the accord, as well as thousands of individuals from 100 countries and six continents, helping to raise awareness about eco-friendly design while giving designers a concrete way to engage clients in conversations about sustainability—today, a commonplace practice.

Now, the designer Sarah Krasley is trying to create a new kind of accord, this time for those in the business of making images. She calls it the Retouchers Accord, a Hippocratic oath for authenticity in images. The first draft of the five-part oath, modeled after the Designers Accord, places an impetus for change on the entire system, from casting directors to graphic designers to photographers to businesspeople. It recognizes the role of images in body image and self-confidence—like how Photoshopping razor-thin models to look even more frighteningly skinny can impact perceptions of beauty for adolescents. It also asks those who sign on to emphasize practicing empathy and integrity, learn more retouching techniques that embody the accord's values, and become evangelists for the cause.

"The downstream impacts of the design decisions that postproduction artists and retouchers are making are causing public health problems," Krasley says. "You have young women and men looking at those pictures and thinking their body needs to look like that in order for them to be beautiful, to be loved or accepted."

Krasley, who runs the design consultancy Unreasonable Women and launched a line of customizable swimwear for women in 2015, began to think about unhealthy image-making practices when she and her team were photographing models in their swimsuits.

She contemplated airbrushing the models' cellulite, believing this might make her products more appealing to customers, but felt unsure about if that was ethical. Krasley began to look around for best practices for retouching images, but had no luck. She decided to leave her models' cellulite alone and instead host a symposium of people from different areas of the image-making industry in order to start a conversation and create the code of ethics she felt was missing.

In January, the group of retouchers, postproduction artists, graphic designers, models, industry businesspeople, editorial decision-makers, stylists, and photographers met to discuss what the accord should encompass. Now, their first draft is online, and Krasley is soliciting comments from the public. When the comment period closes on February 28, she will convene with the organization's board of directors and finalize the oath, then open it up to companies and individuals to voluntarily sign on. She says she already has several large institutions on board, though she declined to share which ones.

"A voluntary pledge is a really amazing first step," Krasley says. "You're promising to do something and then relying on your own creativity and the collective knowledge of the community you're part of to help you make good on the thing you promised to do."

Better Design Could Hold the Key to Less Retouching in Images

Retouching itself isn't inherently bad. It's often used for fixing things like a cord that ends up in the shot or flyaway hairs, helping make shoots go faster, thus making them more cost-effective. For the female-led retouching studio Feather Creative, retouching mostly means adjusting lighting and color. "The reality of retouching is more mundane," says Linn Edwards, one of the studio's cofounders. "We make samples look right, make photos fit page layout, remove tourists from the background of a shot."

Still, when retouchers are directed to drastically alter women's bodies, the results are not only embarrassing, studies have shown that doctored images that only depict idealized, unattainable forms of beauty can really impact body image among adolescents.

Krasley hopes that the Retouchers Accord will help raise awareness on an industry-wide level and encourage more people involved in the process to rethink the images they're creating.

However, the Retouchers Accord isn't just about body image—a lack of image authenticity can be misleading in other ways if used without any ethical guidelines. For Lance Green, a freelance graphic designer who attended the Retouchers Accord Symposium, image manipulation in product design needs to be rethought as well.

"With product design, the end product images, the hero image, those are highly manipulated as well. It's hard when someone higher up is asking to create a fantasy of a product and an image, when you know it's a complete lie," Green says. "It's tough to put that out there and have people believe it. But that's often how it's done. You sell the idea before the end product."

Green says that the conversation about being more authentic in images is a difficult one to have with clients, and that having a framework like the Retouchers Accord would give him a starting place. And as a freelancer, the oath would give him something to indicate his set of values. "If you could be sought out by companies for this, if it's something that a company shows off too, then designers might be more interested in working for that company."

The Designers Accord provides helpful precedent for how the Retouchers Accord might work in practice. DA founder and influential designer Valerie Casey established a set of five simple steps that gave designers a more tangible way to act on their values. Casey now sits on the board of the Retouchers Accord, giving Krasley strategic advice based on her experience. But Casey's influence wasn't the only reason that half

a million people signed on to the Designers Accord—it also had good timing. A 2003 report from California's Sustainable Building Task Force found that a 2 percent increase of upfront investment in green design for buildings results in an average of 20 percent savings over the course of the building's life. By the time the Designers Accord arrived in 2007, the cultural shift toward sustainability—likely influenced by the green-building rating system LEED—was already underway. Today, promoting eco-friendly design is no longer a difficult conversation to have with clients—it's a well-established practice that designers and companies are proud to uphold.

Perhaps, the Retouchers Accord will give the image-making industry a similar way to take actionable steps toward standing up for their values around retouching. The body positivity movement and outrage against magazines and advertisements that retouch models in unnatural ways have been around for years, and social media has helped reveal the downsides of retouching to a larger audience and empowered people to speak up about it. If timed right, the Retouchers Accord could be the tipping point toward real change.

Ultimately, the Retouchers Accord is a symbolic gesture. Time will tell if the oath will have the same kind of reach as its predecessor, but in a highly visual world where photos can no longer be trusted to tell the truth, the Retouchers Accord could serve as an antidote to our post-truth time.

Critical Thinking

1. When is retouching an image ethically acceptable? Unacceptable? Why?

2. Research images that have been retouched. Provide an ethical assessment of each retouching.

3. Describe ways individuals violate ethical norms regarding personal image "retouching," for example, resume embellishment. How can we safeguard against such ethical violations?

Internet References

Ethics in Graphic Design
http://www.ethicsingraphicdesign.org/tag/photo-retouching/

Mashable
https://mashable.com/2017/03/27/retouchers-accord-photoshop-body-positivity/#apG4SIRhIiq0

The New York Times
https://lens.blogs.nytimes.com/2015/02/17/world-press-photo-manipulation-ethics-of-digital-photojournalism/

KATHARINE SCHWAB is an associate editor based in New York who covers technology, design, and culture.

Article   Prepared by: Eric Teoro, *Lincoln Christian University*

How VW Paid $25 Billion for Dieselgate—And Got Off Easy

Volkswagen Paid Huge Government Penalties in the United States, but Virtually Nothing in Europe. Two Things Now Seem Clear: Some Very Senior Officials Knew of the Wrongdoing—and They're Not Likely to Face Meaningful Prison Time

ROGER PARLOFF

Learning Outcomes

After reading this article, you will be able to:

- Outline major events of Volkswagen's Dieselgate.

- Understand how German and U.S. courts have responded to some of the charges against Volkswagen and certain VW employees.

On December 6, former Volkswagen engineer Oliver Schmidt was led into a federal courtroom in Detroit in handcuffs and leg irons. He was wearing a bloodred jumpsuit, his head shaved, as it always is, and his deep-set eyes seemed to ask, "How did I get here?" As Schmidt's wife tried to suppress tears in a second-row pew, U.S. District Judge Sean Cox sentenced him to what, had it been imposed in Schmidt's native Germany, would rank among the harshest white-collar sentences ever meted out: seven years in prison.

Schmidt was being punished for his role in VW's "Dieselgate" scandal, one of the most audacious corporate frauds in history. Yet his sentence brought no catharsis, least of all to Cox, who at times seemed pained while imposing it. Sometimes, he told Schmidt apologetically, his job requires him to imprison "good people just making very, very bad decisions."

Schmidt was a henchman, everyone understood, and his sentence, a stand-in. The judge was addressing a set of people in Germany who are beyond the reach of U.S. prosecutors because Germany does not ordinarily extradite its nationals beyond

European Union frontiers. Above all, the Detroit courtroom was haunted by the shadow of an individual who was absent: Martin Winterkorn, who was VW's CEO during almost all of the fraud. His name was uttered only twice, yet his aura loomed over the entire hearing.

The outlines of the scandal are well known. For nearly a decade, from 2006 to September 2015, VW anchored its U.S. sales strategy—aimed at vaulting the company past Toyota to become the world's No. 1 carmaker—on a breed of cars that turned out to be a hoax. They were touted as "Clean Diesel" vehicles. About 580,000 such sedans, SUVs, and crossovers were sold in the United States under the company's VW, Audi, and Porsche marques. With great fanfare, including Super Bowl commercials, the company flacked an environmentalist's dream: high performance cars that managed to achieve excellent fuel economy and emissions so squeaky clean as to rival those of electric hybrids like the Toyota Prius.

It was all a software-conjured mirage. The exhaust control equipment in the VW diesels was programmed to shut off as soon as the cars rolled off the regulators' test beds, at which point the tailpipes spewed illegal levels of two types of nitrogen oxides (referred to collectively as NO_x) into the atmosphere, causing smog, respiratory disease, and premature death.

At first, Volkswagen insisted the fraud was pulled off by a group of rogue engineers. But over time the company has quietly backed away from that claim, increasingly focusing on protecting a small cadre of top officials. The crime may well have started among a relatively small number of engineers afraid to admit to feared top executives that they couldn't reconcile the company's goals and the law's demands.

Over the past two years, prosecutors in the United States and Germany have been tracing who was aware of the scheme and have identified more than 40 people involved, spread out across at least four cities and working for three VW brands as well as automotive technology supplier Robert Bosch. In a new, potentially explosive move, some U.S. prosecutors are pushing to indict Volkswagen's former CEO. Such a step would be largely symbolic—the United States has no power to extradite them—but it would send a message that the misconduct was egregious and directed from the top.

And it would highlight a stark contrast in punishment. U.S. authorities have extracted $25 billion in fines, penalties, civil damages, and restitution from VW for the 580,000 tainted diesels it sold in the United States. In Europe, where the company sold eight million tainted diesels, it has not sustained any major fines, nor offered snookered owners a single Euro in compensation.

There's no doubt that Schmidt was guilty. He admitted that he'd been part of a cover-up. Yet he was far from the mastermind. Schmidt claimed not to have learned of the cheating until June 2015, just three months before the decadelong conspiracy ended, though he admitted that he "suspected" it in 2013.

Schmidt, now 48, was an engineer who for several years was VW's main point of contact with U.S. environmental regulators. He had only recently been promoted to a midlevel officer (making about $170,000 a year) when he got involved in the cover-up. Everything about him exuded a car-oriented company man. Born in Lower Saxony, the VW-dominated state where about 110,000 of the company's 600,000 employees work, Schmidt came to the company in 1997, straight out of military service. About 50 personal letters submitted through his attorney—"I don't think I've ever seen as many," Cox observed—extolled him as a loyal and loving son, brother, husband, uncle, and friend. In his spare time, the letters recounted, Schmidt enjoyed collecting old slot-car racing sets and restoring classic VW Beetles. When Schmidt got married, in 2010, he and his wife—herself an automotive engineer—held the ceremony in the showroom of a friend's Volkswagen dealership in Miami. Schmidt was an all-too-loyal VW lifer.

His punishment was designed to further "general deterrence," Cox explained at the hearing. In other words, the point was to send a message to other corporate officials that following illegal orders is no defense. It doubtless reflected frustration as well.

Schmidt had committed his crime, Cox told him, "to impress . . . senior management and the board." He was talking about Winterkorn, who was not only CEO from 2007 until the scandal brought him down in 2015 but also chairman of the company's management board. Schmidt and a second employee had made presentations to Winterkorn and other senior officials at a meeting on July 27, 2015, according to versions of the facts endorsed by both Schmidt's counsel and the prosecutors.

Winterkorn was a notorious micromanager—he was known for carrying a micrometer with him, so he could personally measure VW parts and tolerances down to the hundredth of a millimeter—and an imperious martinet. He was also then the highest paid CEO in Germany, having made $18.6 million the previous year, more than 100 times Schmidt's pay.

Schmidt and a colleague had been summoned before Winterkorn to help solve a crisis. U.S. regulators had taken the drastic action of refusing to permit the sale of VW's model year 2016 diesels—so crucial to its U.S. strategy—and the CEO wanted Schmidt to explain what was going on. As Schmidt would lay out, regulators with the California Air Resources Board (CARB) and the U.S. Environmental Protection Agency had discovered a serious anomaly: VW Clean Diesels complied with NO_x-emissions standards when tested in the lab, but then discharged up to 40 times the legal limit when driven on a road. Dissatisfied with more than a year of evasions and stonewalling, the regulators had decided to bar VW's 2016 diesels from the United States until they got better answers.

The July 2015 meeting with Winterkorn delved into detail about the company's misbehavior, legal filings allege. "An unindicted coconspirator presented certain technical aspects of the defeat device," according to Schmidt's sentencing memo. ("Defeat device" is the phrase used to describe the software that enabled VW diesels to fool emissions tests.) Schmidt warned attendees of "the potential severe consequences to VW if regulators discovered the cheating." A slide in his presentation raised a disturbing prospect—"Indictment?"—according to the FBI agent's affidavit that initiated the charges against Schmidt.

Schmidt and his colleague explained to the group "in unmistakable terms that Volkswagen had been cheating, how they were cheating," prosecutor Benjamin Singer told Cox at the sentencing. (The prosecutors and Schmidt's attorney, David DuMouchel, declined to be interviewed.)

If one believes the prosecutors and Schmidt—that Winterkorn was unmistakably informed of the cheating at the meeting—the CEO's response to that information looked suspiciously like a cover-up. Winterkorn did not direct his subordinates to notify authorities about the cheating or launch an investigation to determine exactly what had happened.

Instead, he sent Schmidt on a mission to persuade U.S. regulators to allow the sale of 2016 VWs.

Winterkorn "directed Mr. Schmidt to seek an informal meeting with a senior-ranking CARB official he knew from his time in the United States," according to Schmidt's sentencing memo. "Rather than advocate for disclosure of the defeat device to U.S. regulators," the FBI agent alleged in his affidavit, "VW executive management authorized its continued concealment."

Before leaving on his mission, Schmidt "sought and obtained approval for the 'storyline' he intended to convey during his meeting with CARB," Schmidt's memo asserted. The script was approved by at least four senior VW officials below Winterkorn, according to the memo, which added, "Mr. Schmidt was instructed not to disclose the defeat device or any intentional cheating."

In August 2015, Schmidt flew from Germany to Michigan, where he successively lied to two CARB officials. He e-mailed "detailed updates" to his boss in Germany and 10 other "senior people," conveying that "he was following the script of deception and deceit that VW, with Schmidt's input, had chosen," prosecutor Singer stated.

Finally, a different VW engineer, unable to stomach the deceit any longer, went off-script and confessed to CARB during a meeting on August 19. A VW supervisor formally conceded use of the defeat device to regulators on September 3, and the EPA and CARB made VW's confession public on September 18, 2015.

Winterkorn stepped down five days later, asserting that he was "stunned" by the events of "the past few days," adding that he was "not aware of any wrongdoing on my part." The company's supervisory board exonerated him the same day, stating that he "had no knowledge of the manipulation of emissions data." In testimony before the German Parliament in January 2017, Winterkorn insisted he had never even heard the phrase "defeat device" until the scandal erupted publicly. On four occasions that day he declined to answer legislators' questions, citing ongoing criminal inquiries by German prosecutors.

So far, the Schmidt sentencing in Detroit is the ex-CEO's closest brush with American criminal justice. Twenty-seven months after the conspiracy was exposed, Winterkorn has not been charged with any offense in either the United States or Germany. (His U.S. counsel declined comment for this article.)

Will he ever be? Will anyone higher up the ladder than Oliver Schmidt ever answer for this remarkable crime?

It's very unclear. U.S. prosecutors want to indict Winterkorn, but have not yet received approval from the brass at the Department of Justice, according to two sources familiar with the process.

That would seem like a huge step. Yet in truth, a U.S. indictment of Winterkorn or other top VW figures is increasingly becoming moot simply because the prosecutors can't gain access to most of the key figures in the case. Winterkorn hasn't set foot in the United States since the scandal broke and, after Schmidt's crushing sentence, is not likely to do so anytime soon.

Among the eight VW engineers charged in the United States, only Schmidt and James Liang, a non-supervisor sentenced to 40 months this past August, are actually in the United States, and only one other—an Audi engine development

supervisor, Zaccheo Giovanni Pamio, who happens to be an Italian national—is extraditable.

That means the judicial focus is shifting to Germany. There, three sets of prosecutors are certainly going through the proper motions. The authorities in Braunschweig—acting for the state of Lower Saxony, where both the parent company, VW AG, and its VW brand passenger car unit are based—say they are investigating 39 individuals for fraud in connection with Dieselgate, one for obstruction of justice and three for financial market manipulation (which in this instance would mean the failure to promptly disclose the gestating crisis to shareholders). In Munich, Bavarian prosecutors are looking at 13 individuals at VW's Audi unit, based in Ingolstadt, for fraud and false advertising. And in Stuttgart, three executives are under scrutiny for market manipulation.

The two market manipulation inquiries focus on Winterkorn and three very senior current VW officials. The Braunschweig prosecutors, for instance, are looking at supervisory board chairman Hans Dieter Pötsch (who was CFO when the scandal broke) and current VW brand manager Herbert Diess, while the Stuttgart authorities are scrutinizing Pötsch and current CEO Matthias Müller. (VW declined to comment on the record for this article other than to provide a written statement in which it asserted that its executives fully complied with disclosure laws.)

Yet progress is strikingly slow. There have been only two German arrests so far. One was of Pamio; the other was of Wolfgang Hatz, a senior supervisor at, successively, Audi, VW, and Porsche. German prosecutors do not confirm the identities of detained individuals or what they're charged with, but the Munich probe is focusing on fraud and false advertising, the office says.

We may not see many criminal prosecutions in Germany, let alone convictions, or lengthy sentences. The country's law presents many serious hurdles. There's no criminal liability for corporations, for starters. There's no statute barring a criminal conspiracy, no relevant criminal clean air law, and no law against lying to regulators or investigators. (The latter is actually protected by the robust German right to silence, according to Carsten Momsen, a law professor at Berlin's Free University.) Prosecutors' tools to reward and turn perpetrators into state witnesses are weaker than those wielded by their American counterparts. And some of the criminal laws that do exist—written to catch individuals who swindle other individuals—may be ill-suited to capturing the corporate machinations that happened in this case.

The result is breathtakingly different outcomes for both the company and its customers in the two countries. In the United States, the system has delivered swift consequences. Facing harsh corporate criminal sanctions, flexible and draconian criminal laws, and streamlined consumer class-action procedures,

Volkswagen quickly capitulated. Within nine months—breakneck speed in the legal realm—it agreed to pay roughly $15 billion in civil compensation and restitution to consumers and federal and state authorities for the 2.0-liter cars involved, and the sum has since crept up to more than $25 billion, as deals were reached for the 3.0-liter cars, and for criminal fines and penalties. Volkswagen has bought back or fixed most of the offending vehicles, and customers have received thousands of dollars per car in compensation for a variety of losses, including the deception itself and diminished resale value. The company pleaded guilty in April to federal criminal charges of conspiracy, fraud, making false statements, and obstruction of justice.

VW gave U.S. prosecutors liberal access to the fruits of an investigation it commissioned by the Jones Day law firm, which conducted more than 700 interviews and collected more than 100 million documents. (The inquiry is ongoing, according to VW.) VW also helped recover forensically thousands of pages of documents that had been deleted by scores of VW employees in the final days of the conspiracy. In return, U.S. prosecutors gave the company credit for cooperation, slicing 20 percent from its criminal fine, which came to $2.8 billion even after the reduction.

In Canada, too, the company has paid compensation, including a $290 million deal for 3.0-liter cars just reached in January. And in South Korea, Volkswagen also paid dearly, receiving record fines and seeing eight local VW and Audi officials charged criminally, with one now serving an 18-month prison term.

Yet in Germany and Europe, it's been a totally different story. There, VW has not offered compensation to any customer. In Germany, where the key decisions were made and all the decision makers reside, no criminal or administrative fines or penalties have yet been imposed.

VW's "cooperation," which so impressed American prosecutors, hasn't extended beyond U.S. borders. Volkswagen has not shared the Jones Day materials with German prosecutors, for instance. And last April, the company revealed that it would be breaking its repeated promise to issue a report summarizing the results of the Jones Day inquiry. VW said the public statement of facts that accompanied its guilty plea revealed the inquiry's key findings and that any further announcement would risk undermining ongoing investigations or conflicting with its plea agreement. But the plea bargain document is just 30 double-spaced pages, identifies nobody by name, and, as prosecutorial documents often do, plays its cards close to the vest. It includes only one sentence, for instance, about the July 27, 2015, meeting that was so central to the Schmidt prosecution. (It states that a meeting took place, but gives no hint of what was discussed or that senior executives were present.)

Even when German law enforcement has taken aggressive action, it has been stymied so far. Last March, Munich authorities raided Jones Day's German offices and seized materials from the firm's VW investigation. But the Federal Constitutional Court has temporarily blocked their examination, at Jones Day's request, while it sorts out issues of attorney–client privilege and the privacy rights of interviewed employees. German court precedents are deeply divided on these questions, according to professor Momsen.

The definitions of "defeat device" in the United States and EU are nearly identical. Nevertheless, VW contends the software was lawful outside North America. Germany's Federal Motor Transport Authority, or KBA—notoriously lax in its diesel oversight policies—rejected this theory in December 2015.

The company has also insisted non-American customers suffered no injury. Because of more lenient NO_x limits abroad, it maintains, most of those cars could be fully addressed with simple software fixes. Yet many engineers can't fathom how software alone could possibly repair a NO_x problem without correspondingly reducing fuel economy and undermining the durability of the emissions control equipment—the very problems that led VW to cheat in the first place. The KBA and other national regulators have approved these fixes, but haven't released any test results shedding light on what the recalls achieved. "VW could not do miracles regarding NO_x emissions without replacing the hardware," argues Yoann Bernard of the International Council on Clean Transportation, which commissioned the 2014 study by West Virginia University that first revealed VW's use of a defeat device.

Plaintiffs' lawyers abroad are suing VW over the affected diesels there. But, like the criminal authorities, they are hampered by a slew of handicaps. Under EU rules, all eight million EU customers who bought Dieselgate cars could theoretically sue in Lower Saxony, where VW AG is based. But in Germany, there are no consumer class actions. In addition, plaintiffs have very limited discovery rights; lawyers are prohibited from accepting contingency fees; and plaintiffs who sue run the risk that if they lose, they will have to pay not just their own legal fees, but a portion of their adversary's, as well.

To be sure, VW isn't yet in the clear. It may yet be hit with penalties worth hundreds of millions of euros, imposed by German state prosecutors or by the BaFin, the Federal Financial Supervisory Authority (something like the U.S. Securities and Exchange Commission).

And two groups of plaintiffs—VW shareholders and owners of VW diesels—are attempting to overcome the obstacles to civil litigation. The bigger threat comes from German shareholders, who allege that VW failed to disclose the budding scandal. Plaintiffs' lawyers are using a "model" litigation mechanism, a class action analog available only for shareholder suits, which is scheduled to begin in September in the Higher Regional Court of Braunschweig. But that procedure is expected to take years and the amount recovered may be a fraction of the huge sums sought (€9.5 billion, or $11.2 billion), depending on how early or late the court concludes VW should have disclosed the crisis. At the same time, an innovative "group action" was filed in Braunschweig in November on behalf of a German consumer group—to whom 15,347 VW diesel owners had assigned their claims—by the Berlin office of the American law firm, Hausfeld.

In fairness, Volkswagen's obstructive stance abroad may be more defensible when one considers the vast divide between the political, social, and regulatory milieus in Europe and the United States. Since the scandal broke, further testing has made clear that cheating on diesel emissions was endemic across Europe. In December 2016, the European Commission began investigating whether regulatory authorities in Germany and six other EU nations have been lax in their oversight of diesel emissions. Though VW's cheating was, in most instances, more brazen in methodology, its diesels' NO_x emissions outside the United States appear to have been no worse than their competitors'. Moreover, BMW, Fiat Chrysler Automobiles, Daimler (maker of Mercedes), PSA (maker of Peugeots and Citroëns), and Renault–Nissan have all come under scrutiny over the past year by either German or French authorities for possible diesel emissions irregularities. (The manufacturers deny wrongdoing.)

Even in the United States, it's become clear, VW's conduct—though still the most egregious—was not unique. In May, the Justice Department sued Fiat Chrysler for having allegedly placed a species of defeat device on 104,000 model year 2014–2016 Jeep Grand Cherokees and Dodge Ram 1500 pickups, the most popular diesel pickup sold in America. (FCA, which denies wrongdoing, is in settlement negotiations.)

European and, especially, German industrial, labor and even environmental policy favored the production of diesel cars. Regulatory oversight was slight, penalties for violations were trifling, and national regulators were disinclined to handicap their home country's carmakers vis-à-vis those of neighboring countries, whose regulators were presumed to be winking at the same gamesmanship.

Dieselgate's $25 billion consequences in the United States have transformed the political landscape in Europe, however. The scandal has drawn attention to a long simmering public health issue that, it turns out, was not caused by Volkswagen alone, but rather by the diesel car industry and the political culture that nurtured and protected it. For example, a European government report has found that 72,000 EU residents die prematurely each year because of NO_x emissions.

In February, the Administrative Law Court in Leipzig will decide a case brought by an advocacy group called Environmental Action Germany that could eventually result in diesel car bans in as many as 70 German cities. Diesel auto sales are dropping precipitously in anticipation, and in December,

VW CEO Matthias Müller shocked the automotive world by suggesting in a newspaper interview that the time had come for Europe to abandon key tax subsidies that have long supported the diesel industry.

The regulatory, environmental, and cultural gap between the EU and the United States is closing. But it was that chasm that spawned Dieselgate and that chasm that Schmidt toppled into. So there is some injustice in the fact that Schmidt will pay so dearly. Yet there will be even greater injustice if he is the only one to do so.

The key contours of the Dieselgate affair emerged soon after the scandal broke. Since then, the slowly accumulating evidence amassed and presented (or leaked) from criminal, civil, and media investigations has only made the breadth of VW's conspiracy clearer. Examining the chronology of the company's behavior in light of that information leaves little doubt that knowledge of the wrongdoing reached high up the ranks, repeatedly coming within a whisker of CEO Winterkorn himself.

In 2006, Volkswagen initiated a strategy to revive its then-moribund U.S. sales by marketing a clean diesel car. The challenge was that diesels produce more NO_x than gasoline engines, and American NO_x regulations were far more stringent than Europe's—permitting only about ⅙ of what Europe then allowed. Most ways of cleaning NO_x reduced fuel economy, harmed performance, took up space, increased cost, or required frequent servicing. (Environmentally, Europe had focused on reducing greenhouse gases, including carbon dioxide. Diesels, due to their excellent fuel economy, were great at reducing carbon emissions. But diesels also produced NO_x, which causes smog. Because of the history of smog problems in Los Angeles, regulators from CARB and the EPA had long been more sensitive to the health dangers posed by NO_x than their European counterparts.)

VW's U.S. strategy was born under then-CEO Bernd Pischetsrieder and continued when Winterkorn replaced him in January 2007. In early 2008, Winterkorn announced a 10-year plan that called for tripling the company's U.S. sales by 2018, enabling it to surpass General Motors and Toyota to become the world's leading automaker. Clean Diesel was the linchpin of the plan, which, by mid-2015, had succeeded.

Winterkorn was the protégé of the chairman of VW's supervisory board, Ferdinand Piëch. (German companies have two boards: a management board, composed of top executives, and a nonexecutive supervisory board.) Piëch, who had been CEO himself from 1993 to 2002, was considered the most influential figure in the company's history. A gifted engineer and prophetic leader, he was also ruthless; Piëch boasted about his willingness to fire executives if they didn't deliver quickly.

VW had an arrogant culture, shielded by the vital role the company plays in its nation's economy; its officials' cozy relationship with German politicians; and its unusual quasi-public status (the state of Lower Saxony controls 20 percent of its voting stock). Piëch had survived major scandals, including a corporate espionage debacle in the 1990s, which led to a $100 million settlement with General Motors, and a nearly decadelong labor scandal that surfaced in 2004, in which the company made illegal payments to labor representatives and politicians. The company had a "corrupt corporate culture," lacking in "openness and honesty," former Deputy U.S. Attorney General Larry Thompson, who became VW's outside monitor in June under the terms of its U.S. guilty plea, told a German newspaper in December.

In Winterkorn, Piëch selected a PhD engineer and former quality assurance chief with a reputation for perfectionism and micromanagement. Just a few years later Forbes would comment with wonder at how, in 2011, he visited the VW factory in Chattanooga, Tennessee—where some diesels were manufactured—"no less than seven times" to oversee the U.S. launch of the 2012 Passat. "He drove early prototypes," the article continued, "and pored over initial quality, using a micrometer he carries in his pocket to measure the tiniest of gaps between body panels. Even minor paint flaws didn't escape the former quality manager, one American executive recalled. 'He finds everything.'"

Under Pischetsrieder and then Winterkorn, two sets of engineers attacked the riddle of how to build a diesel passenger car for the U.S. market. It was a tall order, given how draconian U.S. environmental regulations were, at least in the company's view. A high-level VW supervisor, Wolfgang Hatz (since arrested in Germany), was captured on video in 2007, complaining about California's rules in a widely repeated remark that would come to be seen as prophetic. "The CARB is not realistic," he said. "We can do quite a bit, and we will do a quite a bit. But impossible we cannot do."

And so the two sets of VW engineers, located in different cities, embarked on their missions. One group would design the 2.0-liter engines for VW and Audi cars. A second set, from Audi, would design the 3.0-liter engines for SUVs and luxury vehicles for both brands.

Both groups quickly homed in on the same solution: a defeat device. It is unclear whether they acted independently; to date, U.S. prosecutors have not alleged coordination. Each group was aware of, and adapted, a variant of the cheating software that Audi had developed as far back as 1999 and had in its diesel V6 SUVs in Europe from 2004 to 2006.

At the time that the earlier cheating software was allegedly being implemented on Audis in Europe, Winterkorn was already just a couple steps from the action. He was CEO of Audi, while Hatz—reportedly a Winterkorn confidant—was Audi's head of engine development. When Winterkorn became

CEO of VW AG in 2007, he promoted Hatz to head engine development for VW AG.

A succession of four top supervisors for engine development for the VW Brand, serving from 2006 to 2015, all knew about the cheating software, as did, from as early as 2006, the head of exhaust control measures for all of VW AG, according to U.S. prosecutors. Three of these five individuals have been indicted in the United States, for conspiracy to commit wire fraud and making false statements. But all are in Germany, beyond the prosecutors' extradition powers. (None have filed papers in the Detroit criminal proceedings. Lawyers for two of them declined comment, and the others could not be reached by ProPublica.) None of the five have been charged in Germany.

News of the fraudulent software reached "senior Audi managers" as early as 2008, according to U.S. prosecutors. In January 2008, they assert, members of that team sent a presentation to the head of the group, Zaccheo Pamio, and other senior Audi managers, warning that the software solution was possibly illegal and "highly problematic in the United States" In July 2008, a member of Audi's environmental certification team wrote Pamio that the software was "indefensible." The plan went forward, nonetheless. (Last July, Pamio was charged in federal court in Detroit with conspiracy, wire fraud, and making false statements. That same month he was arrested by Munich authorities. His lawyers declined comment.)

In 2011, the cheating spread to a third VW brand in another city, seemingly creating still more opportunities for word to leak up to executives. VW had just acquired Porsche, and Porsche engineers in Stuttgart sought to adapt Audi's 3.0-liter diesel engine for use in a Porsche Cayenne SUV for the U.S. market. That September, Audi engineers explained to Porsche engineers how the cheat software worked, according to a civil complaint filed by the New York State Attorney General's office, and Porsche adopted the fraudulent technology. By this time, Winterkorn had moved Hatz to Porsche as head of research and development. He served on Porsche's management board, where he worked alongside VW's current CEO, Müller.

Meanwhile, in Wolfsburg, problems with the 2.0-liter diesel exhaust systems were forcing knowledge of the cheat software further up the corporate hierarchy to people who knew Winterkorn personally and well. Engineer Liang had learned of unusually high numbers of hardware failures involving the NO_x treatment equipment. The problem, as he diagnosed it, stemmed from the fact that the equipment was being used too much—not just during lab testing, but sometimes on the road. He proposed refining the cheat software to ensure that full exhaust treatment would be triggered solely during testing.

In July 2012, he and other engineers met with Hans-Jakob Neusser and Bernd Gottweis, according to U.S. prosecutors.

Neusser was then head of engine development at the VW brand. Gottweis was a member of the powerful Products Safety Committee, answering to the head of quality management at VW AG, Frank Tuch. Tuch met weekly with Winterkorn, according to an account in VW's in-house magazine. Gottweis was a close confidant of Winterkorn and was sometimes referred to as "the fireman" at VW—someone who put out fires.

Liang's solution was approved, and his more finely tailored defeat device was installed on the next generation of VW diesels, which arrived in mid-2013. In addition, a recall was carried out in 2014 to retrofit older models with the tweaked software. Customers and regulators were told that the recall was to fix a dashboard warning light and address certain environmental issues. (Neusser and Gottweis have been charged in the United States with conspiracy to commit wire fraud and making false statements in the United States; neither has been charged in Germany. Neusser's attorney declined comment, and Gottweis could not be reached.)

In late 2013, the fact that cheat software was being used in 3.0-liter engines reached the top echelons of Audi, according to U.S. prosecutors, presenting still another opportunity for someone to blow the whistle. An Audi engineer, prompted by the concerns of a manager in the environmental certification department, had his people prepare a presentation to a "then-senior executive and member of Audi's brand management board," describing in detail how the software worked. The engineer who sent the presentation advised every recipient to delete the e-mail and attachment after downloading it.

That same month, Schmidt saw a different presentation about Audi's fraudulent software. "It would be good if you deleted us from the cover page," Schmidt e-mailed afterward. "If such a paper somehow falls into the hands of the authorities, VW can get into considerable difficulties."

In March 2014, the biggest clue about the criminal conduct festering within VW began filtering out into the automotive community, soon reaching Gottweis, Tuch, and, through them, Winterkorn. At an industry conference, researchers at West Virginia University presented a study, which would be published in May. They had studied the emissions of three randomly selected diesel cars available in the United States. A BMW X5 had done fine, but a VW Jetta and VW Passat had each performed suspiciously, passing the test in the lab, but emitting up to 35 times the lawful NO_x limit during real-world driving.

In Wolfsburg, VW engineers, led by Neusser, Gottweis, and others, formed an ad hoc committee to address the study. Their goal, according to prosecutors, was to concoct evasive and misleading responses to regulators' anticipated questions.

On May 23, 2014, Gottweis wrote a now infamous report about the West Virginia study, which Tuch forwarded to Winterkorn the same day, as part of his regular weekend package of reading materials. (VW suspended Tuch in October 2015,

and he resigned in February 2016. He could not be reached for comment.)

The memo, revealed by Bild Am Sonntag in 2016, has been regarded as a smoking gun by Winterkorn's critics. "A thorough explanation for the dramatic increase in NO_x emissions cannot be given to the authorities," Gottweis wrote. "It can be assumed that authorities will then investigate" to see if VW used a "defeat device," he continued, explaining what a defeat device was. A team is working on software changes that can "reduce the real driving emissions," he noted, "but this will not bring about compliance with the limits either."

For its part, Volkswagen asserts that nothing in the Gottweis report should have caused its CEO to suspect that anything more than a routine product defect was afoot. "This memo merely raised the prospect that U.S. regulators would investigate whether a defeat device was in use," the company's lawyers wrote in its motion to dismiss U.S. shareholder litigation in August 2016; "it did not state or imply that a defeat device had actually been installed, or what it meant if a defeat device were found by U.S. authorities, much less the potential magnitude of any associated financial risks resulting from such a finding."

Winterkorn admits receiving the report, according to papers his attorney filed in U.S. civil litigation, "but does not recall whether he read [it] that weekend." He also admits being aware of the West Virginia University study by May 2014—15 months before the conspiracy ended—but says, according to the same filing, that "he believed a task force of Volkswagen employees were working to address the situation."

One was. At its behest, VW engineers, including Liang, lied to CARB and EPA regulators for more than a year. They even promised regulators that they'd address the problem with a software fix, carried out through yet another recall in late 2014.

In November, Winterkorn was advised of this recall in a one-page memo that estimates the fix would cost just €20 million to effectuate—a negligible sum for a company whose 2014 net operating profit would come to €12.7 billion. Winterkorn, in his testimony before the German Parliament, said the memo reassured him that the problem had been addressed.

But by early 2015, CARB had discovered that the recalled vehicles still exceeded NO_x limits during real-world driving.

By that time, Schmidt, who'd been at VW's environmental office in Auburn Hills, MI, for three years, had been promoted. In February 2015, he had returned to Wolfsburg to become one of three deputies to Neusser, who, by then, had become chief of development for the VW Brand, overseeing 10,000 employees.

In July, CARB told VW engineers that it would refuse to certify the company's 2016 diesels until it got better answers. That precipitated the July 27, 2015, meeting at which Schmidt and a colleague made their presentations to Winterkorn and other top executives, including Herbert Diess, then and now the highest executive in charge of its VW brand passenger car unit, and a member of VW's management board.

"Winterkorn admits," his attorney wrote in a U.S. legal filing, "that on July 27, 2015, after a regular meeting about damage and product issues, he, Diess, and other VW AG personnel participated in an informal meeting during which there was a discussion regarding approval for the sale of model year 2016 diesel vehicles." However, the attorney, Gregory Joseph, continues, "Winterkorn denies that he knew the cause or significance of the issues related to diesel emissions before September 2015."

To date, the company has been vague and noncommittal about the July 27 meeting, and it declined to comment on it for this article. "Individual employees discussed the diesel issue on the periphery of a regular meeting about damage and product issues," the company said in a March 2016 press release, its last and fullest public discussion of matter. "It is not clear whether the participants understood already at this point in time that the change in the software violated U.S. environmental regulations. Mr. Winterkorn asked for further clarification of the issue." (The company is expected to describe its perspective on the meeting more fully in late February in a filing in German securities litigation, though such filings are not public.)

The lying to US regulators continued until August 19, when an engineer confessed to CARB regulators. Later that month, after word of this development reached Wolfsburg, a high-level in-house attorney notified employees that a "litigation hold" would be issued on September 1, after which they would not be permitted to destroy pertinent documents. About 40 Volkswagen engineers took this as a directive to start deleting immediately. Some notified Bosch engineers, who did the same.

Top VW officials clearly sensed trouble. By August, they had asked the American law firm Kirkland & Ellis to look into possible regulatory liability for use of a defeat device. VW received the reassuring news that the largest fine that had ever been meted out for a Clean Air Act violation had been just $100 million, in 2014, for an incident involving 1.1 million cars—more than twice as many vehicles as were then known to be implicated in VW's Clean Diesel problems.

Yet the incident being used as a benchmark was hardly similar. In that instance, Hyundai-Kia, which never admitted wrongdoing, had overstated fuel economy by 1–6 miles per gallon because it used figures obtained in the most favorable tests it had run, rather than by averaging results from a large number of tests. But the cars' emissions were never illegal, no recalls were required, and no lying to regulators had been alleged.

The text of the Kirkland memo suggests that the lawyers hadn't been informed that the company had been lying to regulators for a decade. The lawyers urged VW to find out if statements made to regulators had been "complete and not misleading."

Given the lack of information, the memo concluded that "we are currently unaware of any facts that suggest any such [criminal] issues in the present situation." (Kirkland & Ellis did not return calls and e-mails seeking comment on the memo, which became public when plaintiffs' lawyer Michael Melkerson filed it in a lawsuit on behalf of diesel owners who opted out of the federal class action.)

On September 3, 2015, a VW supervisor confessed to CARB in writing the use of a defeat device, formalizing his subordinate's earlier oral admission. Winterkorn was notified the next day, VW has acknowledged. Still, despite German laws requiring that material market information be disclosed immediately, VW shareholders were given no inkling that anything was amiss. They learned only when CARB and EPA stunned the world on September 18 with the news that the company had admitted using an illegal defeat device on close to 500,000 2.0-liter cars sold in the United States. The Justice Department announced a criminal investigation the next day. Three days after that, VW revealed that some 11 million cars worldwide were equipped with the dual-mode software that the U.S. regulators had discovered. Over that week, the company's shares lost about €32.5 billion in value ($38.5 billion at today's rates). In the ensuing months, the total decline ballooned to about €55.6 billion ($66 billion).

Volkswagen argues that it had no obligation to disclose anything until U.S. regulators announced they were issuing a "notice of violation" in September 2015. "Volkswagen believes that it duly fulfilled its disclosure obligation under capital markets laws," the company asserted in a written statement for ProPublica. "Right up until the publication of the notice of violation, the board of management believed, based on the advice of its U.S. external legal counsel and numerous precedents, that Volkswagen could resolve the issue consensually with U.S. regulators."

As the Dieselgate investigation slowly churned, allegations of a much vaster conspiracy unexpectedly emerged this summer. Der Spiegel reported then that since 1999, all five German carmakers—Audi, BMW, Daimler, Porsche, and Volkswagen—had been colluding in ways that may have violated competition laws. (VW, which owns three of the brands, and Daimler have admitted to EC competition authorities that some discussions might have been improper; BMW maintains they were lawful.)

The participants held more than 1,000 meetings relating to 60 working groups on different aspects of automotive production, including emissions control. As early as 2007, according to the magazine, the emissions group began colluding on specifications for exhaust equipment that was used to control NO_x emissions in some of the diesel engines. This new scandal could hurt VW executives by bringing even more scrutiny to their actions—or help them by suggesting every car company was doing the same thing.

In early 2018 came yet more news that sullied German automakers, as filmmaker Alex Gibney's "Dirty Money" documentary and *The New York Times*' Jack Ewing reported that research organizations funded by those manufacturers—including VW—had, in 2014, gassed monkeys with diesel exhaust fumes from a modern-day, allegedly Clean Diesel VW and an old Ford diesel pickup truck, each running on rollers in a lab, in order to show their relative effects. When the news broke in January, VW CEO Müller wrote to employees, calling the tests "unethical, repulsive, and deeply shameful" and apologizing for "the poor judgment of individuals who were involved." The CEO said the company is investigating and "we will be coming to all the necessary conclusions." VW's stock price fell when the reports of the monkey tests emerged. But that was a minor bump in a resurgence of the company's shares: they're now priced just above where they were when Dieselgate was revealed.

That Liang and Schmidt—and perhaps eventually Pamio—would end up being the only ones to take the fall for Dieselgate in the United States is happenstance. Though Liang was working in Wolfsburg when the conspiracy began in 2006, he was transferred in 2008 to VW's Oxnard, CA, test center, near Los Angeles, to help with the Clean Diesel launch. He was still working there in October 2015 when the FBI knocked on his door in the nearby affluent community of Newberry Park.

Liang began cooperating immediately, according to the government. A slight, mild-mannered man with a wife and three children, Liang, now 63, had worked for VW for 34 years. He was never a supervisor. Still, because of his long involvement in the scheme—from start to finish—Judge Cox sentenced him last August to 40 months in prison, a lengthier term than prosecutors had requested.

Schmidt's presence in the United States was strange, even reckless. Acting without counsel, he contacted FBI agents in November 2015, offering aid with their investigation. The FBI flew him from Wolfsburg to London to meet with him there. U.S. prosecutors flew there, too, to participate. But the agents and prosecutors later determined that Schmidt lied extensively at the five-hour debriefing, falsely exonerating himself and his superiors, and setting back their probe.

Evidently imagining that he was still on good terms with the government, in December 2016, Schmidt had his U.S. lawyer notify the FBI that he and his wife would be travelling to Florida later that month for their annual Christmas vacation. (He owned some rental properties in Florida, and had hoped to retire there.) On January 7, 2017, as they headed home to Germany, eight officers converged on Schmidt in a men's room at the Miami International Airport. They brought him out in

shackles and then led him away. His wife was left alone, crying amid a pile of luggage.

Had Schmidt remained in Germany, it's unclear whether he could have been charged under German law, and it's inconceivable that the result would've been a seven-year sentence. Prosecutors would be hard-pressed to bring a major case against him and the same is true for the VW suspects still in Germany. One possible charge is false advertising, but that is narrow, not necessarily apt—it is aimed primarily at unfair competition—and carries a two-year maximum term, according to two German law professors who have studied corporate crimes: Michael Kubiciel, of the University of Augsburg, and Momsen of Berlin's Free University. (Momsen is associated with a law firm that represents a VW employee in the inquiry, but says he is not personally working on that case.)

The relevant German fraud statute, in turn, is generally designed to capture individuals who swindle others out of money. "Fraud requires proof of a concrete financial loss on the part of an individual consumer," writes Kubiciel in an e-mail. "Proving that a manipulation of the diesel engine caused concrete financial damage is not easy, if possible."

"You need to be able to figure out," says Momsen in an interview, "what is the damage in dollars or euros?" That's challenging, he continues, because the cars were roadworthy and safe. It's not clear whether German judges will consider the fact that a vehicle was polluting more than the consumer realized to constitute the sort of financial damage the law recognizes. As VW put it in its statement to ProPublica concerning its civil liability in Europe, "Customer satisfaction is our highest priority and the modification we have provided our customers in Europe entails no change to performance, fuel economy, or other key vehicle attributes, as confirmed by our regulator."

Indeed, scores of consumer lawsuits have been tried in Germany and Volkswagen appears to be winning most of them, according to newspaper accounts and interviews with three European plaintiffs' lawyers. Even when judges have ruled that VW used an illegal defeat device, many have still concluded that consumers suffered no compensable injury.

The main remaining criminal statute in play is the one barring market manipulation. VW executives might appear to have been astoundingly tardy in notifying the market of the building crisis at their company. Yet there are hurdles here, too. Executives can point, for instance, to the Kirkland & Ellis report—predicting modest sanctions in the vicinity of $100 million—and argue that that didn't sound like a "material" loss that needed to be disclosed.

Perhaps, despite the many daunting obstacles, German prosecutors will yet manage to obtain some convictions. It sounds as if Oliver Schmidt will be rooting for them. In a letter to Cox before his sentencing, he described how he had pored over the government's VW evidence "during my many sleepless nights in my prison cell." As Schmidt put it, "I've learned that my superiors that claimed to me to have not been involved earlier than me at VW knew about this for many, many years. I must say that I feel misused by my own company."

Critical Thinking

1. Describe the ethical breaches committed by Volkswagen with respect to Dieselgate.

2. What forms of punishment do you think should be administered to individuals associated with Dieselgate? To Volkswagen as a corporation? Why?

3. What safeguards should Volkswagen employ to prevent any future occurrences similar to Dieselgate?

Internet References

International Journal of Science and Engineering Applications
http://ijsea.com/archive/volume5/issue4/ijsea05041004.pdf
Wiley
https://onlinelibrary.wiley.com/doi/pdf/10.1111/misp.12060

Article

Prepared by: Eric Teoro, *Lincoln Christian University*

Case Study: Deutsche Bank Money-laundering Scheme

Michelle Chan

Learning Outcomes

After reading this article, you will be able to:

- Outline facets of the Deutsche Bank money-laundering scandal.

- Outline ethical violations committed by Deutsche Bank.

The Deutsche Bank Money-laundering Scandal

After Russia's incursion into Crimea, sanctions by the European Union and the United States against Russia forced President Putin to declare "offshorization" illegal in an attempt to keep Russian businesses at home and prevent the declining exchange rate of the ruble from damaging the Russian economy. As a result, Russian billionaires resorted to a more discreet way of funneling money offshore via mirror trading whereby a relatively small amount is traded in each transaction,[1] thus, creating the Deutsche Bank money-laundering scandal. This scandal raises questions about the effectiveness of systems and controls implemented to prevent the occurrence of these types of unethical violations.

Key Players

The central players in the Deutsche Bank money-laundering scandal, which gained media attention in late 2016 include:

Deutsche Bank AG

Deutsche Bank is a global German banking and financial services company with more than 100,000 employees in over 70 countries and a large presence in Europe, the Americas, and Asia-Pacific. The company is headquartered in the Deutsche Bank Twin Towers in Frankfurt and was the largest foreign exchange dealer in the world with a market share of 21 percent in 2009. The company offers financial products and services for corporate, institutional, private, and business clients. Deutsche Bank provides services that include sales, trading, research, origination of debt and equity, mergers and acquisitions, risk management products, such as derivatives, corporate finance, wealth management, and transaction banking. Deutsche Bank's core business is investment banking representing 50 percent of equity, 75 percent of its leverage assets, and 50 percent of its profits.[2] Deutsche Bank Ltd (Russia) was established in 1998. Deutsche Bank Russia offers a full range of banking services including commercial and investment banking services to local and international clients.[3]

U.S. Department of Justice

The U.S. Department of Justice (DOJ) is a federal executive department of the U.S. government, responsible for the enforcement of the law and administration of justice in the United States, equivalent to the justice or interior ministries of other countries.[4] The Department is headed by the United States Attorney General, who is nominated by the President and confirmed by the Senate and is a member of the Cabinet.[5] The current Attorney General is Jeff Sessions.

New York State Department of Financial Services

The New York State Department of Financial Services (DFS) is the department of the New York state government responsible for regulating financial services and products, including those subject to the New York insurance, banking, and financial services laws. The department's mission is to foster the growth of the financial industry in New York and spur economic development through judicious regulation and vigilant supervision. The department aims to achieve its goals by ensuring the continued solvency, safety, and prudent conduct of the providers of financial products and services, ensuring fair and equitable fulfilment of the financial obligations of such providers and by protecting users of financial products and services from financially impaired or insolvent providers of such services.[6]

Organized Crime and Corruption Reporting Project

The Organized Crime and Corruption Reporting Project (OCCRP) is an impartial and nonpartisan consortium of investigative centers, media, and journalists that operates internationally in Eastern Europe, the Caucasus, Central Asia, and Central America. It is the only existing full-time investigative reporting organization that specializes in organized crime and corruption in the world. The organization's goal is to help people around the world understand ways in which organized crime and corruption resides in their countries and governments.[7] OCCRP's mission statement says, "Our world is increasingly polarized. The world's media channels are rife with propaganda, misinformation, and simply wrong information. We must all strive to understand how our increasingly complex society works. We must be able to find the truth to make the kinds of decisions we need to. We are committed in our small way to telling the truth the best we can" (OCCRP, 2007).[8]

Transactions

In a press release published on the 30th of January 2017, the New York State DFS states it found Deutsche Bank and several of its senior managers responsible of neglecting opportunities to detect, intercept, and investigate a long-running mirror-trading scheme facilitated by Deutsche Bank's Moscow headquarters and involving its New York and London branches.[9] Deutsche Bank employees used a mirror-trading scheme to help wealthy Russians move $10 billion out of that country from 2011 to 2014.

Mirror trading is an automated forex strategy that allows investors to imitate international forex trading behaviors and make trading decisions that are independent of any emotional biases. The system uses a forex brokerage's trading platform to examine various trading strategies and allows the trader to choose a trading strategy based on various options such as the trader's investment goals, risk tolerance, investment capital, and desired currencies. When originators of the trading strategies execute their trades, these trades are duplicated in the mirror traders' accounts using automated software that operates uninterrupted for 24 hours a day, seven days a week.[10]

Specific companies that were clients of the Moscow equities desk operated through the equities desk at Deutsche Bank's Moscow branch. They issued orders to purchase Russian blue chip stocks. These companies would always pay for the stocks in rubles. Through Deutsche Bank's London branch, a related counterparty would then sell the identical Russian blue chip stock sometime thereafter in similar quantities and at the same price in US dollars.[11] The counterparties involved were mostly U.K. Limited Partnerships or Limited Liability Partnerships. They were often linked by common beneficial owners, management, or agents, with "designated members" registered in tax havens and trade stocks in similar quantities between the Russian company and the offshore company.[12] These trades were regularly approved by the bank's Deutsche Bank Trust Company of the Americas (DBTCA) unit. The selling counterparties were usually registered in an offshore territory and paid for shares in U.S. dollars. At least 12 entities were involved, and none of the trades demonstrated any legitimate economic rationale.[13]

Mirror trading is unethical because, when done in large quantities, it can be used to facilitate money-laundering practices, which is the act of transferring large sums of money obtained from illegitimate and often illegal practices to tax havens around the world. This is usually done to evade any legal repercussions and taxes, which, in return, contributes to on-going illegal activities viewed as profitable and without legal consequences. Money-laundering practices take place through mirror trading as mirror trades bypass currency controls, anti-money-laundering (AML) laws, and, possibly, tax controls when moving money overseas.[14]

The investigation carried out by the New York State DFS exposed Deutsche Bank for violations that include the following:

- The bank conducted its banking business in an unsafe and unsound manner, failing to maintain an effective and compliant AML program.[15]
- The bank failed to maintain and make available true and accurate books, accounts, and records reflecting all transactions and actions.[16]
- The DBTCA unit was unresponsive to efforts made by outside sources to stop the mirror-trading scheme. In addition, the senior compliance employee did not take any steps to investigate the basis for the European Bank's inquiry.[17]
- The bank's Know Your Customer (KYC) processes were weak, functioning merely as a checklist with employees mechanically focused on ensuring documentation

was collected. Virtually all of the KYC files for the companies involved in the scheme were insufficient.[18]
- The bank failed to accurately rate its country and client risks for money laundering throughout the relevant time period and lacked a global policy benchmarking its risk appetite.[19]
- The bank's anti-financial crime, AML, and compliance units were ineffective and understaffed.[20]

The DFS worked closely with the Financial Conduct Authority of the United Kingdom on the investigation to uncover Deutsche Bank's failure to detect, investigate, and stop the mirror-trading scheme due to extensive compliance failures.[21] This negligence allowed the scheme to continue for years.

Outcomes

So far, three Deutsche Bank employees have been suspended, two Co-CEOs of the bank have announced their resignation and new Co-CEO, John Cryan, has announced the forthcoming closure of all investment banking activity in Russia.[22] Currently, the bank is under investigation by the U.S. DOJ, the New York State DFS, and financial regulators in the United Kingdom and in Germany for allegations of money laundering in Deutsche Bank's Moscow office.[23]

On January 30, 2016, Financial Services Superintendent Maria T. Vullo announced that Deutsche Bank AG and its New York branch will be required to pay a $425 million fine and hire an independent monitor.[24] This $425 million dollar fine seems a drop in the ocean in comparison to billions of dollars bank employees have profited from the aforementioned unethical practices.[25] As part of a consent order entered into with the New York State DFS for violations of New York AML laws involving a "mirror-trading" scheme among the bank's Moscow, London, and New York offices that laundered $10 billion out of Russia, Deutsche Bank must engage an independent monitor within 60 days of the consent order. This independent monitor must be approved by DFS to conduct a comprehensive review of the bank's existing AML compliance programs, policies, and procedures that refer to or affect activities conducted by or through its DBTCA subsidiary and the New York branch.[26]

Furthermore, within 30 days of the selection of the independent monitor, Deutsche Bank, DBTCA, and the New York branch must submit to DFS an engagement letter, for DFS's approval, that provides for the independent monitor to review and report on, among other things:

- The elements of the bank's corporate governance that contributed to or facilitated the improper conduct and allowed it to go on for such a long time.

- Relevant amendments or reforms to corporate governance that the bank has made since the time of the improper conduct and whether those changes or reforms are likely to significantly enhance the bank's AML compliance programs going forward.
- The thoroughness and comprehensiveness of the bank's current global AML compliance programs.[27]

In addition, Deutsche Bank must submit a written action plan to enhance its current global AML compliance programs that pertain to or affect activities conducted by or through DBTCA and the New York Branch.[28]

Ethics Violations
Failure in Its Duty to Detect, Investigate, and Stop Illegal Practices within the Institution

Deutsche Bank failed in its fiduciary duty to act on the various opportunities to detect, investigate, and stop the mirror-trading schemes taking place throughout the years by its employees. Deutsche Bank's failure to uphold its duty compromised the integrity of financial institutions that should provide preventive services and should not, under any circumstances, have allowed for or tolerated illegal practices, such as money laundering and fraud, to take place without reporting the illegal behavior. Among the systematic issues present within the bank that have contributed to this scandal are its internal reviewing process and the malpractices of its London and Moscow compliance departments. Elaboration of these points are provided in this section.

A "counterparty" is a new fund intending to trade with Deutsche Bank. In Deutsche Bank's London and Moscow headquarters, each new fund is subjected to a "double check" by compliance departments to ensure all required documentation is in order. Evidently, all the counterparties wishing to trade with Deutsche Bank passed both internal reviews. Deutsche Bank was also required to complete a "KYC" assessment to determine if the client intending to trade is trustworthy by uncovering any taint of criminality the client may have had in its past. However, the KYC processes set in place were weak and Deutsche Bank did not perform a thorough interrogation of the source of funds of its clients.[29] It seems Deutsche Bank was negligent in ensuring any illegitimate funds from their clients were not secretly introduced into the financial system as the KYC procedure put in place at the bank was fixated on the collection of proper documentation and consisted of sales traders requesting counterparties to state the source of their funds without much further questioning on the legitimacy of their claim. Thus, the information provided by potential clients for the companies involved in the KYC files was inadequate to detect an earlier ongoing mirror-trading scheme. Moreover, in an article published on the August 29, 2016, *The New Yorker* claimed that a Moscow employee who oversaw the illicit mirror trading was also actively participating in the onboarding and KYC documentation of companies involved in the scheme (Caesar, 2016).[30]

Finally, the anti-financial crime, AML, and compliance units within Deutsche Bank's Moscow branch were ineffective and understaffed. Compliance staff had difficulty accessing appropriate resources, leaving existing personnel scrambling to perform multiple roles.[31] *The New Yorker* wrote that at one point, an attorney who lacked any compliance background had to serve simultaneously as the Moscow bank branch's head of compliance, head of legal, and as its AML Officer (Caesar, 2016).[32] This failure was unethical as these processes were put in place to ensure safe, legal transactions and should have been carried out properly, using correct procedures to uphold AML, corruption, and anti-terrorism funding policies.

The compliance departments in Deutsch Bank's Moscow and London branches that were supposed to be in charge of ensuring safe and legitimate transactions also failed to perform their intended duty. To illustrate, the companies involved in this scandal were supposedly subjected to a rigorous "client review" process, and all of them were deemed satisfactory by a Deutsche Bank compliance team.[33] But there was a pattern suggesting malfeasance. Clients of the scheme consistently lost small amounts of money. The differences between the Moscow and London prices of a stock were often not in the client's favor, and clients had to pay Deutsche Bank a commission for every transaction. The commission cost was between ten hundredths and fifteen hundredths of a percentage point per trade.[34] The apparent willingness of counterparties to lose money again and again should have signaled the true purpose of the mirror trades was to facilitate capital flight. However, these signals went by undetected or were wilfully ignored by the compliance department.

The compliance department within Deutsche Bank also failed to effectively tackle allegations of fraud when approached by outside sources. For example, when contacted by a European financial institution about contradictory information on one of the companies involved in the trading scheme, a senior compliance employee who supervised special investigations at the DBTCA unit never responded. In addition, the senior compliance employee did not take any steps to investigate the basis for the European Bank's inquiry, later explaining that the employee had "too many jobs" and "had to deal with many things and had to prioritize."[35] The neglect and irresponsibility of Deutsche Bank's compliance department is unethical as it facilitated mirror-trading schemes and corruption with a nonchalant attitude toward incidences of money laundering, contributing to this 10-billion-dollar scandal.

Institutional Corruption and Conflict of Interest Issues

Banks owe a duty of care to their customers to ensure the transactions carried out on behalf of their clients are legal. However, when the culture of corruption is rife within an institution, conflicts of interest between providing services to benefit a client and abiding by legal regulations arises within the institution. Institutional corruption within the Deutsche Bank Moscow, London, and New York headquarters conjured up a host of conflict of interest issues arising from the mirror-trading schemes. These schemes go against the fundamental values of AML laws and further instill the culture of dishonesty further adding to corruption within the institution.

Many regulators found Deutsche Bank guilty of banking misconduct. In fact, the Financial Conduct Authority of the United Kingdom sent a letter to Deutsche Bank in March 2016 informing the institution that its London branch had some serious systemic AML, terrorist funding, and sanctions failings. However, when a lawyer who sat on the bank's integrity committee was brought in, specifically to improve the controls put in place and analyze any former misconduct, Deutsche Bank executives relieved him of his duties. He apparently had an argument with executives at a board meeting when he attempted to probe the links between senior executives and misconduct at the bank.[36] Hence, it is fair to deduce senior management at the institution failed to act impartially and transparently when faced with institutional corruption and conflict of interest issues that arose from unethical mirror-trading schemes.

On the topic of mirror-trading schemes, Deutsche Bank has not commented on whose money was expatriated through the mirror trades. The CEO, John Cryan, has insisted the bank has not knowingly provided services to Russians on the sanctions list.[37] However, as Deutsche Bank officials did investigate thoroughly the legitimacy of their clients' KYC process claims, it is difficult to determine whether the source of funds came from a legitimate law abiding source or otherwise. Moreover, the bank failed to accurately rate its country and client risks for money laundering throughout the relevant time period and lacked a global policy benchmarking its risk appetite.[38] This has resulted in material inconsistencies and no methodology for updating the ratings. Hence, Deutsche Bank was not in line with peer banks, which rated Russia as high risk well before Deutsche Bank did in late 2014. In an interview in March 2016, Cryan said, "To our knowledge, the individual transaction steps in themselves were innocuous. However, the case raises questions about how effective our systems and controls were, especially with regard to the onboarding of new clients, an area where we experienced difficulties in collecting sufficient information."[39] This euphemistic language belies the brazen nature of the scheme.

Reports of Deutsche Bank's internal investigation into mirror trades do not inspire confidence as people struggle to comprehend the level of corruption and unethical behavior that is rife in the banking industry. Mirror trades that have occurred for at least two years before anyone raised any concerns and were only acted on months after the red flags first appeared depict a bank culture that emphasizes employee compliance over sovereign laws. According to Bloomberg News, the internal report notes that, in early 2014, a series of inquiries about the propriety of mirror trades had been logged by multiple parties, including Hellenic Bank, in Cyprus, the Russian Central Bank, and back-office staff members at Deutsche Bank itself. However, when Hellenic Bank executives contacted Deutsche Bank and asked about the unusual trades, they did not hear back from the compliance department. Instead, their inquiry was fielded by the equities desk that was performing the mirror trades. Deutsche Bank's Moscow branch reassured Hellenic Bank that everything was in order.[40] Deutsche Bank's failure to maintain an effective money-laundering program and their failure to maintain accurate books, accounts, and records reflecting all transactions and actions is not only irresponsible but also dishonest.[41]

Policy Recommendations

As stressed in the DFS's 30th January 2016 press release, the DFS's new risk-based anti-terrorism and AML regulation, which became effective on January 1, 2017, is significant in regulating financial institutions and preventing similar scandals involving financial institutions from reoccurring. DFS's regulation requires regulated institutions to maintain programs to monitor and filter transactions for potential AML violations and prevent transactions with sanctioned entities. It also requires regulated institutions to submit an annual board resolution or senior officer compliance finding confirming the steps taken to ascertain compliance with the regulation. In addition, DFS has proposed a first-in-the-nation cybersecurity regulation, effective March 1, 2017, requiring DFS regulated institutions to establish and maintain a cybersecurity program designed to protect consumers and ensure the safety and soundness of New York's financial services industry.[42] In order to ensure safe and honest transactions, Deutsche Bank officials should consider applying the aforementioned regulations as proposed by the DFS.

Conclusion

Bottom line, based on the information in this case study of the Deutsche Bank money-laundering scandal, Deutsche Bank acted unethically because:

- The institution failed to act impartially and transparently when faced with institutional compliance and legal

governance conflict of interest issues arising from mirror-trading schemes. These schemes aided corruption and criminal activity because they normalized the act of money laundering in financial institutions.
- The institution failed in its fiduciary duty to act on the various opportunities to detect, investigate, and stop the mirror-trading schemes taking place throughout the years by its employees.

Notes

1. Caesar, Ed. "Deutsche Bank'S $10-Billion Scandal." The New Yorker. N.p., 2016. Web. 18 January 2017.
2. Lee, Peter. "Can Cryan Halt Deutsche Bank's Decline?" EuroMoney. N.p., 2016. Web. 18 January 2017.
3. "Deutsche Bank—History." Deutsche Bank Russia. Web. 18 January 2017.
4. "Organization, Mission & Functions Manual: Attorney General, Deputy and Associate, Department of Justice." The United States Department of Justice. N.p., 2014. Web. 18 January 2017.
5. Ibid.
6. "NYSDFS: Mission and Leadership." New York State Department of Financial Services. Web. 18 January 2017.
7. "About Us." Organized Crime and Corruption Reporting Project. N.p., 2007. Web. 18 January 2017.
8. Ibid.
9. New York State Department of Financial Services (DFS),. DFS FINES DEUTSCHE BANK $425 MILLION FOR RUSSIAN MIRROR-TRADING SCHEME. 2017. Web. 25 January 2017.
10. "Mirror Trading." Investopedia. Web. 18 January 2017.
11. Caesar, Ed. "Deutsche Bank'S $10-Billion Scandal." The New Yorker. N.p., 2016. Web. 18 January 2017.
12. Smith, Richard. "Deutsche Bank and a $10Bn Money Laundering Nightmare: More Context Than You Can Shake a Stick At." Naked Capitalism. N.p., 2017. Web. 18 January 2017.
13. New York State Department of Financial Services (DFS),. DFS FINES DEUTSCHE BANK $425 MILLION FOR RUSSIAN MIRROR-TRADING SCHEME. 2017. Web. 25 January 2017.
14. Caesar, Ed. "A Big Fine, And New Questions, On Deutsche Bank's 'Mirror Trades.'" The New Yorker. N.p., 2017. Web. 22 February 2017.
15. Williams-Grut, Oscar. "Deutsche Bank Is Paying $628 Million in Fines over Its $10 Billion Russian 'Mirror Trade' Scandal." Business Insider Australia. N.p., 2017. Web. 19 January 2017.
16. Ibid.
17. New York State Department of Financial Services (DFS),. DFS FINES DEUTSCHE BANK $425 MILLION FOR RUSSIAN MIRROR-TRADING SCHEME. 2017. Web. 25 January 2017.

18. Ibid.

19. Caesar, Ed. "Deutsche Bank'S $10-Billion Scandal." The New Yorker. N.p., 2016. Web. 18 January 2017.

20. Ibid.

21. New York State Department of Financial Services (DFS),. DFS FINES DEUTSCHE BANK $425 MILLION FOR RUSSIAN MIRROR-TRADING SCHEME. 2017. Web. 25 January 2017.

22. Caesar, Ed. "A Big Fine, and New Questions, on Deutsche Bank's 'Mirror Trades.'" The New Yorker. N.p., 2017. Web. 22 February 2017.

23. Caesar, Ed. "Deutsche Bank'S $10-Billion Scandal." The New Yorker. N.p., 2016. Web. 18 January 2017.

24. New York State Department of Financial Services (DFS),. DFS FINES DEUTSCHE BANK $425 MILLION FOR RUSSIAN MIRROR-TRADING SCHEME. 2017. Web. 25 January 2017.

25. Caesar, Ed. "Deutsche Bank'S $10-Billion Scandal." The New Yorker. N.p., 2016. Web. 18 January 2017.

26. New York State Department of Financial Services (DFS),. DFS FINES DEUTSCHE BANK $425 MILLION FOR RUSSIAN MIRROR-TRADING SCHEME. 2017. Web. 25 January 2017.

27. Ibid.

28. Ibid.

29. Caesar, Ed. "Deutsche Bank'S $10-Billion Scandal." The New Yorker. N.p., 2016. Web. 18 January 2017.

30. Ibid.

31. Ibid.

32. Ibid.

33. New York State Department of Financial Services (DFS),. DFS FINES DEUTSCHE BANK $425 MILLION FOR RUSSIAN MIRROR-TRADING SCHEME. 2017. Web. 25 January 2017.

34. Caesar, Ed. "Deutsche Bank'S $10-Billion Scandal." The New Yorker. N.p., 2016. Web. 18 January 2017.

35. New York State Department of Financial Services (DFS),. DFS FINES DEUTSCHE BANK $425 MILLION FOR RUSSIAN MIRROR-TRADING SCHEME. 2017. Web. 25 January 2017.

36. Caesar, Ed. "Deutsche Bank'S $10-Billion Scandal." The New Yorker. N.p., 2016. Web. 18 January 2017.

37. Ibid.

38. New York State Department of Financial Services (DFS),. DFS FINES DEUTSCHE BANK $425 MILLION FOR RUSSIAN MIRROR-TRADING SCHEME. 2017. Web. 25 January 2017.

39. Caesar, Ed. "Deutsche Bank'S $10-Billion Scandal." The New Yorker. N.p., 2016. Web. 18 January 2017.

40. Farrell, Greg, Keri Geiger, and Suzi Ring. "Deutsche Bank Said Near Mirror-Trade Deal With U.K., N.Y.". Bloomberg (2017): n. pag. Web. 20 January 2017.

41. New York State Department of Financial Services (DFS),. DFS FINES DEUTSCHE BANK $425 MILLION FOR RUSSIAN MIRROR-TRADING SCHEME. 2017. Web. 25 January 2017.

42. Ibid.

References

Lee, Peter. "Can Cryan Halt Deutsche Bank's Decline?". EuroMoney. N.p., 2016. Web. 18 Jan. 2017. Available at: http://www.euromoney.com/Article/3534126/Can-Cryan-halt-Deutsche-Banks-decline.html

"Deutsche Bank – History." Deutsche Bank Russia. Web. 18 Jan. 2017. Available at: https://www.db.com/russia/en/content/765.htm

"Organization, Mission & Functions Manual: Attorney General, Deputy And Associate, Department Of Justice." The United States Department of Justice. N.p., 2014. Web. 18 Jan. 2017. Available at: https://www.justice.gov/jmd/organization-mission-and-functions-manual-attorney-general

"NYSDFS: Mission And Leadership." New York State Department of Financial Services. Web. 18 Jan. 2017. Available at: http://www.dfs.ny.gov/about/mission.htm

"About Us." *Organized Crime and Corruption Reporting Project*. N.p., 2007. Web. 18 Jan. 2017. Available at: https://www.occrp.org/en/about-us

"Mirror Trading." Investopedia. Web. 18 Jan. 2017. Available at: http://www.investopedia.com/terms/m/mirror-trading.asp

"Task Force: ELIGO Factsheet." Australian Crime Commission, Australian Federal Police, AUSTRAC. Web. 18 Jan. 2017. Available at: http://www.austrac.gov.au/sites/default/files/documents/eligo_ml_fact_sheet.pdf

Caesar, Ed. "Deutsche Bank'S $10-Billion Scandal." The New Yorker. N.p., 2016. Web. 18 Jan. 2017. Available at: http://www.newyorker.com/magazine/2016/08/29/deutsche-banks-10-billion-scandal

Smith, Richard. "Deutsche Bank And A $10Bn Money Laundering Nightmare: More Context Than You Can Shake A Stick At." Naked Capitalism. N.p., 2017. Web. 18 Jan. 2017. Available at: http://www.nakedcapitalism.com/2016/09/deutsche-bank-and-a-10bn-money-laundering-nightmare-more-context-than-you-can-shake-a-stick-at.html

"US Doj Hits Deutsche Bank With Record $14Bn Fine." The Local Germany (2016). N.p., 2017. Web. 18 Jan. 2017. Available at: https://www.thelocal.de/20160917/us-doj-hits-deutsche-bank-with-record-14bn-fine

Farrell, Greg, Keri Geiger, and Suzi Ring. "Deutsche Bank Said Near Mirror-Trade Deal With U.K., N.Y." Bloomberg (2017): n. pag. Web. 20 Jan. 2017. Available at: https://www.bloomberg.com/news/articles/2017-01-30/deutsche-bank-said-to-be-near-mirror-trade-deal-with-u-k-n-y

Williams-Grut, Oscar. "Deutsche Bank Is Paying $628 Million In Fines Over Its $10 Billion Russian 'Mirror Trade' Scandal." Business Insider Australia. N.p., 2017. Web. 19 Jan. 2017. Available at: http://www.businessinsider.com.au/deutsche-bank-russian-mirror-trades-settles-uk-fca-new-york-regulator-2017-1?r=UK&IR=T

New York State Department of Financial Services (DFS). DFS FINES DEUTSCHE BANK $425 MILLION FOR RUSSIAN MIRROR-TRADING SCHEME. 2017. Web. 25 Jan. 2017. Available at: http://www.dfs.ny.gov/about/press/pr1701301.htm

Caesar, Ed. "A Big Fine, And New Questions, On Deutsche Bank's 'Mirror Trades.'" The New Yorker. N.p., 2017. Web. 22 Feb. 2017. Available at: http://www.newyorker.com/business/currency/a-big-fine-and-new-questions-on-deutsche-banks-mirror-trades

Critical Thinking

1. What do you think of the author's analysis of Deutsche Bank's ethical violations?

2. What ethical lessons can be drawn from the Deutsche Bank money-laundering scandal?

3. How can companies build corporate cultures that help prevent the type of ethical breaches committed by Deutsche Bank?

Internet References

Deutsche Bank
 https://www.db.com/ir/en/download/Code_of_Business_Conduct_and_Ethics_for_Deutsche_Bank_Group.pdf

Forbes
 https://www.forbes.com/sites/iese/2014/12/22/10-ways-banking-sector-ethics-can-stop-being-an-oxymoron/#6d72089460fc

The New Yorker
 https://www.newyorker.com/magazine/2016/08/29/deutsche-banks-10-billion-scandal